TO Sarah [illegible]

FROM Ben [illegible]

Best Wishes

Lightning Ben

I Flew with Eagles

C. Ben Basye

Edited by Von Pittman, Ph.D. Two Mules Editing
Book designed by Yolanda Ciolli

Published by AKA-Publishing
Columbia, Missouri
www.akayola.com
www.aka-publishing.com

ISBN: 978-1-936688-24-1

Lightning Ben

I Flew with Eagles

The Autobiography of C. Ben Basye

C. Ben Basye

Author in Grumman F6F Hellcat cockpit
Hellcat has wings folded to save storage space on aircraft carriers.

Preface

This is my autobiography, the story of my life's journey. I served over four decades in the U. S. Navy and Naval Reserve and almost four decades as an engineering professor. Because proper education and military performance are crucial for the welfare of our nation, and because I have significant experience and concern in both areas, I critique both after this chronicle.

Some readers will conclude that certain incidents recalled herein recount unacceptable behavior by young—and not so young—service members. To the best of my recollection, I have included these incidents exactly as they occurred many decades ago, in some cases up to sixty-seven years ago. Profanity—part of that traditional military culture—is included, as it was then. The traditional military culture associated with these incidents is that of some of the U. S. Navy pilots who participated in winning the greatest war in our history. That traditional military culture is far superior to the sterile and 'politically correct' culture imposed on today's 'new military' by civilian and military bureaucrats, with their mania for diversity and feminization.

My Navy nickname was "Lightning Ben," hence the title of this book.

This book is written for my four sons and for future generations. The future of freedom depends on the vision and courage of those generations, and freedom is under assault as never before. All opinions stated herein are my own. They do not represent the U. S. Navy, the University of Missouri, or any other organization.

C. Ben Basye and his wife, Joanne, and four sons,
Scott Basye; Portland, OR, Chuck Basye; Rocheport, MO,
Randy Basye; St. Charles, MO, and George Basye; Yorba Linda, CA.

Dedications and Acknowledgements

This book is dedicated to my brother, Ensign George Levon Basye, who lost his life in an accident while performing dive bombing practice as the pilot of a U. S. Navy F4U Corsair at El Centro, California on 12 July 1951. It is also dedicated to the many other U. S. Navy pilot friends and acquaintances killed in training accidents or in combat. They include Lilburn Edmonston, Jay Reed, Hal Avants, Don Oblad, Jesse Brown, J. B. Morris, Jim Verdin, Dave Tatum, Bill Bauhof, and several others whose names I cannot recall, even though I vividly remember the accidents and combat situations. It is also dedicated to Cliff Fanning, a Kansas farm boy who attended a one-room country school, and a true American hero. Cliff was my first Navy Commanding Officer in the Pacific Fleet.

I would especially like to recognize and thank Joanne Basye, my wife of fifty-seven years, who was always there to care for our sons while I was involved in the activities described herein.

I owe a great debt of gratitude to my wonderful parents. A wise man once said that his parents were the greatest book he ever read. I can truthfully and enthusiastically say the same.

Photographs of several of the airplanes I flew and of some individuals noted herein are courtesy of Wikimedia Commons.

George Levon Basye

Table of Contents

Part One: The Early Years

Preceding page: Charles Bradley Basye and Dorothy Elizabeth Basye, the author's parents

The author's sisters, Billy Ann Ballard-Turner and Betty Jane Smythe

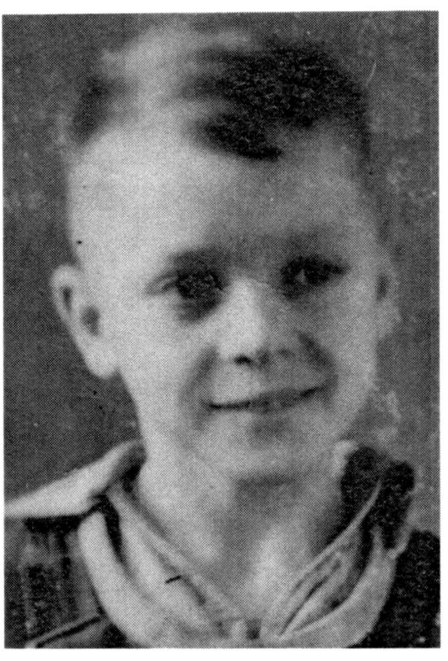

The author's grade school photo

George Basye, brother of the author

Chapter 1: Childhood and Family

My life's journey began at 2:50 in the morning on June 10, 1927, on a farm in southeast Howard County, Missouri. Five-year old twin sisters Betty Jane and Billy Ann preceded me. George Levon, the last child in our family, arrived twenty months later. Our father Charley was a farmer, carpenter, blacksmith, mechanic, sheep-shearer, and just about anything else he needed to be, for whatever task was at hand. He had enlisted in the U. S. Army in 1918. Assigned to the Tank Corps, he served at Fort Riley, Kansas and in North Carolina. I recall him discussing the terrible flu epidemic and how hard it was on the soldiers.

We baled hay for our neighbors. Dad pulled a hay baler with his truck. It was hard and dirty work. One of my elderly friends recalled an incident from when Dad was about twenty years of age. A neighbor, Mr. Billy Shipe, owned a mule that no one had succeeded in riding. Dad rode up on his horse and said "Mr. Billy, do you want him rode"? Mr. Shipe gave his blessing. Dad removed the saddle from the horse and secured it to the mule. He mounted the mule and all Hell broke loose. When the dust cleared, the mule was exhausted; Dad still sat on his back. He took off his hat and beat the mule over the ears with it to get him to buck some more. The mule had been through enough. He called off the proceedings.

My mother, the former Dorothy Elizabeth Crews, was a housewife who cared for her family during the Great Depression. She was the kindest person I have ever known. I can remember her saying "When I am old, I do not want to be a burden on my children." She was an outstanding student at New Franklin, Missouri, High School. She taught school, and at times served on the Board of Directors of Union School. She also served as Clerk of the district.

We always had a nice vegetable garden because of her efforts. We shared many Thanksgiving meals with neighborhood widowers so that they would not be alone on that holiday. Each Christmas during the Depression, Mother bought a gallon of cherries for the family. Each child received a one-dollar bill from Mother's brother, Herbert Crews, a bachelor who lived in Texas. We were most thankful.

Food was scarce during the depression. If a piece of meat remained at the end of a meal, Mother never wanted it; she saved it for one of the children to eat. Thus it has always been with mothers. Sadly, girls today often overlook the most important task of all; that is to be the mother who is always there for her children. The fact that caring for children is today—and will forever be—the most important role, does not mean that mothers who work outside the home should be criticized. In many cases, economic reality necessitates it. I am most thankful that my mother and my wife were full-time housewives who recognized the importance of being present for their children.

The Great Depression—which would be an extremely hard time on the farm—was fast approaching when I was born. Calvin Coolidge was President. He was a man of few words who rarely issued unnecessary public statements. He understood that "empty wagons make the most noise," and was cherished for upholding the virtues of the founding fathers. He understood the importance of the truth. What a contrast between Coolidge and several recent Presidents and presidential candidates.

Baling hay in the summer on the family farm in Missouri. The author is wearing a straw hat and his brother George is on the opposite side of the baler. His sister, Betty is on the hay rake, and the author's father is leaning on the pitchfork. The nearest horse was named Helen; the other, Lady

Chapter 2: Elementary and High School 1932-1943

In the fall of 1932, shortly after my fifth birthday, I began my education at Union School, a one-room country school. Iva Dean Blakemore, who later married Bill Ray, taught the first two years. By the end of the second year, and before my seventh birthday, I had completed the first three grades. I never asked my mother why she placed me on this fast track. She and Miss Blakemore probably made the decision jointly. It did not cause me any academic difficulty, but it did mean that all through high school I was two years behind other class members in social development. Apparently, it turned out all right. My brother George also navigated a similar fast track.

Union School was about two miles from our farm. Most of the time, we walked. There was no electricity or running water. The bathroom facilities were outside and a large wood stove provided heat. My grandfather's sister-in-law, Ada Basye, who lived only about 200 feet from the school building, started the fire early each school day.

Augustus and Ada Basye

Following Miss Blakemore, Dad's sister Bennie Basye taught the next two years. Then came Lois Virginia Smith for two years. Mary Lucille Innes taught the 1938-1939 school year. All of them were outstanding teachers who understood the importance of reading, writing, and arithmetic, unlike many of today's teachers, who often present information that is worthless, or sometimes even destructive. As long as America continues to accept the myth that College of Education attendance is necessary—or even desirable—for school personnel, no progress will be made. Government school unionization, particularly the National Educational Association (NEA), is also responsible for much of this disaster.

Grandparents, George and Sarah Basye

I entered Fayette High School in the fall of 1939. Our farm sat on a dirt road, three miles from the point where the gravel road ended, and the school bus turned around. Sometimes we walked to the bus. A large hollow sycamore tree stood close to the bus turnaround. The tree had a vertical opening, about six feet high, with an opening large enough for George and me to enter. This tree provided shelter while we waited for the bus. Sometimes George and I rode one of our horses to the bus. If we turned our horse Lady loose and told her to go home, she would do just that, then help Dad with the farm work.

Fayette attorney Jasper Thompson permitted me to live in his home on Watts Avenue my senior year in high school. He had grown up on the Thompson family farm, across the road from Union School. He was the same age as my grandfather, George Samuel Basye, and they were boyhood friends. Before Union School was built on a corner of my great-grandfather's farm in 1892, an earlier school had existed on a corner of the Thompson family farm.

Union School

As a high school freshman, I took algebra.

Mr. Raymond McIntyre, the principal and a fine man, was the teacher. Mr. Sutton, the superintendent, taught physics my senior year. I doubt that many government school administrators today could pass traditional algebra or physics, much less teach them.

High school was an interesting time. Several of us farm boys took vocational agriculture together all four years. We all belonged to the Future Farmers of America (FFA). The girls took home economics and joined Future Homemakers of America (FHA). Today, the girls seem to be moving away from home economics and appear to be striving to take over FFA, and otherwise enter traditonally male roles in many areas of American society.

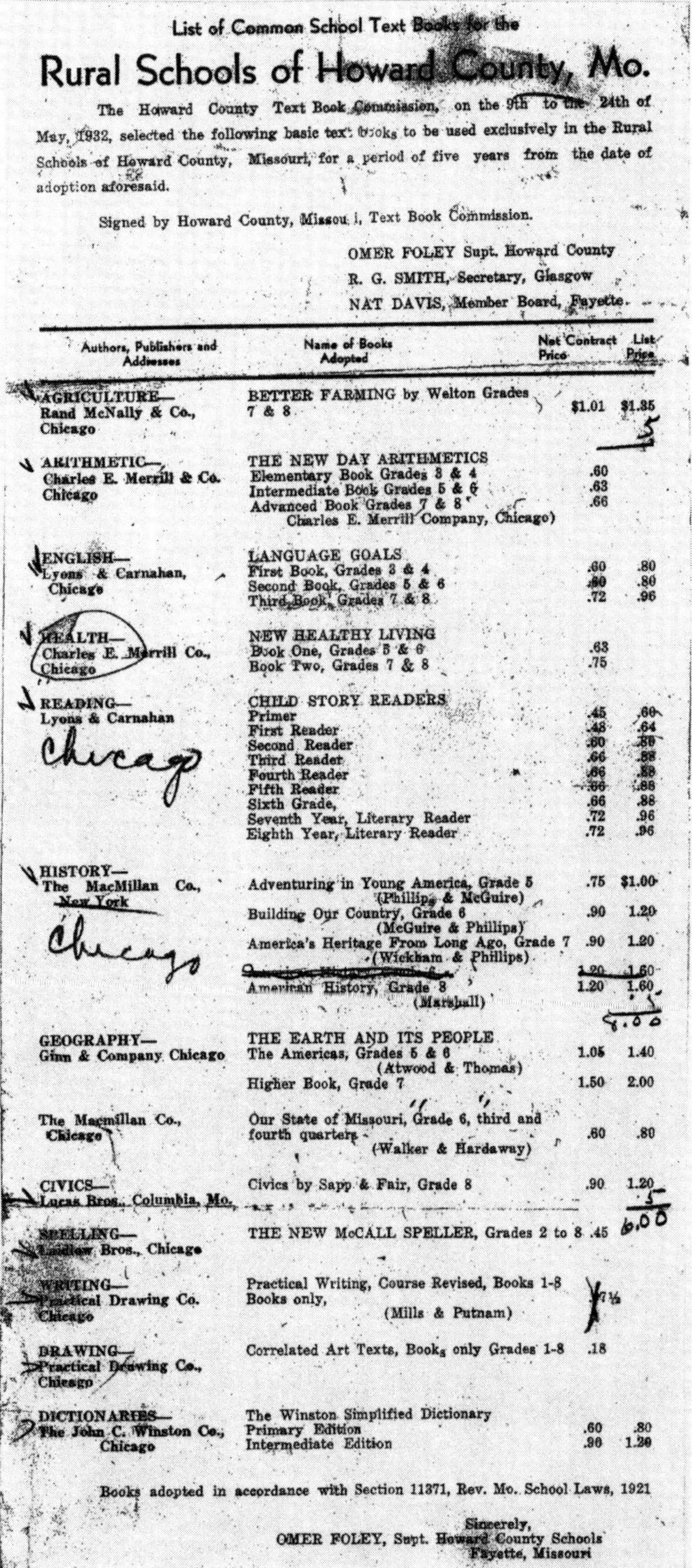

List of Common School Text Books for the

Rural Schools of Howard County, Mo.

The Howard County Text Book Commission, on the 9th to the 24th of May, 1932, selected the following basic text books to be used exclusively in the Rural Schools of Howard County, Missouri, for a period of five years from the date of adoption aforesaid.

Signed by Howard County, Missouri, Text Book Commission.

OMER FOLEY Supt. Howard County
R. G. SMITH, Secretary, Glasgow
NAT DAVIS, Member Board, Fayette.

Authors, Publishers and Addresses	Name of Books Adopted	Net Contract Price	List Price
AGRICULTURE— Rand McNally & Co., Chicago	BETTER FARMING by Welton Grades 7 & 8	$1.01	$1.35
ARITHMETIC— Charles E. Merrill & Co. Chicago	THE NEW DAY ARITHMETICS		
	Elementary Book Grades 3 & 4	.60	
	Intermediate Book Grades 5 & 6	.63	
	Advanced Book Grades 7 & 8	.66	
	Charles E. Merrill Company, Chicago)		
ENGLISH— Lyons & Carnahan, Chicago	LANGUAGE GOALS		
	First Book, Grades 3 & 4	.60	.80
	Second Book, Grades 5 & 6	.60	.80
	Third Book, Grades 7 & 8	.72	.96
HEALTH— Charles E. Merrill Co., Chicago	NEW HEALTHY LIVING		
	Book One, Grades 5 & 6	.63	
	Book Two, Grades 7 & 8	.75	
READING— Lyons & Carnahan	CHILD STORY READERS		
	Primer	.45	.60
	First Reader	.48	.64
	Second Reader	.60	.80
	Third Reader	.66	.88
	Fourth Reader	.66	.88
	Fifth Reader	.66	.88
	Sixth Grade,	.66	.88
	Seventh Year, Literary Reader	.72	.96
	Eighth Year, Literary Reader	.72	.96
HISTORY— The MacMillan Co., New York	Adventuring in Young America, Grade 5 (Phillips & McGuire)	.75	$1.00
	Building Our Country, Grade 6 (McGuire & Phillips)	.90	1.20
	America's Heritage From Long Ago, Grade 7 (Wickham & Phillips)	.90	1.20
	[illegible]	1.20	1.60
	American History, Grade 8 (Marshall)	1.20	1.60
GEOGRAPHY— Ginn & Company Chicago	THE EARTH AND ITS PEOPLE		
	The Americas, Grades 5 & 6 (Atwood & Thomas)	1.05	1.40
	Higher Book, Grade 7	1.50	2.00
The Macmillan Co., Chicago	Our State of Missouri, Grade 6, third and fourth quarters (Walker & Hardaway)	.60	.80
CIVICS— Lucas Bros., Columbia, Mo.	Civics by Sapp & Fair, Grade 8	.90	1.20
SPELLING— Laidlaw Bros., Chicago	THE NEW McCALL SPELLER, Grades 2 to 8	.45	
WRITING— Practical Drawing Co. Chicago	Practical Writing, Course Revised, Books 1-8 Books only, (Mills & Putnam)		
DRAWING— Practical Drawing Co., Chicago	Correlated Art Texts, Books only Grades 1-8	.18	
DICTIONARIES— The John C. Winston Co., Chicago	The Winston Simplified Dictionary		
	Primary Edition	.60	.80
	Intermediate Edition	.90	1.20

Books adopted in accordance with Section 11371, Rev. Mo. School Laws, 1921

Sincerely,
OMER FOLEY, Supt. Howard County Schools
Fayette, Missouri

This is the list of textbooks for Howard County country schools in 1932.

Note that there are books for English, History, Geography, Civics, Writing, and Spelling. Much of this valuable curriculum has been replaced by 'Social Studies' and 'Language Arts,' which partially explains the dismal performance of government school graduates over the last several decades.

Union School students in 1940: Left to right, back row: Josephine Skaggs, George Basye, Clara Skaggs, Leon Skaggs, James Walje, Alice Wyatt. Front row: Duane Snell, Harriet Hollon, Don McKee, Paul Skaggs, Darlene Wyatt

Union School students in 1938: From the left;
Duane Snell, George Basye, Jim Snell,
James Walje, Ben Basye,
Don McKee, Harriet Hollon

Fayette High School Class of 1943—The author is in the middle back row.

Chapter 3: North American Aviation, 1943-1944

I graduated from high school in May of 1943, before my 16th birthday. Our country was at war. Many of the boys in my high school class were entering the military, via either enlistment or Selective Service. The draft age was eighteen and the minimum age to enlist was seventeen. Too young to join the military, I asked myself what I could do to help the war effort.

North American Aviation was building the B-25 Billy Mitchell medium bomber at a plant in northeast Kansas City, Kansas. This was the famous airplane used to attack the Japanese home islands in April, 1942, less than four months after the December 7, 1941 attack on Pearl Harbor. Jimmy Doolittle, then a Lieutenant Colonel, led a flight of sixteen B-25s taking off from the aircraft carrier USS Hornet.

B-25 Billy Mitchell
Medium Bomber

The B-25 was named for a famous Army officer named Billy Mitchell. Very early in the history of military aviation he became convinced that airplanes could sink battleships, and that the U. S. military was moving too slowly in the utilization and development of airpower. He pushed his ideas so aggressively that he alienated many people. He was involved in dramatic bombing tests in 1921 and 1923. He sank several obsolete U.S. ships and captured German battleships in these tests.

Mitchell became publicly critical of the country's naval and military leadership to the point that he was court martialed and found guilty of insubordination. But by the outbreak of World War II, he was widely recognized as a man of vision and foresight.

On 10 December 1941, only 3 days after the Pearl Harbor attack, Japanese military aircraft sank the British battleship Prince of Wales and the battle cruiser Repulse off the coast of Malaysia. The British ships had no air cover. They were the first capital ships to be sunk by air attack on the high seas. Winston Churchill and President Roosevelt had held meetings on the Prince of Wales only a few months earlier. The Prince of Wales was completed in early 1941, less than one year before Japanese air power destroyed it. This traumatic naval catastrophe vindicated Mitchell's warnings.

When I applied to North American, they hired me to be a riveter. On day three of the one-week training program, someone came to our training area and asked for volunteers to train to become inspectors. I raised my hand. The man looked puzzled and asked my trainer if I should be considered, "since he is only 16." The trainer said, yes, he should be considered. So, I spent the next 14 months as an inspector on the center sections of the B-25s. My work shift was from 5:42 in the late afternoon until 4:24 in the morning, with a forty-two-minute lunch break. It was a ten-hour shift, Monday through Saturday. So it was a sixty-hour week, week after week. With a day shift also putting in sixty hours per week, the plant turned out 150 B-25s each month. That is correct; 150 bombers each month from one plant. Many of the riveters were women. I don't remember the pay amount, but seemed like a lot to a young farm boy.

I was issued a metal stamp to use to indicate approval. If parts were okay, I struck the stamp with a hammer, leaving an indentation. This stamp was somewhat like a blacksmith punch. The part that made the indentation was a circle about ¼ inch in diameter. Inside were ANK and 916. ANK indicated North American, Kansas and my number was 916. North American also had plants in Texas and California. I later learned that stamps like this can lead to initiation of fatigue cracks in structures, if used at certain critical locations.

Upon turning seventeen in June, 1944 and now being old enough to be in the military, I applied for pilot training in the Army Air Corps.

B-25 Production Plant in Kansas City, Kansas during World War II

Part Two: Military Career

NAME (Print) Charles (First) Benjamin (Middle) Basye (Last) Lcdr (Rank)

DATE PHOTOGRAPH TAKEN: November, 1963 514556 (File Number) 1355 (Designator)

INSTRUCTIONS FOR SUBMISSION OF PHOTOGRAPH
IN ACCORDANCE WITH ARTICLE B-2210 BUPERS MANUAL

1. This sheet may be used in lieu of a letter of transmittal by stapling or otherwise attaching photograph, prepared as indicated below, in center and filling in spaces indicated.

2. Photographs shall ... e Naval Reserve, regardless of status,

(a) Upon origina

(b) Upon accepta

(c) In any event

(d) Upon transfe

3. The photograph sh ... n a uniform other than the working unif ... in width and 5 inches in height.

4. Group pictures a

5. Print on back of ... ank and approximate date photograph was

6. Photographs submi ... and may be used for official release.

7. Secure photograph ... ef of Naval Personnel (Attention Pers-E221

8. Label container

9. The Navy Photogr ... tivities having an established photogra ... graphs for this purpose.

OFFICER PHOTOGRAPH SUBMISSION SHEET
NAVPERS 2669 (REV. 2-59)

Chapter 4: U. S. Army Air Corps, 1944-1945

I joined the U. S. Army at Fort Leavenworth, Kansas in late September, 1944, ninety-eight years after my great-grandfather, Michael Mauzy Basye, enlisted at the same base. He was in the mounted cavalry in the Mexican War and took part in the battles of Moros and Taos. After completing the voluminous required paperwork, I was assigned to the pre-engineering program at the University of Nebraska.

In Lincoln, my fellow recruits and I lived in a new building, Love Memorial Library. The Army appropriated it before it could be used for its intended purpose. Our sleeping area was on the east side of the second floor. We slept on steel bunks. One soldier snored so loud that it was hard for the rest of us to sleep. One night eight soldiers carefully picked him and his bunk up. While he snored away, they carried him down the stairs and sat his bunk out the front door in the snow. What a way to wake up!

The program operated on a quarter system schedule, with classes running three months. We stayed there six months, completing the second quarter at the end of March, 1945. Our mathematics professor seated us alphabetically and called alternate rows, front to back, odd and even. He wrote examination problems on the board, one problem for the odd row and a different problem for the even one. I remember being able to complete both sets of problems in a fraction of the allotted time.

The first quarter classes were Chemistry, English, History, Mathematics, military training, Physics, and physical training. Geography replaced History as the only change in the second quarter classes.

The chow hall was across the street from Love Library. One evening, several of us took some ice cream from the chow hall, something we were forbidden to do. We went to a dark attic in Love Library to consume it. Our Captain knew we had it and where we were. There was only one entrance to the attic and suddenly he was standing in it. He said "I know you are in here eating the ice cream. Come on out."

He could not identify us because we were in the dark. One of my friends decided to follow orders. He bolted through the door at full speed. When I passed the Captain, also at full speed, he was still spinning from the initial impact of my friend. He never identified us. It was sad because the Captain was such a kind person. But he probably had a laugh over it. He may have even admired our audacity.

The (USO) United Services Organization, located a short distance from the campus, was a nice place to spend time. The USO arranged for a friend and me to spend Christmas, 1944 with a farm family. Nebraska was a pleasant place and the Nebraskans were great people.

In April, 1945, the Army transferred us to the University of Wyoming to continue our college education. A mathematics professor there was extremely kind. She took several of us out to neighboring mountains on weekends to enjoy the scenery. Our English professor cried the day President Roosevelt died. Mathematics and English are the classes I recall.

In the early part of June, the Army notified us that it had discontinued our program. I had not yet reached my 18th birthday. Because we had entered the program at age 17, below the 18 year draft age, the Army gave us three options—infantry, aerial gunner, or a discharge. Because I still wanted to be a military pilot, I accepted a discharge. En route from Wyoming to my home in Missouri, I stopped at the U. S. Navy Recruiting Office in Kansas City and enlisted for naval pilot training.

The author in U. S. Army uniform while at the University of Nebraska

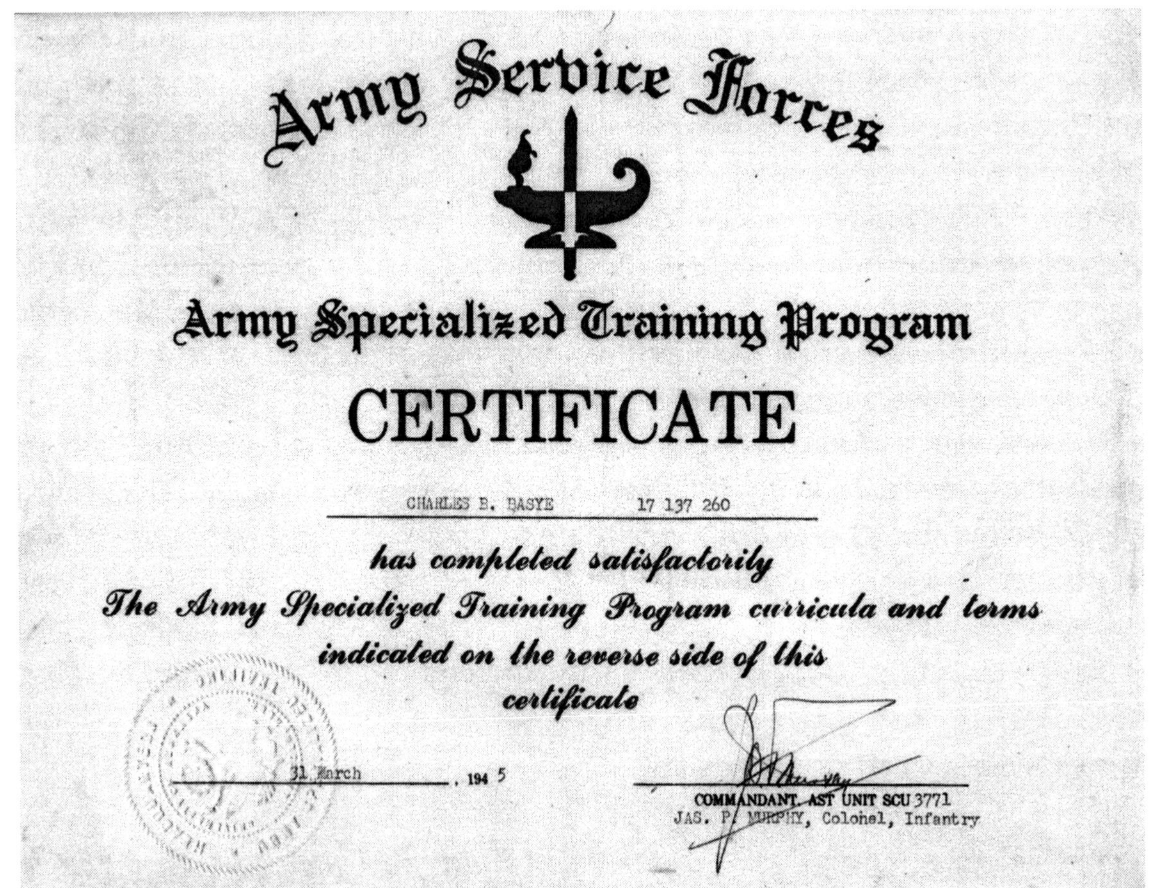
Army Service Forces

Army Specialized Training Program

CERTIFICATE

CHARLES B. BASYE 17 137 260

has completed satisfactorily
The Army Specialized Training Program curricula and terms
indicated on the reverse side of this
certificate

31 March , 1945

COMMANDANT, AST UNIT SCU 3771
JAS. P. MURPHY, Colonel, Infantry

Graduation Certificate for University of Nebraska Army Program

Chapter 5: U. S. Navy Pilot Training, 1945-1948

My first duty station as a member of the U. S. Navy was located at Central Missouri State College, in Warrensburg. This assignment lasted from July through October, 1945. The war against Japan ended in August, 1945, after the dropping of the atomic bombs on Hiroshima and Nagasaki. The coursework at Central Missouri State was primarily pre-engineering. Those of us in the pilot training program were identified by the Navy as being in a V-5 program, although the program was referred to as a V-12 program. We lived in Yeater Hall. Our chow hall was in the lower level. Two other men and I were assigned a room on the first floor.

It was hot and the classrooms were not air-conditioned. A physics class met just after noon. Try as hard as I could, I could not remain awake. I felt sorry for the professor, who had to watch someone sleeping, especially since I was sitting in the front row. He must have understood. I received an "A" in his class. I was enrolled in Descriptive Geometry, Analytic Geometry, English, Physics, History and Background of The Present War, Naval Organization, and physical training.

We made extensive use of the large swimming pool on the campus. Naval aviation cadets were required to pass a rigorous swimming test, called the AAA swimming test, in order to complete the program. As I recall, the requirements included swimming a mile with clothes on, and also jumping in the deep end of the pool clothed, then removing and inflating the trousers. The trousers were inflated by holding them partly submerged and beating air into the waist. This was done after each lower pant leg was tied into a knot at the lower end. The trousers could then be used as a floatation device. The swimming requirements were more difficult for me than academics or flying. One of the training devices at Pensacola was the notorious "Dilbert Dunker."

The cockpit model slides down the rails and inverts when it hits the water. Occupant, with a parachute on, must swim downward out of the cockpit. This simulates the case of an emergency ocean landing with the plane inverting when it hits the water.

The Dilbert Dunker

Several sailors with extended time in the fleet had entered this program. It was not easy for some of them to show proper respect to the young officers, without military experience, who were our instructors. The experienced sailors concluded that these young officers were incompetent.

After four months at Warrensburg, our next stop was Brown University, an Ivy League institution in Providence, Rhode Island. I began the trip by hitchhiking to St. Louis. At that time, motorists were willing—or even eager—to give rides to servicemen in uniform. There was no concern about crime, as there is today. From St. Louis, I had a choice between the Pennsylvania Railroad or the Baltimore and Ohio. I was enrolled in Astronomy, Biology, Naval History, Physics, Psychology, and Naval Organization at Brown.

The Navy gave us time off to go home for Christmas, 1945. On my way back to Brown, I stopped in New York City to take in New Year's Eve at Times Square. It was wild since it was the first New Year's Eve since the end of the war. People were packed like sardines on the street. I was with one of my Navy friends, Wes Clark, whose father was a Methodist minister in Cincinnati. People offered us drinks. We slept on concrete benches in Grand Central Station before going on to Providence.

I recall going to a watering hole in Providence named 'The Pirates Den.' Several sailors got in a big brawl and the Shore Patrol showed up. The next thing I knew, one of the brawl participants had a Shore Patrolman in a headlock. I decided that my departure was overdue.

After completing our assignment at Brown, I enjoyed a visit home, then reported to Naval Air Station (NAS) Memphis, Tennessee, for a critical evaluation. In just sixteen days there, cadets had to demonstrate to the flight instructors that we had the potential to become naval aviators. This evaluation determined which cadets would continue in the program. The 15.8 hours of flight time in the N2S Yellow Peril at Memphis included a forty-five-minute solo flight. The N2S was an open cockpit, bi-wing airplane, and it was a pleasure to fly. It was extremely rugged. About the only way to damage it was to hit the landing surface with something other than the landing gear. It was rugged enough to tolerate being subjected to a "snap-roll." In this maneuver, one suddenly jerked the stick all the way to the rear, causing the plane to stall. Then the pilot suddenly applied full rudder and the plane quickly rotated about the longitudinal axis. To recover from the "snap-roll," the pilot thrusts the stick all the way forward to exit the stall, then hit the opposite rudder to stop the rolling. Snap rolls would overstress the wings on most airplanes, and could cause wing separation from the fuselage.

Stearman N2S Yellow Peril

Author with N2S at NAS Memphis in 1946

The instructor rode in the front N2S cockpit and the student in the rear. The instructor had a rubber tube that he could talk through to the student's ear covers. The instructor could look at the student through a mirror mounted under the top wing. The student could nod yes or no to questions as to whether or not he understood the instructions.

One of my friends, Lee Hall, was a flight instructor who used the Yellow Peril. He wanted to make a parachute jump, but the Navy told him he could not do it. After being refused permission to jump several times, he took the initiative. In a flight with a student who was far enough along to have several solo flights, Lee was in the front cockpit, with the student in the rear. Lee unbuckled his seat belt and directed the student to do a slow roll. As expected, when the plane was upside down, out he went, to the horror of the student. The student circled him all the way down. The Navy was unable to prove that his loose seat belt was deliberate. Lee was proud of himself.

The next stop on the journey was Navy Pre-Flight School, at NAS Ottumwa, Iowa. I remember admiring the northeast Missouri scenery as we rode the train from Memphis to Ottumwa. The Mississippi River ran along the east side of the railroad tracks.

Pre-flight training lasted sixteen weeks. Four hours each day were devoted to academics, including navigation with memorization of prominent navigation stars. The curriculum also covered aerology, which is a Navy term for meteorology, and weather. The instructors addressed survival training and its importance. Such things as aircraft controls, engine mechanics, and oxygen breathing apparatus received significant attention. During the latter part of this training phase, we were left out by the Des Moines River in southeastern Iowa for a few days for a survival exercise. We had to forage for our food. The instructors had told us which bugs, snakes, and plants were edible, but a better op-

This shelter was home for three of us during a survival exercise at Iowa Pre-Flight program, 1946. Black Bottom, the dog, was the base mascot.

Left to right: Harris Hinnant, Dwight Merritt, the Author, and Futrell (Futrell did not belong in the picture)

tion presented itself. Several farm gardens were not too far away and they were frequently unguarded. Stolen cabbage, tomatoes, and lettuce beat worms and snakes any day.

In addition to academics, we devoted four hours a day to athletics. Among the activities—for two weeks at a time—were swimming, track, boxing, wrestling, gymnastics, and several others. It was no-nonsense training and we ended up in excellent physical condition. They had a large rope anchored about twenty-five feet above the floor, which by then we call the "deck." Each cadet would sit on the surface straddling the rope. When the instructor rang the bell, we were timed on our climb to the top. I could climb faster by not using my legs than by using them.

The instructors divided the Cadets into four groups of about fifty, then further divided each group by weight. Then, the instructors arranged wrestling contests. I won the contest for my weight class for my group, and lost to the eventual base champion for that weight. My friend Don Oblad won the weight class contest for his group, and also lost to the individual who beat me. I remember talking to Don after he had lost his match. Don was killed in a training flight over the Pacific

Ocean three years later. Mark Bitter was his best Navy friend. Mark and Don's sister later married. I can picture Don's grief-stricken parents and his sister at our mess hall in San Diego after his accidental death. Mark escorted them. Everyone wanted to console them, but found it awkward. We didn't know how.

At the successful completion of Pre-Flight, it was on to NAS Corpus Christi, Texas. I arrived in Corpus Christi in mid-August, 1946. As there were more cadets than instructors or training facilities, we had about three months in which nothing of consequence happened. I was assigned a barracks to look after, which I did with a civilian base employee, a black man, who took care of our maintenance and janitorial work. We became friends during this time. One day during this period, a call went out for volunteers to ride a Navy transport plane to Norman, Oklahoma, where a Navy facility was closing. Volunteers were needed to drive Navy road vehicles back to Corpus Christi. It was to be a three-day trip from Norman to Corpus Christi in a fifty-vehicle convoy. Each cadet was responsible for his own food on the trip.

Studying radial aircraft engines. Author is second from right

On the night before the beginning of the return trip, my friend Kenny Key and I were in Oklahoma City. After spending almost all our money, we were down to $1.07. We were impersonating sailors, one could say. We were assigned to drive a station wagon-panel truck type vehicle. It only had one seat, under the steering wheel. We took a seat out of a Navy ambulance and placed it in the front passenger location for the non-driver. Four cot size mattresses taken from a barracks served as our beds. There was no money for motels. Bread was inexpensive, so we made it the first day on jam sandwiches. Take a piece of bread and jam it against another piece before consuming.

Late the first day, just north of the Texas border, near Marietta, Oklahoma, someone in the convoy applied brakes. It was raining and the pavement was slick. Kenny was driving. As we were about to slide into the vehicle in front of us, he drove onto the right shoulder. The right front tire sank into the mud; we spun around and rolled down the road bank. Both of us, the ambulance seat, the four mattresses, and our suitcases were bouncing around the back of the vehicle until it came to rest, on its wheels, headed back toward Norman. But we could not get it started. The Chief in charge of the convoy had to buy a new battery. After prying the fenders off so the wheels could turn, we drove on to Denton, Texas, to spend the night. The sides of the vehicle were bent about ten degrees from upright. We were both sore and stiff.

We parked next to the curb at a service station and were inside loafing when two Mexican men drove in with a large load of watermelons. The passenger jumped out of the truck while it was still rolling and ran to the back to guard the load. After the truck was serviced, the passenger waited by the back of the truck until it was rolling. Then he ran up to the cab and jumped in. Kenny saw his chance. He jumped up on the back of the truck and took a five-finger discount on a monster watermelon. Kenny put the melon behind the gas pump, which—luckily—was large enough to hide it. The Mexicans reached the street and turned. They looked back and determined to their satisfaction that no melons were missing. One could say that this watermelon transaction was on the honor system; the Mexicans had the honor and Key had the system. We gave the Mexicans a friendly wave as they departed. The service station man was speechless, which is most unusual for a Texan.

We survived the next two days on jam sandwiches and watermelon. When we turned the vehicle over to the motor pool in Corpus Christi, they wondered why the Okies would send them a vehicle in such a damaged condition. We did not explain.

My turn to fly finally came. On 27 November I again started flying the N2S Yellow Perils. This lasted until 31 March 1947. From 15 April until 2 July 1947, I flew the SNJ Texan.

North American SNJ Texan

To kill boredom on weekends, many cadets would hitchhike to different locations on Saturday, then hitchhike back on Sunday. Three of us made such a trip to Laredo, TX. We asked Laredo firemen if we could sleep in the fire station on Saturday night. I slept in the front seat of the Fire Chief's car, another cadet slept in the back seat, and the other one slept on some fire hose coiled up on a fire truck. This practice made for inexpensive weekends. On another weekend, Robert Smith and I hitchhiked to Galveston and decided to sleep in a nice city park on park benches. We were awakened by a city policeman tapping the bottom of our shoes with his nightstick. He chased us out of the park and was upset when we told him that we had witnessed things much more appropriate for his attention than chasing well-behaved service men out of the park. Robert Smith was from Marshall, Texas, and ended up flying the SB2C Helldiver dive bomber. Some fighter pilots referred to the Helldiver as son-of-a-bitch-second class because of the S, B, 2, and C. The SB actually stood for Scout Bomber. It was the second scout bomber manufactured by

Author and J. C. Sapp on USS Wright, 9 October, 1947

Author in SNJ cockpit. Corpus Christi, TX, 1947.

the Curtiss Aircraft Company.

Some South American cadets were in training with us. One—from Brazil or Argentina, I believe—bailed out of his SNJ during night flying. He landed in Corpus Christi Bay in water about four feet deep. Not knowing which direction shallow water and the shore lay, he stood there all night. When daylight arrived, he walked out of the bay.

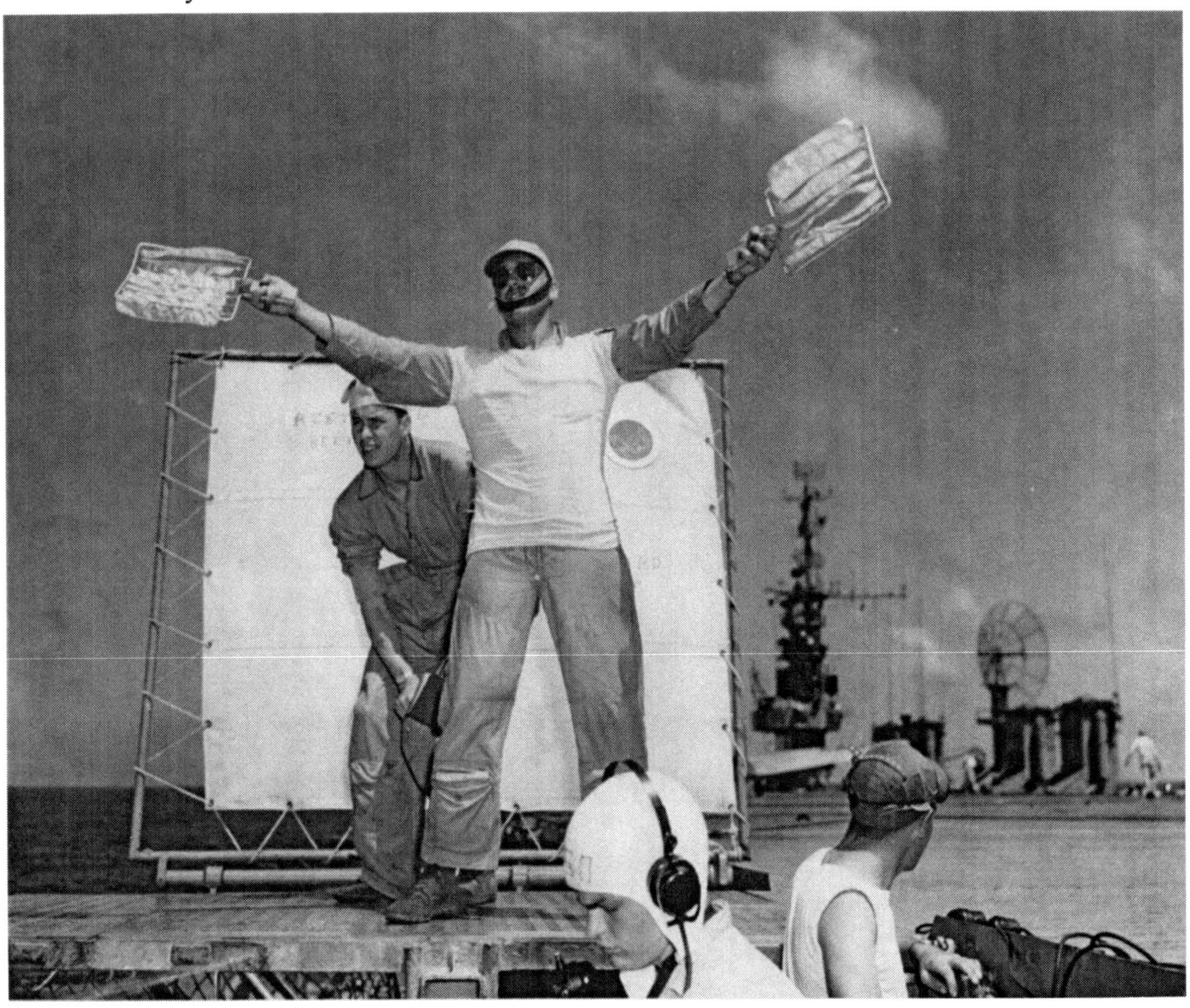

LSO (landing signal officer) on USS Wright in Gulf of Mexico

We frequently witnessed unusual situations on Saturday night bus rides from downtown Corpus Christi to the Naval Air Station. One remains etched in my mind, even though it happened sixty-five years ago. The bus seats filled quickly and then more riders packed the aisles like sardines. A sailor had had more than his share of adult beverages and was sick; he leaned over in the bus seat and threw up violently between his legs, splashing it on the floor. A Marine in dress blues,

An SNJ has just caught a wire on the USS Wright.

USS Wright in Gulf of Mexico:
See the six SNJ's on the flight deck.

with red stripes on the legs, was standing in the isle next to him. Close to the Marine, a round chrome-plated pipe ran from the floor to the ceiling, firmly bolted at both ends. To escape the splashing vomit, the Marine pulled himself up the pipe until he could go no further. He remained up against the ceiling for several miles. Another sailor witnessed the entire episode while eating a jar of pickled pig's feet. He never missed a bite. The bus driver, a Texan, ignored the incident entirely.

We flew SNJs at Pensacola between 21 July 1947 and 9 October 1947. On 9 October, I made six carrier takeoffs from and six carrier landings onto the light carrier USS Wright. The Landing Signal Officer (LSO) is an experienced carrier pilot who directs incoming pilots' speeds and flight paths. When the pilot is in close enough, the LSO gives the cut sign and the pilot must cut the engine back to idle. This is a mandatory signal which the pilot must obey. Hopefully, the plane's hook will catch a wire and stop the plane on the deck. When the engine is cut to idle, as directed by the LSO, one of three things will happen: (1) the hook will catch a wire and stop the plane on the rear part of the flight deck; (2) the hook will bounce over the wires or break, and the plane will crash into parked aircraft or a safety barrier; or, (3) the plane and pilot will go over the side and into the ocean. The canted deck aircraft carrier has taken most of the excitement out of carrier landings. I will discuss carrier operations in greater detail later in the book.

While we were flying SNJ's at Pensacola, a cadet from New York City apparently lost control and crashed into the Gulf of Mexico. This was the first of several fatalities associated with naval aviation that I witnessed.

Pilot trainees with a PBY Catalina at Pensacola in October, 1947

I took my first flight in the PBY Catalina on 15 October 1947. The PB indicated patrol bomber and Y was the Navy identification for Consolidated Aircraft, the manufacturer. The maiden flight of an early PBY traveled a record 3443 miles nonstop in 1936. The PBY was a valuable contributor to the war effort. PBY scout planes blanketed the Japanese approach to Midway Island in June 1942. They were slow

Author in PBY cockpit at Pensacola, 1947
The cadet in front is Dick Huntington from Chicago.

but dependable, and could remain aloft a long time. I am standing, fourth from the left, in the photograph of the PBY with the pilot trainees. Mark Bitter is standing, third from the right. As was noted earlier, Mark later married Don Oblad's sister after Don's fatal accident over the Pacific. Jay Reed, the cadet to my left, was killed when his fighter crashed into the Pacific while we trained at San Diego. The tall cadet standing fifth from the right—Joe Dobronski—was a test pilot for McDonnell Aircraft in St. Louis for many years. Jack Dewenter, fourth from the right, attended Central College in Fayette, Missouri in 1945, while I was at Warrensburg.

We completed the PBY phase of training on 17 November 1947. In the last part of the PBY training phase, we flew the aircraft "solo." This did not mean that cadets were alone in the plane. It meant there was no instructor with us. But two cadets and a required flight engineer came along on these "solos." The flight engineer's station was below the wing, in the structure that attached the wing to the fuselage.

There were two ways to land the PBY on the water. The first was called a "full stall" landing. The pilot approached the water at a low power setting and pulled the nose up to lose speed. The object was to stall the aircraft just above the water and let it drop onto the surface. The wings must be kept level or the lower wingtip float will dig into the water. Because there are no physical objects on the water's

PBY making water landing

surface, it is difficult for the novice to judge height above the water. Depth perception utilization on land enables much better height estimates. The other landing method was to set up a 200 feet-per-minute rate of descent at ninety knots airspeed and to be certain to keep the wings level. Instead of being too concerned about height, pilots just waited until they hit the water. This was much easier for a novice than the "full stall" method.

There were three strict rules for the cadets on solo flights. The first was for the cadet acting as pilot to always occupy the seat in the cockpit that he was accustomed to. The instructor always was in the left seat, the cadet in the right seat. Therefore the cadet acting as pilot was to be in the right seat. The two solo cadets were to trade seats when it was the other man's turn to act as pilot. The second rule was that neither cadet create a simulated emergency for the other. Third, there were to be no "full stall" landings. On one solo flight the two cadets broke all three rules in one incident.

Ed Brown

The cadet acting as pilot was in the left seat. As he got airborne and got a little altitude, the other cadet pulled the throttle back to idle on one engine. The pilot landed in "full stall" fashion. His wings weren't kept level and the lower float dug in and jerked the plane around. The impact knocked the radios out and broke the plastic bubble surface on the top rear side of the fuselage. They could not radio for advice or assistance and the rear of the fuselage had taken on quite a bit of seawater. They decided to fly it back, seawater and all. Surprisingly, they had an uneventful return trip.

Ed Brown, my wife's first cousin, served as a PBY pilot during World War II. Ed attended Central College in Fayette in 1938 and 39 and then graduated from Central Missouri State in Warrensburg. He enlisted in the Navy for flight training on 4 July 1942. Ed was in Black Cat Squadron 33. His plane sank a Japanese ship and made an open ocean landing in order to successfully rescue a downed crewman of a Douglas A-20 Havoc. Ed's decorations included two Air Medals. He served in Australia, the Dutch East Indies, and the Philippines and flew scout and bombing missions all over the South Pacific. See Ed's picture below.

Another humorous incident occurred in the mess hall at NAS Pensacola. As we went through the chow line, each cadet had a rectangular food tray, with five compartments to keep food separated. Food servers put the appropriate food item in the proper compartment. As each cadet passed the server for that food item, the server placed that item on the tray. The meat item was a delicious looking steak or pork cutlet. One of my friends told the meat server to put an extra piece of meat on his tray. The server said "The Chief said no one gets seconds." My friend reached over the counter and grabbed about five pieces of meat and slapped them on his tray. The server yelled to the Chief that this guy put his hand in the meat and took about five pieces. The Chief had been in the mess hall business for many years; his profile confirmed it. He came charging out from behind the servers, where he had been admiring his kingdom. The race was on. There was a swinging double door, like movie saloon doors, to the outside. The cadet was in front holding the food tray in front of his chest. The Chief was a good distance behind him. Luckily, the doors opened. Off they went. The Chief lost ground with every step; the cadet was in shape and he was not. The escape was complete. There were no repercussions for the great meat theft incident.

Beech SNB Kansan

I took my first flight in the SNB Kansan on 24 November 1947. These flights were out of Whiting Field, northeast of Pensacola. My last SNB flight was on 16 December 1947. Three days later, on 19 December, my class went through the graduation ceremony. I was now an ensign and could proudly wear the "Wings of Gold." Most Navy pilots did not go through a training program this long. Even though I was destined to end up as a fighter pilot, I also trained in multi-engine land and multi-engine sea aircraft, which was not the usual scenario. Because almost all Navy pilots wanted to be fighter pilots, I felt fortunate.

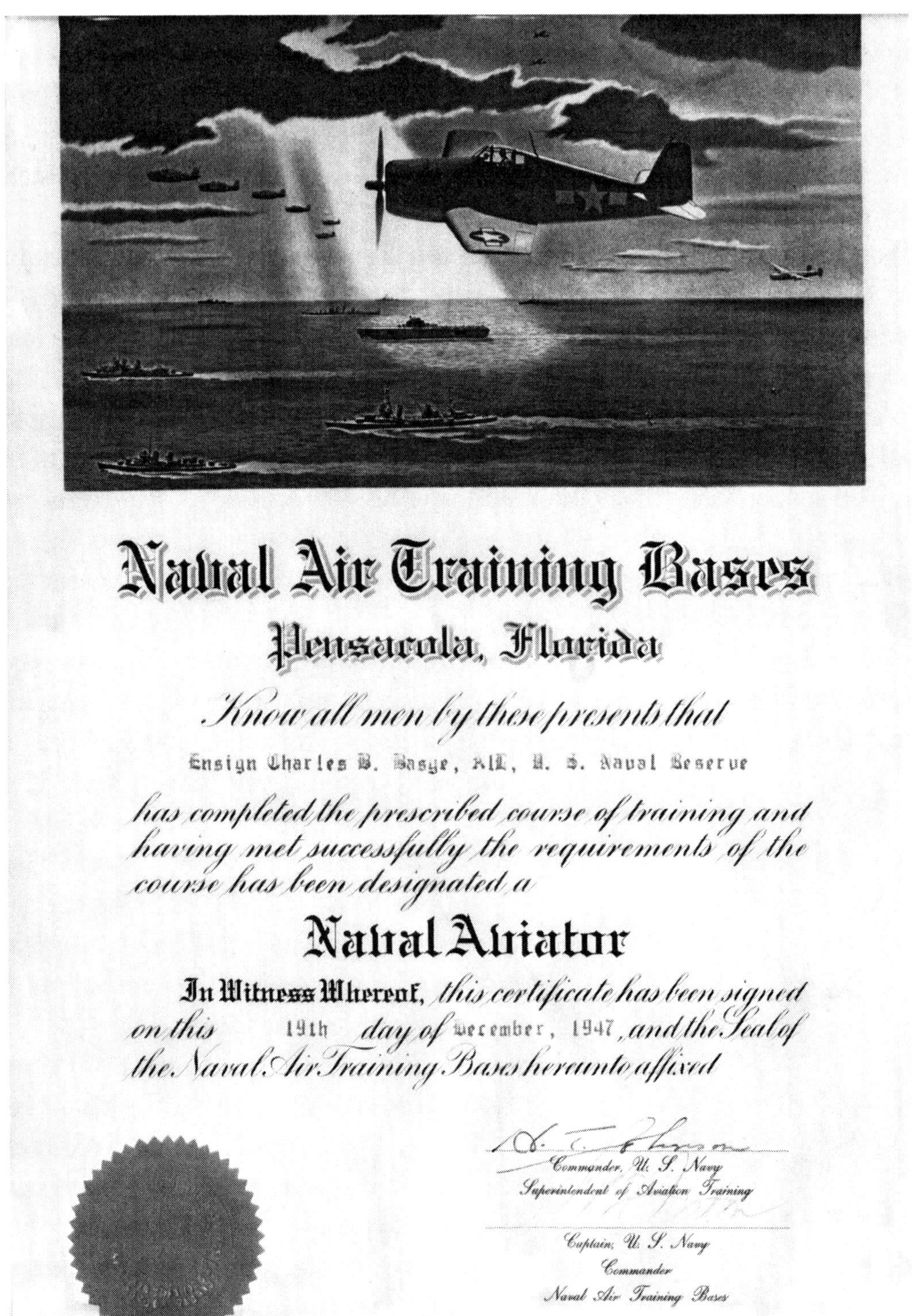

Naval Air Training Bases
Pensacola, Florida

Know all men by these presents that

Ensign Charles B. Basye, A1L, U. S. Naval Reserve

has completed the prescribed course of training and having met successfully the requirements of the course has been designated a

Naval Aviator

In Witness Whereof, this certificate has been signed on this 19th day of December, 1947, and the Seal of the Naval Air Training Bases hereunto affixed

Commander, U. S. Navy
Superintendent of Aviation Training

Captain, U. S. Navy
Commander
Naval Air Training Bases

This Naval Aviator Certificate is the reward for so much training and hard work. This is presented to the new Naval Aviator with his wings.

Advanced Flight Training, NAS Jacksonville, FL, 1948:
Standing, left to right; Ken Burrows, Bill Banks, Jack Davidson, Max Thompson.
Kneeling; the Author, Marcus DuPree, Mark Bitter, Bill Hembree

Next came NAS Jacksonville, Florida, for advanced training. Seven of us were designated as Flight 540 of VF-ATU #2. The "F" in VF indicates fighter aircraft and ATU indicates Advanced Training Unit. Bill Banks was the instructor. This was the first time that a group had trained together for an extended period of time. Three of the seven—Marcus DuPree, Max Thompson, and Jack Davidson—were Annapolis graduates. Marcus, Ken, Bill, Mark, and I were together in the PBY photograph, so we knew each other well before the advanced training at Jacksonville. We flew the Grumman F6F Hellcat during this training. This plane had acquitted itself quite well against the Japanese.

I vividly remember my first Hellcat flight, on 6 February 1948. On the landing approach when I throttled back to slow down to land, it seemed that the plane wanted to maintain high speed; it seemed not to want to decelerate. All went well, however. I brought it down successfully. We practiced instrument flying, formation flying, gunnery using only gun camera film, actual gunnery, dive bombing, fighter tactics, rocket firing, over-water navigation, night flying, cross country flying, and field carrier landing practice. The LSO would be stationed on a surface which simulated the deck of an aircraft carrier. We did the latter in preparation for landing the Hellcat on the USS Wright.

In a sense, we were on our own. There was no two-seat trainer version of the Hellcat. In fact, all eight Navy fighters I flew were single-seat aircraft. A two-seat trainer version of one of them, the F-80, came along later.

On 12 May 1948, I made seven carrier take offs and landings, again on the USS Wright in the Gulf of Mexico.

During this training, I received the CAA (Civil Aeronautics Administration) Commercial Pilot License. I was qualified for single and multi-engine land and multi-engine sea ratings. All that was required was proof of the Navy flight training and passing a written examination. This license was valid for life. To use this license as a commercial pilot required periodic physical examinations.

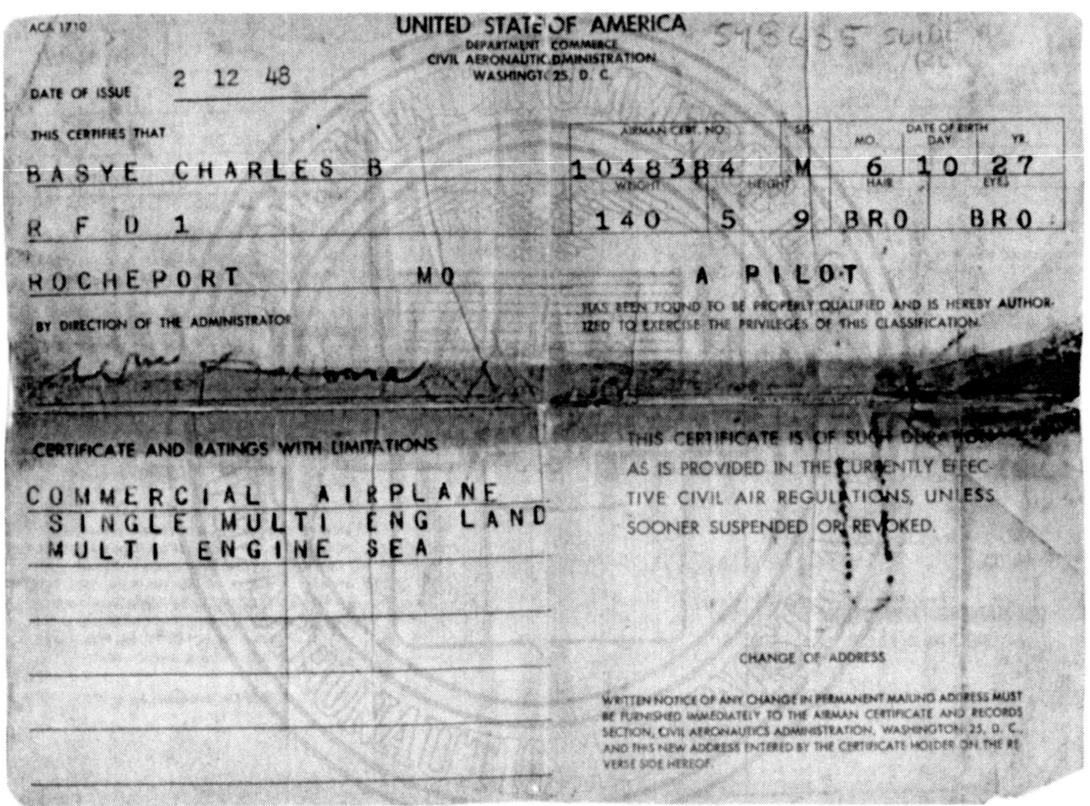

ACA 1710

UNITED STATES OF AMERICA
DEPARTMENT COMMERCE
CIVIL AERONAUTIC ADMINISTRATION
WASHINGTON 25, D. C.

DATE OF ISSUE 2 12 48

THIS CERTIFIES THAT

BASYE CHARLES B
R F D 1
ROCHEPORT MO

AIRMAN CERT. NO.	SEX	DATE OF BIRTH MO.	DAY	YR.
1048384	M	6	10	27

WEIGHT	HEIGHT	HAIR	EYES
140	5 9	BRO	BRO

A PILOT

HAS BEEN FOUND TO BE PROPERLY QUALIFIED AND IS HEREBY AUTHORIZED TO EXERCISE THE PRIVILEGES OF THIS CLASSIFICATION

BY DIRECTION OF THE ADMINISTRATOR

CERTIFICATE AND RATINGS WITH LIMITATIONS

COMMERCIAL AIRPLANE
SINGLE MULTI ENG LAND
MULTI ENGINE SEA

THIS CERTIFICATE IS OF SUCH DURATION AS IS PROVIDED IN THE CURRENTLY EFFECTIVE CIVIL AIR REGULATIONS, UNLESS SOONER SUSPENDED OR REVOKED.

CHANGE OF ADDRESS

WRITTEN NOTICE OF ANY CHANGE IN PERMANENT MAILING ADDRESS MUST BE FURNISHED IMMEDIATELY TO THE AIRMAN CERTIFICATE AND RECORDS SECTION, CIVIL AERONAUTICS ADMINISTRATION, WASHINGTON 25, D. C., AND THIS NEW ADDRESS ENTERED BY THE CERTIFICATE HOLDER ON THE REVERSE SIDE HEREOF.

Civil Aeronautic Administration (later named the FAA)
Commercial Pilot License: Received 12 February 1948

To conclude this record of my Navy flight training, a copy of 'A Navy Flyer's Creed' is shown. This summarizes what one should be aware of and strive to uphold.

A NAVY FLYER'S CREED

I am a United States Navy flyer.

My countrymen built the best airplane in the world and entrusted it to me. They trained me to fly it. I will use it to the absolute limit of my power.

With my fellow pilots, air crews, and deck crews, my plane and I will do anything necessary to carry out our tremendous responsibilities. I will always remember we are part of an unbeatable combat team - the United States Navy.

When the going is fast and rough, I will not falter. I will be uncompromising in every blow I strike. I will be humble in victory.

I am a United States Navy flyer. I have dedicated myself to my country, with its many millions of all races, colors, and creeds. They and their way of life are worthy of my greatest protective effort.

I ask the help of God in making that effort great enough.

— a Naval Aviator

A Navy Flyer's Creed

At the completion of the advanced training program, the Navy assigned me the Pacific Fleet at San Diego, California. I did not have a car at this time, so I rode to San Diego with Max Thompson. Max stayed one night at my parent's farm in Missouri and I stayed one night at his home in South Dakota. I rode a bus from Missouri to South Dakota. Max had been tagged with two different nicknames—'The Big Wind' and 'Big Max.'

Chapter 6: U. S. Pacific Fleet, 1948-1950

From 22 June until 8 July 1948 those of us in the next photograph and several of our other friends were undergoing Airborne Electronic Warfare (AEW) training at the Naval Auxiliary Air Station, Ream Field. This facility is south of San Diego, a few miles from the Mexican border at Tijuana. My class spent a total of about thirteen hours in the back of R4D-5 aircraft loaded with electronics. The R4D is better known as the Air Force C-47. Personnel in the photograph are—from left to right—Rudy Peterson, Don Brown, Glen Allen, Stan Hayes, Dick Gosnell, Jay Reed, myself, and Jack Dewenter. Dick and I were Ensigns while the other six were midshipmen. The midshipmen were destined for the regular Navy while Dick and I, by choice, remained in the Naval Reserve. Admiral James L. Holloway, Jr. was the Superintendent of the Naval Academy at Annapolis from 1947 to 1950. He was the guiding force behind the establishment of the NROTC (Naval Reserve Officer Training Corps) program at civilian universities and also the program in Naval flight training where individuals could train for the regular Navy as midshipmen. The midshipmen in this photograph were part of that program. Information on this program and individuals in the program can be found on the Internet at TheBrownShoes.org. The training of the midshipmen and that of those of us who chose to remain reservists were completely identical. As noted earlier, Jay Reed was later killed in an accident over the Pacific.

My nickname was 'Lightning Ben' and Dick Gosnell's was 'The Uncultured Vulture.' Once one of these nicknames got attached to you, regardless of how vulgar or insulting, it usually stayed. The individual with the nickname might not even know who hung that tag on him. Dick was the light heavyweight boxing champion of the entire group of cadets in pre-flight training. He was, and is today, one of my closest friends. He is a retired chemical engineer and lives in Quincy, IL.

Following the Ream Field training came two weeks of amphibious warfare training at the U. S. Navy Amphibious Base in Coronado, California. Two weeks

Left to right—Rudy Peterson, Don Brown, Glen Allen, Stan Hayes,
Dick Gosnell, Jay Reed, the author, and Jack Dewenter
Naval Auxiliary Air Station-Ream Field, San Diego CA, 1948

of training in air support for the Marines followed. Some of this training included duty on the ground at the Marine Base at Camp Pendleton, California. We maintained radio contact with Navy pilots flying simulated air support for ground troops.

It is interesting—even surprising—to note that in 1948, only three years after the conclusion of World War II, the U. S. Navy only had two Essex-class carriers in the entire Pacific Fleet, the Boxer (CV-21) and the Valley Forge (CV- 45). They were the only carriers available for both West Coast training and Western Pacific (WESTPAC) duty.

This sorry state of affairs is illuminated by reviewing the "Revolt of the Admirals," a name given to an episode in which several Navy Admirals publicly disagreed with the strategy and plans of President Truman and Secretary of Defense Louis Johnson. In December 1949, Johnson stated "There's no reason for having a Navy and Marine Corps. General Bradley tells me that amphibious operations are a thing of the past. We'll never have any more amphibious operations. That does away with the Marine Corps. And the Air Force can do anything the Navy can do nowadays, so that does away with the Navy." The folly of this line of thinking was exposed in only a few short months when the Korean War started in June 1950.

This San Diego training was preliminary to assignment to our first fleet squadron. I soon received orders to fighter squadron VF-211, one of the squadrons of All-Weather Air Group 21 at NAS Seattle. We were not required to report to Seattle until about 1 October 1948, which left us in San Diego without much to do. The NAS San Diego Hobby Shop had a fully equipped automobile shop. One of my friends who had been an auto mechanic volunteered to overhaul the engine of a 1936 Ford I had recently purchased. He did an excellent job. I drove it to Seattle, back to San Diego, and later back to Missouri.

Max Thompson and I were roommates in San Diego before we went to Seattle. One afternoon, while I was relaxing in the room, he charged in and announced that he was going to "work me over." He was about half full of beer and made a high speed charge at me. I was able to step aside, as bullfighters do, and knocked him off balance as he went by. When he crashed into the wall, he said that he was going to remove his dress uniform and then I would "really get it." I stepped outside the room and shut the door. I was getting a drink from a water fountain by our door and thinking about my best course of action when the problem solved itself. Ken Burrows came sauntering down the hall. He must have been having a nice day as he was whistling and humming. Ken said, "Is Big Max in there"? I answered yes. Ken did not hesitate or knock, and before I could say anything else, he opened the door. Max hit him at full speed and the two of them went crashing into the bulkhead on the other side of the passageway. It was about two or three minutes before either of them could turn the other one loose. It was quite a scene—fists, elbows, snorting, kicking, and cussing! I still cannot decide which was the most unpleasant; watching it or listening to it. When they got through with each other, Big Max had lost all interest in "working me over." The three of us flew together all through the advanced flight training in Jacksonville.

Also about this time, Dick Gosnell, Max, and I went to a watering hole in San Diego one night. Our current nicknames were 'The Uncultured Vulture', 'Big Max', and 'Lightning Ben', respectively. One should have expected trouble. We were sitting with an attractive girl named Pat Murphy. Pat was a night club singer. She had a badly sprained ankle and had it wrapped. Max and I decided to go somewhere else and leave Dick and Pat there. Instead of leaving quietly, Max decided to use some Navy terminology. He said to Dick, "Stand by for a shakedown, because you are going to get your ashes hauled tonight." Pat immediately took offense and called Max some things that I had not heard before. She said some things about his mother that I knew to be untrue. I had met Max's mother and knew that she was a nice lady. Pat started at Max with a partly full bottle of beer and he headed for the exit at flank speed. With her bad ankle, she was losing the race, so she threw the bottle of beer at him as hard as she could. Luckily, it only grazed his right ear as it sailed past his head. A direct hit in the back of his head would probably have brought him down. Note that "shakedown" means a new ship's first cruise. "Ashes" was a reference to the by-product of combustion on the coal burning ships many decades earlier.

Jack Dewenter was a torpedo bomber pilot. On 7 September 1948, I rode in the tail gunner/radio operator station for a three-hour flight Jack piloted. The plane was a Grumman TBF Avenger, which fighter pilots nicknamed the "Turkey." Jack flew around Catalina Island at an altitude of about fifty feet. I expected him to be placed on report for flying too low, but nothing came of it.

Later, John (Jack) Dewenter was a member of the famous Navy Blue Angels aerial demonstration team. Following a long and extremely distinguished career, he retired as a regular Navy Captain in 1978.

LCDR Lilburn (Babe) Edmonston

Early in our Seattle adventure, LCDR Lilburn (Babe) Edmonston did not return from a flight. The NAS was located at Sand Point, on the west side of Lake Washington, in the northeastern part of Seattle, a location now called Warren G. Magnuson Park, named after a long-serving U.S. senator from Washington. Babe's flight was on a Tuesday afternoon. I had talked to him that morning. All pilots in the Air Group were at the ready before daybreak the next morning. Each of us had a sector to fly over to try to locate the downed airplane. It was so foggy that it was impossible to take off. The same was true the following day.

On Friday, in response to news that a farmer had reporting hearing a loud noise, we went out in a ground party. There were perhaps thirty of us in a Navy bus. A Coast Guard helicopter told us which direction to travel through the vegetation, which was so dense that you could only see about 10 feet. We reached the wrecked plane and LCDR Edmonston's body late Friday afternoon. It was obvious that he had died instantly and did not suffer for any extended time. Dick Gosnell and I were the only officers in the ground

"Big Ed" (Babe) Edmonston is on the left.

party. Babe was Dick's Commanding Officer.

Babe was born on 26 December 1916. He was a football lineman for Central College in Fayette and graduated in 1940. He taught history for a time before going through Navy flight training. He had an outstanding record as a combat pilot while assigned to VF-34. His decorations included two Distinguished Flying Crosses and four Air Medals. His Navy nickname was 'Big Ed.' He was a large, friendly, and kind man. His son, Lilburn Kingsbury Edmonston, was three years old when Babe was killed and does not remember his father. Babe's uncle, Lilburn Kingsbury, was well known around central Missouri as a historian. Here are two photographs of Babe. He was wearing his dress blue uniform in the formal photograph taken in the early 1940's. He is in the foreground in this photograph and is wearing Navy flight gear. It is easy to understand why his Navy friends called him 'Big Ed.'

Crashed Navy Plane, Pilot's Body Found

The crashed navy plane and body of Lt. Cmdr. Lilburn A. Edmonston, missing since a take-off from Sand Point Air Station last Tuesday afternoon, were found yesterday afternoon.

The wreckage was spotted 18 miles northeast of Sand Point and a half mile west of Devil's Lake in logged-off land between Woodinville and Duvall.

It was sighted from a navy PBY amphibian piloted by Lt. V. O. Hatfield of Everett, on duty at Sand Point. Spotting the wreckage were Chief Aviation Machinst's Mate W. R. Miller, Radioman J. L. Burris and Technical Devices Man 3C W. B. Ging.

A navy ground party brought the body to Sand Point last night, 13th Naval District headquarters reported.

Commander Edmonston, whose home is in Louisville, Ky., was commander of Flight Squadron 212, Carrier Group 21. He took off from Sand Point at 1:57 p. m. Tuesday and had been sought continuously by navy, air force and coast guard parties after his failure to return.

Seattle Newspaper report of crash

One of the pilots in the Air Group complained of

neck and high back pains the two days while we waited for the fog to lift. He died from polio the same day that the wrecked plane was located.

The write-up in the Seattle newspaper stated that the F6F-5N wreckage was spotted by a PBY. I remember it being spotted by a Coast Guard helicopter. The important thing was that we recovered Babe's body.

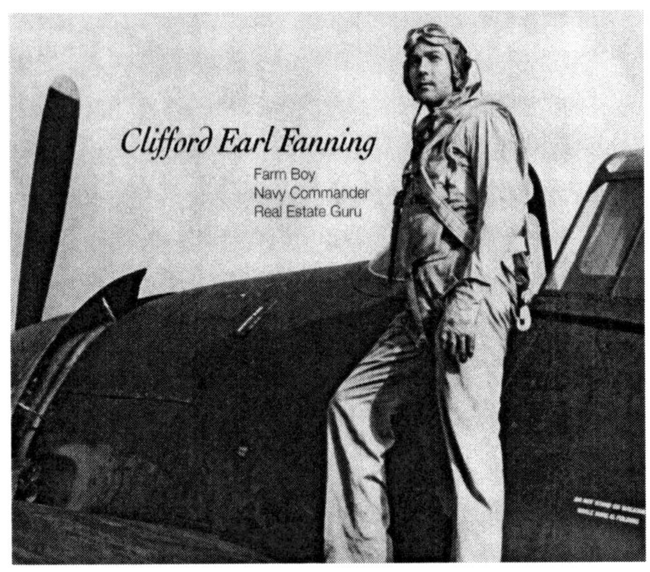

Clifford Earl Fanning
Farm Boy
Navy Commander
Real Estate Guru

Clifford Fanning's memoir © 2011

LCDR Cliff Fanning was the Commanding Officer of VF-211. Cliff and Babe, who commanded the Air Group's two fighter squadrons, were good friends. Babe's home town was New Franklin, Missouri, only a few miles from my home. Cliff accompanied Babe's body home and represented the Navy at his funeral. The service was held in the Kingsbury home where Babe's mother, then a widow, was living. Babe was buried in Mt. Pleasant Cemetery across Highway 5 from the Kingsbury home, just north of New Franklin. Babe's wife, Jean, and infant son returned to Missouri when his body was located.

Cliff Fanning also had an outstanding record as a combat pilot during the war. He was one of 58 Navy pilots on the World War II light carrier USS Bataan, CVL-29. The Bataan was involved in combat at New Guinea, Saipan, Marianas, and the Philippine Sea in 1944. Following repair in the United States, it was in combat at Okinawa and Japan in 1945. It also participated in sinking the giant battleship Yamato. Cliff's decorations included the Distinguished Flying Cross. He later befriended my brother, George, at Pensacola when Cliff was an instructor and George was a cadet.

When Cliff returned to Seattle, he suggested that I drive Edmonston's car home to Missouri, so that Jean would not have to come back to Seattle for it. It was a new Dodge sedan. I left Seattle in the middle of November and drove south into Oregon, and then east across Idaho and Wyoming. It was extremely cold and much snow covered the highways.

I recall passing two hitch-hikers, then after some forty miles or so, there they were again! Apparently someone had picked them up, and then passed me. It was so cold that I did not have the heart to pass them again, even though I had res-

Pilots of VF-211 at NAS Seattle, Washington in March 1949
Standing, left to right: Dunbar, Klindworth, Thompson, Christianson, Fanning, Woodbury, Morris, Hughes, Basye, Pardee;
Kneeling, left to right: Gortney, Kaste, Brown, Wilbur, Struthers, Brannen.

ervations about the wisdom of stopping for them. They were cowboys, and very courteous. I told them that I was going to stop for coffee and asked if they wanted to join me. One of them said "We will watch you drink the coffee." I asked if they did not drink coffee. They replied that they had no money. I pulled into the front of a grocery store and gave them a one-dollar bill, which was worth much more than it is today, of course. They came out with a loaf of bread and some baloney and ate like hungry wolves. They rode with me another 100 miles or so until we got close to the ranch they were heading for.

The car started sliding on a snow covered highway in Wyoming. It was scary, but no harm was done. I delivered the car to Jean. Her parents lived in Boonville.

While visiting Babe's mother to try to ease her grief, she asked me if I could confirm to her that her son's body was in the closed casket. I gave her the details of his accident, of how the ground party found and retrieved his body. I told her I was certain that her son's body was indeed in the casket.

My brother George took me to Fairfax Airport in Kansas City, Kansas. Luckily for me, two Air Force pilots were going from Kansas City to March Air Force Base in Riverside, California in a C-47. They let me ride with them and permitted me fly the C-47 for a time. There were only the three of us on the plane. Riverside was not far from San Diego, and I rode a Navy transport from San Diego back to the base in Seattle.

Grumman F6F-5N Hellcat

The F6F-5N Hellcat we were operating in VF-211 differed from the F6F-5 Hellcat only by the large radar mounted on the right wing. A Navy fighter pilot has many duties; navigator, gunner, flight engineer, radio operator, pilot for carrier landings and take-offs, and anything else that comes up. Now, with this radar system on the F6F-5N, the pilot was asked to assume another demanding task, to monitor and interpret the radar images. Some later Navy fighters had a provision for another crewman to handle some of these duties, thus lessening the load on the pilot. This position was named RIO (Radar Intercept Officer)

One of the non-flying duties assigned to me at Seattle was what the Navy called the "First Lieutenant." This individual is responsible for the maintenance and cleanliness of the squadron spaces. I took custody of a Navy pickup truck and had a sailor assigned full time to assist in these duties. His name was Booker T. Washington, a likeable black man. Since Booker T. had to haul cleaning supplies and get donuts for the pilots ready room every morning, I gave him custody of the pickup truck and keys. Booker T. was popular with the pilots. He always had coffee and donuts at the ready. The Hellcat heaters weren't very efficient and when a pilot landed from a winter flight in Washington State, hot coffee was much appreciated.

I looked out the window one morning and saw that the station police chief had stopped Booker T. The police chief was a Marine Warrant Officer in dress blues. He had been in the Corps a long time. I went out to ask Booker T. what was going on. When he started to answer, it was clear that he had been drinking, although he was not in bad shape. The Marine said, "Oh yes; you are drunk. I'm taking you to sick bay to get a Brogans Test to prove you are drunk. I have me a trophy."

When they left to go to sick bay, I reported to the Commanding Officer, LCDR Fanning, what had occurred. We were not about to let Booker T. be court-martialed. Mr. Fanning said that it would take some time for the Air Station bureaucracy to get court-martial papers to us. He said we will have a Captain's Mast for Booker T. this afternoon. I will call you, his supervisor, as a witness and you can say any nice things about him that you see fit. Mr. Fanning had total authority to conduct the Captain's Mast. He restricted Booker T. to the base for a few days. When we received the Court-Martial papers, we informed the Station that Booker T. had been tried and punished and could not be tried twice for the same offense. Booker T. was saved. The Navy had a decades-old, even centuries-old saying that "loyalty down begets loyalty up." A commanding officer must take care of his men. Mr. Fanning did just that as far as Booker T. was concerned. He was a kind, firm, gentleman and an outstanding Commanding Officer. Cliff retired from the Navy after completing 22 years of duty. He lives at Pensacola. His book titled *Memoirs of Cliff E. Fanning* is copyrighted 2011. It includes an excellent description of life on a Midwestern farm in the 1920's and 1930's during the depression.

F6F Hellcat

F4U Corsair

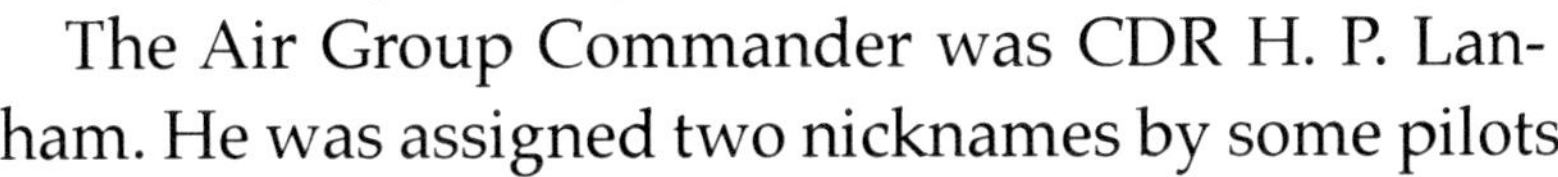

The Air Group Commander was CDR H. P. Lanham. He was assigned two nicknames by some pilots. The first was "Hot Pilot Lanham" because of his initials. The other was "'Living on borrowed time' Lanham." I do not know why someone came up with that one, but it stuck. Anyone using it made certain that Lanham did not overhear them.

CDR Lanham graduated from the Naval Academy in 1937. He was awarded two Distinguished Flying Crosses, a Silver Star, and two Legions of Merit. He was one of the Navy pilots who shared in winning the important Battle of Midway in June of 1942. Lanham was promoted to Rear Admiral before his death in 1973.

The airport runways featured lights, with large glass enclosures, that stood about 18 inches high along each edge. When the F6F Hellcat was on the surface with the tail wheel touching the surface, it was extremely difficult for the pilot to

Chance Vought F7U Cutlass

see outside the plane. The F4U Corsair proved even more difficult. As a result of the vision difficulties, several pilots broke the runway lights by hitting them with landing gear or propeller. CDR Lanham decided to solve the problem. He announced, "The next son-of-a-bitch that hits one of these lights is going to answer to me."

Not long after this edict, he informed our squadron he wanted to fly that afternoon. He told us to prepare a Hellcat for him and to as-

Hal Avants and his seven students at Jacksonville in 1948.
Top: Hal Avants, Robert S. Hamilton, Leo Franz
Middle: William Quarg, Hal Marr, Robert Horton
Bottom: Lee Zeni and Dave Barksdale

sign another Hellcat pilot to accompany him. I lucked out and was assigned to be his flight mate. We taxied out and I was perhaps 150 feet behind him. I saw him headed for a light and hoped he would nail it. He did. The propeller struck the light and glass flew in all directions. He turned his plane sideways so that he could look at me and asked me by radio if his plane was damaged. I told him that his plane looked OK. The tower operator directed him to return to the flight line to get his aircraft inspected. He replied that it was already inspected and he roared down the runway. When we returned, the subject of the broken runway light did not come up for discussion as we walked from the flight line to the hangar. So much for one S. O. B. having to answer to another one.

Hal Avants, a pilot on CDR Lanham's Air Group staff, had been an instructor in the advanced training unit at Jacksonville the previous year while we were at Jacksonville. The photograph shows Hal in the F6F cockpit and also shows his seven student pilots. One morning the phone in our squadron office rang and was answered by pilot Christianson. He yelled to me: "Hey, Basye. What is Thompson's girl's phone number? Avants was with her last night and they can't find him." Hal was killed several years later, while flying a Chance Vought F7U Cutlass. The Cutlass was powered by two Westinghouse J-46 jet engines with afterburners. Hal was flying in a two plane formation with Ron Puckett. I do not know any details about Hal's accident.

Snow covers a significant part of the area east of Seattle and some of it never melts. Many airplanes crash in the snow and are never found. A Navy transport pilot who lived in the same two-room unit as I went out in a SNJ for a local flight. He was accustomed to a much more extensive navigation system in the transports he normally flew than the SNJ possessed. He told the Navy tower he was lost. We never heard from him again. He was from Tennessee. His mother came to the area every summer for several years looking for him. The SNJ, as well as the F6F and F4U, had navigation systems that were markedly inferior to both transports and the newer jet fighters.

The six midshipmen in the Ream Field photograph, along with several others, were promoted to Ensign as a group. An appropriate celebration in the Officers Club marked the happy occasion. At the conclusion of the party, all but one participant went to bed. That one decided to go to downtown Seattle. He rode a bus to the vicinity of the University of Washington and fell asleep in the snow while waiting for a transfer to the downtown bus. Someone called the Seattle police, who deposited him in the Seattle drunk tank. The police called the base and someone went to retrieve him. The pilot assigned to pick him up was informed that he had

Pilots of VF-211 at NAS Seattle, Washington in March 1949—Left to Right: Gortney, Kaste, Brown, Basye, Klindworth, Thompson, Fanning, Christianson, Woodbury, Morris, Hughes, Pardee, Brannen, Wilbor, Struthers, Dunbar

been voted best dressed man in the tank. The other tank inhabitants were impressed that he was to be released so soon. Some pleaded with him to get them released. He assured them that he would have all of them out by morning. Of course, he had no intention, or capability, of securing their release.

In early March 1949, we learned that Air Group 21, which had only existed some six months, was to be de-commissioned. We were to deliver the airplanes to Marine Corps Air Station, El Toro, California, and NAS San Diego. Then we were to report to NAS San Diego for re-assignment. I delivered an F6F-5N to El Toro, then rode a Navy transport back to Seattle. Nine of us were told to take Hellcats to San Diego. Bad weather delayed us several days. Finally, on 22 March 1949, we were told that the weather was good enough to begin the trip to San Diego. Because I was senior in rank, I became the flight leader. The other eight were new ensigns, having recently been promoted from midshipman.

Our first stop was to be at Medford, in southern Oregon. Initially the flight was uneventful. I checked the weather as we passed Portland. The weather station said that we would encounter no bad weather between Portland and Medford. It did not take long to realize that the weather people were sadly mistaken. Before we got to Medford, the clouds descended to the mountain tops. Five of us turned around and went back to Eugene. The other four somehow followed the highway and got to Medford without hitting any mountains. It was quite a feat.

When the five of us got back to Eugene, we were almost out of gasoline. Our flight charts showed a reasonably large airport at the southwest edge of Eugene and a smaller airport some ten miles west. None of us had been to Eugene, so we had no way of knowing that the flight charts were wrong. The large airport was the one which the charts showed to be the small one, and vice versa. We all landed at the small airport. The asphalt runway there was not intended to land airplanes as heavy as the Hellcat. Our main wheels left impressions in the asphalt. We waited there for two or three days, hoping for good weather. A man who operated a service business took us to and from our hotel. We bought some low-octane gasoline from him. We had enough high-octane gas to take off on. We would then switch over to the low-octane fuel, which was adequate for lower power settings. We would then fly the ten miles to the other airport where high-octane gas was available. The airport manager was irritated that we did not buy gasoline from him. He told me that we were forbidden from taking off because it would further damage the asphalt. We ignored this command, of course. Meanwhile, we had gotten acquainted with some lumberjacks at a watering hole in the evenings. They said; "You boys give us an air show when you leave." Al Kaste did just that. He did a low altitude slow roll for their benefit.

We delivered the airplanes to San Diego and returned to Seattle on a Navy transport plane. The Base Commander called us to his office. He had received a letter from the irate airport manager in Eugene. In it, the proprietor said that we disobeyed his orders, did aerobatics on takeoff, tore up his runway, weren't gentlemen and a few other things. Not bad for five young Navy fighter pilots. What might the letter have said had we stayed longer? I told the Captain what had happened and that if we had not flown the Hellcats out as we had done, they would have had to be disassembled and trucked out.

The Captain thought a while and said; "Boys, the only thing you did wrong was that you did not bullshit that son-of-a-bitch out of writing that damned letter. Now I have to fix his damned runway." He then turned his attention to Al Kaste and said; "I am going to see to it that you be assigned to fly torpedo bombers. See if you can slow roll that son-of-a-bitch on takeoff."

28 March 1949 Eugene Register-Guard (OREGON)

BASYE
BROWN
KASTE
ZAJICHEK
JONES

BAD WEATHER DOWNED these U. S. Navy fighters in Eugene Tuesday and temporarily disrupted a flight to San Diego Wednesday. Five Grauman "Hellcats," F6F 5-N, which had taken off from Sand Point Naval Base, Seattle, were turned back to Eugene by foul weather over the Sextons. They landed at the Eugene Airpark where one fighter overran the runway. Navy pilots said they hoped to continue the flight Wednesday.
(Staff photo, Wiltshire engraving.)

Eugene, OR Register-Guard photograph, March 1949
Pilots of the five F6F-5N Hellcats were Don Brown, Bob Zajichek, Al Kaste, Ben Basye, and Jones.
(Jones' first name escapes me.)

We then returned to San Diego for reassignment. Four of us became jet pilots and Kaste was assigned to fly the TBF torpedo bomber, which cannot be slow-rolled.

My next duty assignment was VF-52 at NAS, San Diego. VF-51 and VF-52 were the only two jet fighter squadrons in the Pacific Fleet. CDR Ed Pawka was Commanding Officer of VF-52. He was one of the most experienced fighter pilots in the Navy. VF-52 flew the Lockheed TO-1 jet fighter. This is the designation the Navy used for the F-80 C Shooting Star. The two airplanes were identical. The Navy used the TO-1 only because the Grumman F9F Panther was not yet available. As soon as the Panthers arrived, the TO-1's were assigned to the training command. Everything we did in VF-52 was designed to prepare for a tour to the Far East on the USS Valley Forge, scheduled to embark on about 1 May 1950. Air Group 5 consisted of VF-51, VF-52, and three propeller squadrons. The entire Air Group was scheduled for the far-east tour on the Valley Forge. CDR Lanham was Air Group Commander.

There were no two-seat jet trainers available at this early stage of Navy jet operations. We spent several days in lectures related to the Shooting Star. Finally, on 14 April 1949, I made my first flight in the F-80. I remember it well. When I became airborne and retracted the landing gear, the nose wheel retracted just under my heels. The rotating nose tire rubbed the surface under my feet. The resulting noise and vibration was quite a sensation. This was not a serious problem, and did not cause any concern after I knew what was happening.

On the third day I flew the F-80, several of us were making simulated gunnery runs at one of our jets. We were over the Pacific Ocean, south of San Diego and west of Mexico. One of my fellow pilots served as the designated target plane as we flew south. When it was time to turn around and head north toward San Diego, the flight leader instructed me to assume the target position on the trip back north. I throttled back to lose altitude and take up the target plane position. To my surprise, there was about two or three inches of throttle movement with no change in engine speed. The engine was not decelerating as I expected when I throttled back. We had been told that the engine had a main fuel control and an emergency fuel control. We were told that the emergency fuel control could be turned on at any time something might be wrong with the main control. I turned on the emergency fuel control. The engine flamed out, since the two fuel controls were not calibrated. This was not a good situation—30,000 feet over the Pacific, off the Mexican Coast, and the engine had flamed out. There was no fire in the engine. The recommended practice in this situation is to shut the fuel off, dive, and then pull the nose up, so that hopefully gravity will take excess fuel out through the exhaust. Then, try for an air start. I did succeed in getting the engine started again, but it started extremely hot. Excess fuel in the engine probably caused the hot start. I landed successfully at San Diego. Because the Station had been informed of the situation, there was a big audience when I landed. The engine was sent to overhaul due to the hot start. Thus, as far as I know, I had the distinction of being the only Navy pilot to have a flame out in our F-80's. What I had missed during the lectures was the fact that the jets —as opposed to piston engines—idle much faster at altitude than at sea level. Five of us new jet pilots attended the lectures and only one picked up this point.

Several Lockheed test pilots had bad experiences with the F-80. On 20 March 1945, test pilot Tony LeVier suffered a broken back when he ejected from the Grey Ghost, one of the first F-80's, due to a failed turbine blade. Chief engineering test pilot Milo Burcham was killed on 20 October 1944. Also, Major Richard Bong was killed on 6 August 1945 in an acceptance flight of a production F-80. Major Bong was the highest scoring World War II U. S. air ace, with a score of more than 40 Japanese planes. He had been awarded the Medal of Honor. Both the Burcham and Bong accidents involved fuel system problems with main/emergency questions somewhat akin to the situation I was in over the Pacific. I had the good fortune of being at 30,000 feet, while their problems occurred at low altitude. I had time to analyze the situation.

Major Bong was once grounded for flying down Market Street in San Francisco. The General who reprimanded him said, "If you did not want to fly down Market

Street, I would not want you. But don't do it anymore." Bong was a midwestern farm boy. He was a part of the successful military culture discussed previously. It is truly tragic that today's civilian bureaucrats, as well as many high ranking uniformed military bureaucrats, are determined to eradicate that culture and replace it with a politically correct culture. The results have frequently been catastrophic.

I once spent some 30 minutes answering questions for Tony LeVier about the F-80. I did not know that I was talking to the famous test pilot, although I certainly knew who Tony LeVier was. The Navy invited some 200 individuals from aviation related companies around Los Angeles to spend a day on the Valley Forge and to watch F9F Panther landings and catapult launches. Commander Pawka and several of my other friends were conducting the flying demonstration. We left San Diego on the Valley Forge and traveled up close to Long Beach. Our visitors came out to the ship in boats as I recall. Commander Pawka told me to remain on the hangar deck next to one of our F9F Panthers and answer any questions posed by the visitors. I was a veteran of a number of successful jet carrier landings and catapult launches.

Famed Lockheed test pilot Tony LeVier

A group of about five visitors approached and one of them asked me what I had flown prior to the F9F Panther. When I answered that it was the Lockheed F-80, he became most interested. He asked me question after question about the F-80. They related to safety procedures, operating characteristics, and about everything one could imagine. When he was ready to leave, he said to tell CDR Pawka hello. I asked him to tell me who was saying hello. He answered that he was Tony LeVier. So I enjoy the distinction of conducting a seminar for Tony LeVier, the test pilot who made the first flight not only in the F-80 but in the U-2 spy plane and many other famous Lockheed aircraft. As noted above, he also suffered a broken back in an early F-80 accident. It should be noted that Tony LeVier was a high school dropout.

The Gray Ghost; Tony LeVier was seriously injured when a failed turbine blade caused structural failure in this early F-80 Shooting Star.

Jim Gagnon, a VF-52 pilot,

took off from NAS San Diego one day. His destination was NAS Alameda, just south of Oakland, across the Bay from San Francisco. His F-80 had fuel tanks at the tip of each wing. Each held about 1,000 pounds of fuel. As he was going up the coast over La Jolla, the plane suddenly rotated with the wings up and down. The right tip tank had dropped off and the plane was unbalanced. He said he looked down over the left wing and saw water, so he thought he was over the ocean. To re-balance the plane, he released the left tip tank. Unfortunately, both tanks fell in La Jolla. Jet fuel is not as flammable as gasoline, so neither tank exploded or burned. One fell in a yard between houses and did little damage. A mail delivery man said he looked up and saw the second tank coming at him. He said that whatever direction he ran, the tank followed. The tank ruptured and sprayed jet fuel on him but, other than a laundry bill, he suffered no serious consequences. The mayor of La Jolla was irate about the entire episode. He demanded that the pilot appear in court. The Navy and the town eventually resolved the matter. Jim was a reserve officer, like me. He later became the Director of the El Paso International Airport.

The Navy was developing and testing missiles of various kinds during this time period. The Loon was the Navy version of the German V-1 buzz bomb which terrorized London during World War II. On one occasion, a Loon test missile was to be fired out over the Pacific Ocean from the Navy missile facility at Pt. Mugu, just up the Pacific Coast from Los Angeles and Malibu. There was concern that a malfunction might occur in the missile guidance system, and that the missile might turn and come back into California. The missile was a sub-sonic missile, so the F-80 Shooting Star could keep up with it. I was assigned the task of following the missile and shooting it down if it indeed turned around, instead of going on out to sea. My F-80 had a full complement of ammunition in the six 50 caliber machine guns and my flight path was directed in such a manner that I was behind the missile and following it when it was launched. It went on out to sea as planned, so I did not get to shoot it down, although I followed it until advised to return to San Diego.

Guided Loon Missile
near Pt. Mugu

Our squadron had an officers head (Navy for "bathroom") with two sinks. Above one sink was a nice rectangular mirror with rounded corners and a chrome plated metal border. The other sink had no mirror, but appeared to have had one earlier. CDR Pawka told me, "I want you to get a matching mirror mounted above the other sink." As was the case at Seattle, I had the collateral duty of keeping up our assigned spaces. We were taught as cadets that a request from a senior officer is to be treated the same as a direct order. I took his request in that fashion.

I visited every Navy Supply facility around. There were no matching mirrors. However, an officers head in another unit's assigned space had such mirrors above both sinks. The next time I had security duty from midnight until 4 a.m., I was prepared. I stationed my guards around the airplanes and took my tools to the other head. A farm boy could remove a mirror easily, and I did. I hung it in our head. The next morning Pawka came out of the head absolutely beaming. He said, "You got a mirror. Where did you get it"? I told him. He started cussing and went into a war dance. Then he said: "Jesus Christ! You would steal from your own friends in the Navy." But he did not tell me to return it. It was still there the last time I saw that head.

The nickname everyone used to refer to Pawka was 'Boris.' He had a striking resemblance to Hollywood actor Boris Karloff who played the part of Frankenstein in the horror movies. You made sure that he never heard you say Boris, however. Ed Pawka was awarded the Distinguished Flying Cross, the Silver Star, and several Air Medals for his World War II service.

Several new pilots were assigned to VF-52 after I had been in the squadron for some time. A gunnery flight out over the Pacific was scheduled for five of us—Pawka, three new pilots, and me. Each pilot's ammunition was painted a different color. When we returned, the ground crew could count how many holes in the target had each paint color around them. The new pilots and I were down at the line shack waiting for CDR Pawka when he strolled in. He slapped a half dollar on the counter and told the chief that each of the other four pilots was going to also give the chief a half dollar. He said that whoever had the most hits would get the $2.50. Pawka did not take kindly to losing. He knew that I was his only competition because the three new pilots were more interested in just getting back safely than anything else. He figured that his odds were pretty good. When we returned, I had thirty-nine hits, Pawka had sixteen, and the other three had a total of about five. Each of us fired a total of 120 rounds at the target. It was not a pleasant scene. Some thirty or forty of the enlisted men in the squadron witnessed the counting. It was hard for some of them not to laugh because the Old Man's challenge came back to bite him.

We had a gunnery competition in August 1949. We flew F-80's, since the F9F's were not yet available in sufficient numbers. The F-80 had six 50-caliber machine guns in the nose, while the F9F had four 20-millimeter cannons in their nose. The 50-caliber was 1/2 inch in diameter while the 20-millimeter was about 8/10 inch. The 20-millimeter did significantly more damage to anything that it hit. I received this commendation for my successful participation in the competition.

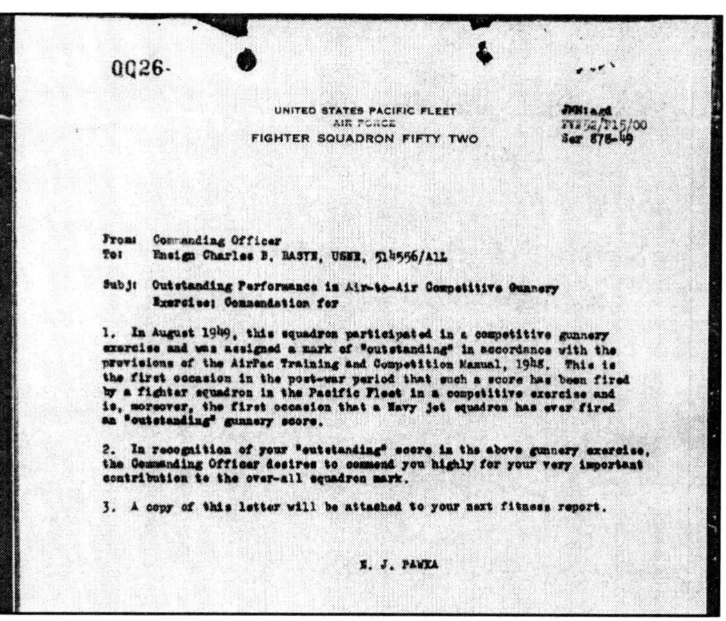

0Q26-

UNITED STATES PACIFIC FLEET
AIR FORCE
FIGHTER SQUADRON FIFTY TWO

JMN:agd
FV52/P15/00
Ser 878-49

From: Commanding Officer
To: Ensign Charles B. BASYE, USNR, 514556/A1L

Subj: Outstanding Performance in Air-to-Air Competitive Gunnery Exercise; Commendation for

1. In August 1949, this squadron participated in a competitive gunnery exercise and was assigned a mark of "outstanding" in accordance with the provisions of the AirPac Training and Competition Manual, 1948. This is the first occasion in the post-war period that such a score has been fired by a fighter squadron in the Pacific Fleet in a competitive exercise and is, moreover, the first occasion that a Navy jet squadron has ever fired an "outstanding" gunnery score.

2. In recognition of your "outstanding" score in the above gunnery exercise, the Commanding Officer desires to commend you highly for your very important contribution to the over-all squadron mark.

3. A copy of this letter will be attached to your next fitness report.

E. J. PAWKA

Gunnery Commendation

By mid-August, the F9F Panthers began to arrive and we immediately started flying them. We were still flying the F-80's, also. The F-80 was the first jet fighter the U. S. Army Air Force used operationally. The F9F Panther was the first jet fighter the Navy used operationally in the Pacific Fleet, while the McDonnell F2H Banshee filled the same role in the Atlantic Fleet. On 26 August 1949, Dick Bates, Dude Brannan, and I were assigned to take three of the F-80's to Pensacola, so that the Training Command could use them. Dick was flight leader because he was senior to Dude and me. We lined up for a formation takeoff with Dick on the left, Dude to his right and slightly behind him, and me to Dude's right and slightly behind him. As we started rolling, I noticed that we were not using full power as we should have been. I only had 93% rpm and it should have been 100%. After a time, I applied full power and passed Dude. I had about 50 feet of altitude at the end of the runway while the two of them were much slower getting airborne. Because we had full wing tip tanks, full power was essential. Dick's nickname was 'Weak Eyes.' We stayed at Kelly AFB in San Antonio for two nights because of a hurricane threatening Pensacola. We travelled from San Antonio to Pensacola on a Sunday morning and went right over Pasadena, TX, which was Dude's home town. Dick and I stayed at an altitude which was legal, but Dude was much lower. He went right over the church his family attended and said he had to look up to see the writing on the town water tower. Everyone in Pasadena knew that he was there.

In September, October, and early November, 1949, we were busy with lots of gunnery practice and practice for landing on the USS Boxer with the new F9F Panthers. The carrier landings were scheduled for mid-November. We practiced extensively by landing on a runway with the painted outline of an Essex Class carrier deck, at Brown Field, southeast of San Diego. Our LSO was an experienced Navy pilot named Peterson. The painted carrier deck was about 1,000 feet up the runway from the ground runway's end. As we approached Peterson and the painted deck, we flew over the 1,000 feet of runway. There were thermal updrafts. If we did not throttle back a little, we would gain either altitude or airspeed due to these updrafts. Pilots developed a habit of throttling back slightly about 1,000 feet before getting to the LSO.

CDR Pawka was assigned to make the first landing of VF-52 pilots on the real Boxer's flight deck on 16 November 1949. We were all at various positions on the carrier island watching as he approached. He got too low and/or slow before he reached the ship. LSO Peterson gave him a wave-off signal. Pawka applied full power and tried not to land. Meanwhile, Peterson dived over the side into a safety net rigged there for the LSO if he thought an approaching airplane was about to hit him. Pawka probably throttled back slightly as we had been doing in the Brown Field practices. Propeller fighters change attitude slightly as they reduce speed in situations like this. There is also a slight noise change. Not so with the jets. That explains why Peterson did not realize that Pawka was getting too low and slow until it was almost too late.

Pawka barely cleared the flight deck's stern. He was so low that his tail hook grabbed a wire even though he was trying not to land. The wire jerked the plane down on the flight deck so abruptly that the nose wheel was driven up through the nose structure of the plane. He was going slightly to the left and came to rest with the left wing sticking out over the ocean. It was quite a demonstration for the rest of us. The next day it was our turn. I made six successful landings and six catapult takeoffs on 17 November 1949. See the entry in my pilot log book verifying my landings and catapult launches on 17 November.

The Los Angeles Times covered these early jet landings and catapult takeoffs on the Boxer. Photographs of VF-52 airplanes, personnel, and the Boxer covered the entire third page of the 17 November 1949 issue. LSO Peterson is shown with his signal flags in the lower center part of this page. Page 2 included a story.

I have included a copy of the Los Angeles Times full page spread. The quality is not perfect, but I have been saving this newspaper for more than 62 years. From it, one can get an idea of the significant coverage of these early jet fighter/aircraft carrier operations.

Los Angeles Times * THURS., NOV. 17, 1949—Part I 3

Jet Planes Shoot Off Giant Carrier in Qualification Flights

HEADED FOR SKY—A Panther jet fighter plane is shown as it is being catapulted from the giant aircraft carrier, the USS Boxer, off the coast of Southern California. Navy's qualification flights were made yesterday.

COMING IN—With hook down, the Panther fighter comes in for landing on the USS Boxer. The craft land at a speed better than 100 miles an hour. The pilot has just received the "cut" signal telling him to "chop" throttle and come in. Precision must be exercised in landing.

HIGH UP—Here the fighter plane circles high above the flat-top in preparation for its return to the "mother" ship. The picture was taken from carrier's flight deck.

LANDING SIGNAL—Lt. H. W. Peterson Jr. gives the pilot the signal that the way is clear for the landing.

CONFERENCE—Lt. W. W. Peterson, Capt. W. W. Fincher and Maj. Ed H. Connor, left to right, gather on the deck after flight to discuss their reactions to maneuvers.

See story Page 2, Part I

Times photos

Panther landing on the USS Boxer

This is a photograph of a Panther landing on the Boxer. It is noteworthy because it shows a perfect landing. The nose wheel is coming down precisely on the striped painted line and the F9F is headed straight up the deck. The tail hook can be seen beneath the plane just before it engaged one of the wires across the deck. Either myself or one of my friends was the pilot; I cannot tell from the photograph. In any case, it was perfect!

As a matter of interest, the Boxer was sold for scrap in the late 1960's. While in Norfolk in 1969, I went aboard the Boxer one last time. It was tied up at the Norfolk Navy Base, in preparation for turnover to the scrap buyer.

The following is a picture cropped from a wide angle picture of all five squadrons of Air Group 5 showing VF-52 personnel in front of an F9F Panther. The sailors standing in front are part of the Air Group Commanders staff. Behind them are the pilots, from the left; Dick Bates, Bill Bauhof, Jim Gagnon, Howard Boydston,

Behind the sailors are the pilots of VF-52:
from the left; Dick Bates, Bill Bauhof, Jim Gagnon, Howard Boydston, CDR Ed Pawka, James Davidson, Fred Cockrel, an unidentified maintenance officer, and Wayne Cheal. From the left in the next row; Dude Brannen, Lou Simmons, Jim Gallivan, Chuck Deasy, myself, Gene Lewis, Bob Zajichek, and Leading Chief Sheehan

CDR Ed Pawka, James Davidson, Fred Cockrel, an unidentified maintenance officer, and Wayne Cheal. From the left in the next row; Dude Brannen, Lou Simmons, Jim Gallivan, Chuck Deasy, myself, Gene Lewis, Bob Zajichek, and Leading Chief

Sheehan.

Several pilots joined the squadron later, including Jim Verdin, Dave Tatum, and Luther Duncan. Bill Bauhof was detached from VF-52 in early 1950 and was a member of Test Pilot Training School Class 4 at the NAS Patuxent River, MD. This class convened in February 1950. Bill was extremely elated to be selected for this test pilot training. Tragically, Bill was killed on 11 May 1950 in the crash of a Lockheed XP2V-1 Neptune at Patuxent River. Dave was from Louisiana and was shot down three times in Korea before being killed. Luther was from Houston, TX. He was stone deaf in one ear but succeeded in keeping the Navy from detecting it. Had examining medical personnel discovered his deafness, he would have been washed out of flight training. His nickname was 'Seawall Grill' because he had been involved in a late night altercation in a greasy spoon restaurant in Corpus Christi called the Seawall Grill.

Bob Zajichek was from Milwaukee. While we were at San Diego after returning from Seattle, Bob married a girl we both knew from Seattle. Her name was Ruth. He did not have the money to buy the ring so I loaned it to him. There was never any interest involved in loans like this. Bob was one of the five pilots involved in the adventure at Eugene, OR. The "Sounding Taps" column in the October 2005 issue of Military Officer Magazine noted the deaths of Bob Zajichek and Ed Pawka.

Most of the senior pilots in VF-52 were decorated combat veterans of World War II. They included Bates, Bauhof, Gagnon, Boydston, Pawka, Davidson, and Cheal. CDR Lanham and his replacement as Air Group Commander, CDR Keats, also

Lockheed F-80 (TO-1) Shooting Star of VF-52—The "S" on tail indicates Navy Air Group Five, NAS San Diego, CA. The "2" in 214 indicates VF-52.

MONTH November YEAR 1949

DAY	AIRCRAFT MODEL	AIRCRAFT BUREAU No.	CHARACTER OF FLIGHT	FLIGHT TIME AS PILOT	CO-PILOT	STUDENT	PASSENGER	TOTAL FLIGHT TIME
1	F9F3	123029	1A6	1.7				1.7
1	"	123040	1A2	1.6				3.3
2	"	123030	1A0	1.1				4.4
3	"	123028	1A6	1.4				5.8
4	"	123028	1A3	.8				6.6
9	"	123042	1A3	.8				7.4
13	"	123027	1A7	2.3				9.7
14	"	123032	1A6	1.8				11.5
14	"	123040	1A3	.8				12.3
17	"	123035	1A4	.3				12.6
17	"	123031	1A4	.6				13.2
21	"	123037	1A2 1A0	1.6				14.8
23	"	123032	1A2 1A0	1.8				16.6
16.6 TOTAL—THIS PAGE								
769.3 BROUGHT FWD.								
785.9 GRAND TOTAL								

16—13816-1

SPECIAL PILOT TIME: INSTRUMENT | MULTI-ENGINE DAY | NIGHT | SINGLE ENGINE NIGHT | NUMBER CARRIER LDGS. | REMARKS

NOV 17 1949

QUAL F9F

USS BOXER 6 LANDINGS

SIX CATAPULT SHOTS

NUMBER CARRIER LDGS.	
6	I certify that the foregoing flight record is correct.
13	[signature] PILOT
19	APPROVED [signature]

16—13816-1

Author's log book showing jet fighter landings and catapult launches on USS Boxer on 17 November 1949

had that background, as did Jim Verdin. CDR Keats was short in stature with short legs. Someone started a nickname of 'Low Crotch' to identify him by. This nickname was used with extreme caution, of course. Dick Bates, Jim Verdin and Bill Bauhof had each received the Navy Cross, which ranks second only to the Medal of Honor. James Davidson had the distinction of being the first Navy pilot to make a series of takeoffs and landings of a jet on a carrier. He did this on 21 July 1946, on the longest aircraft carrier in the fleet at that time, the USS Franklin D. Roosevelt. The aircraft was a XFD-1 (later called the FH-1) McDonnell Phantom, powered by two Westinghouse J-30 jet engines. I am honored to have been an associate of such accomplished naval aviators.

The Boxer deployed to the Far East after the VF-52 operations of 16 and 17 November 1949. The Navy tried to keep either the Boxer or the Valley Forge close to the West Coast for training, and to operate the other in the WESTPAC as much as possible. We conducted flight operations on the Valley Forge from 17 to 24 January 1950, on 17, 18, and 19 February, and on 2, 3, and 6 March. When we were not operating on the carrier, there were other kinds of training. Aerial gunnery got the most attention. We did our the gunnery firing over the Pacific Ocean and at the Chocolate Mountain gunnery range, northeast of El Centro, California.

Author next to exhaust nozzle of Allison J-33 jet engine in F-80

As noted earlier, the F9F Panther was outfitted with the 20-millimeter cannon. The damage done by a 20-mm. round was considerably more severe than that done by the 50-caliber round. I remember one day at El Centro when we shot six out of ten targets loose from the tow plane with the 20 mm cannons. The same tow targets tolerated numerous hits from 50-caliber machine guns without becoming detached from the tow plane. On 20 March 1950, while we were operating out of the Naval Auxiliary Air Station at El Centro, I shot the line that attached the target to the tow plane completely in two. The target incorporated a galvanized pipe about three feet long and an inch in diameter to which the tow line was attached. A rectangular nylon mesh panel about three feet by twenty feet was attached to the pipe. We fired at this mesh panel and it displayed the colored bullet holes. A metal weight was attached to the pipe in such a manner that gravity kept the pipe and target from spinning. When I severed the tow line, air drag slowed the target down so that it appeared to stop right in front of my F9F. When the pipe hit my right wing—about eight feet from the cockpit—I was probably going 400 miles per hour faster than the pipe. The impact of the pipe on the wing probably occurred in less than a second from the instant the tow line parted. There was no time to evade the collision. Only fate prevented the pipe from hitting at the cockpit or engine intake. The consequences in either case could have been immense. As it was, I successfully landed the plane, although about twenty miles per hour faster than usual. NAS San Diego sent a new wing to El Centro by truck.

On another gunnery flight over the Pacific Ocean, off the Mexican coast, I shot the metal weight loose from the pipe and watched it rotate as it descended towards the ocean.

It was extremely hot when we practiced at the Chocolate Mountain gunnery range, in the desert northeast of El Centro. We started flight operations early and stayed in the shade from about 10 am until 3 pm. Then we flew again, at night. During one of the night flights, I was the last jet to land, and there were several Marine pilots flying Grumman F7F Tigercat twin engine propeller fighters who were also ready to land. The control tower operator told the Marines to land after the last jet, which was me. The Marine pilot did not see me, and I did not realize that he landed in front of me. About the time that I recognized the slower moving propeller plane on the runway in front of me, the control tower operator yelled for the Marine to speed up, which he did. I was able to brake enough to avoid running into the Tigercat. It is difficult to see other airplanes at night in situations like this one.

I had considerable success in scoring hits in the early part of the extended gunnery practice. The jets had gun sights that calculated how far to lead the target. The pilot had to keep a projected dot image on the target and the gun sight automatically aimed the plane the right distance ahead of the target to register a hit. The sight used plane speed and tightness of turn among other factors. I concluded that it was crucial to fly a smooth approach turn as opposed to firing when the dot was temporarily on the target during uneven flight. I also allowed about one foot for gravity drop and went in close to the target. These three things seemed to work.

CDR Pawka was impressed by my success but would not ask a lowly Ensign to reveal the technique. Instead, he directed his second in command, LCDR Davidson, to have me explain the secret to the other squadron pilots at an all-pilots meeting. Davidson could then tell Pawka. The World War II Corsairs and Hellcats were not equipped with these more advanced gun sights. The older gun sights projected an image ahead of the plane. The pilot had to use his judgment in leading the target.

One evening while we were operating out of El Centro, several of the older pilots, including Boris (CDR Pawka) decided to go to a Mexican restaurant across the border from El Centro to get large steaks. While they were gone, several of us who stayed behind, removed the sheets and pillow from Chuck Deasy's bed. There was a large heavy refrigerator with a rounded front. It was about the size of a large casket. We placed it on his bed, rounded side up, and made up his bed on top of the refrigerator. The refrigerator weighed at least 400 pounds. We then locked our room doors and went to bed. When they returned, no one would help

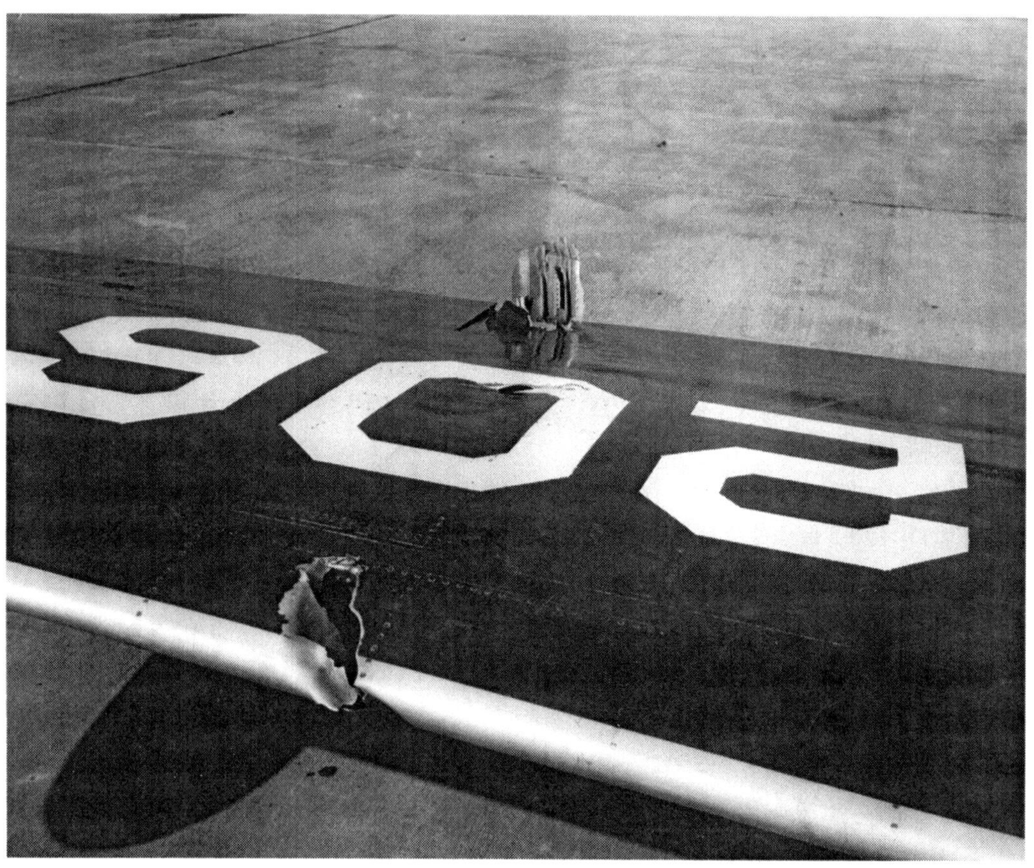

Damaged right wing of Author's F9F Panther caused by impact with gunnery target. 20 March 1950, El Centro, CA

him lift the refrigerator off of his bed. We were treated to quite a volley of Navy cussing. I do not recall where he slept that night.

The next photograph shows the damage to the right wing of my F9F caused by impact with the pipe attached to a gunnery target.

Another photograph shows a piece of the nylon mesh target material that lodged in the cavity in the damaged wing's leading edge. Also note the copy of the entry in my pilot log book, describing the collision with the target.

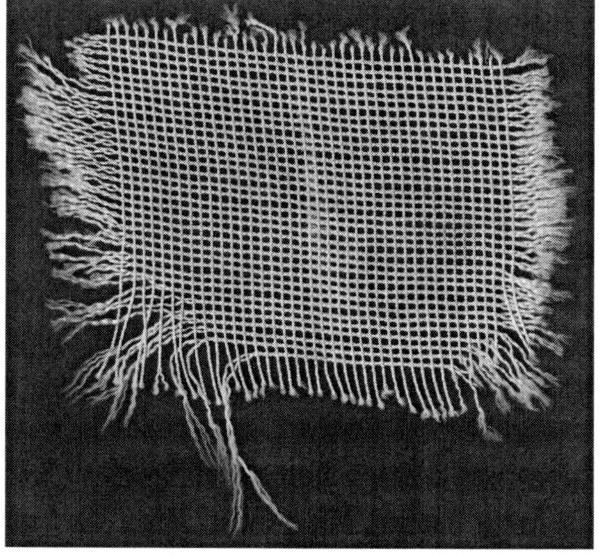

Target material lodged in damaged wing leading edge cavity

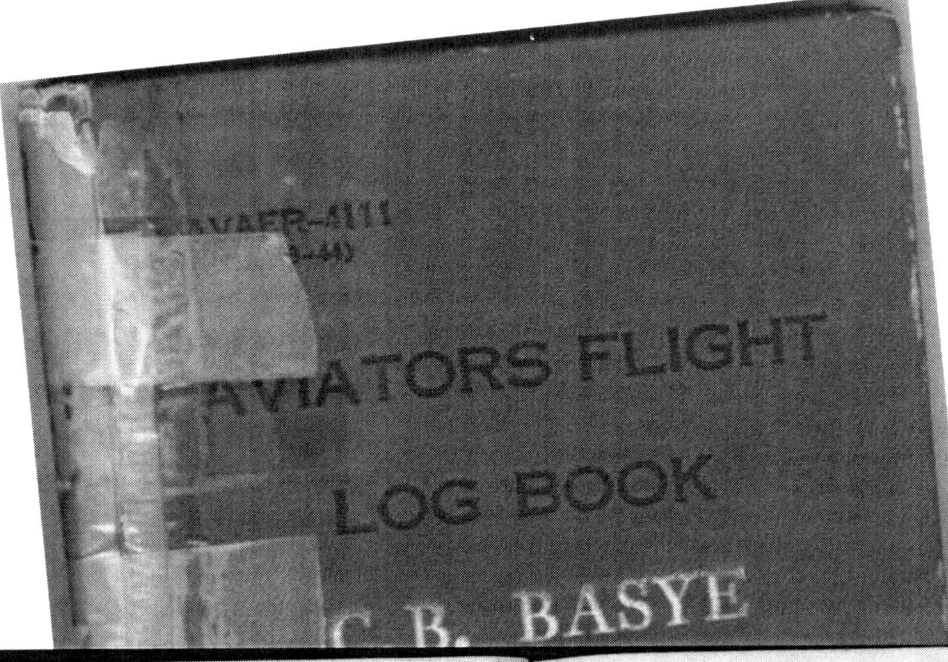

MONTH March YEAR 1950

DAY	AIRCRAFT MODEL	AIRCRAFT BUREAU No.	CHARACTER OF FLIGHT	FLIGHT TIME AS PILOT	CO-PILOT	STUDENT	PASSENGER	TOTAL FLIGHT TIME	INSTRUMENT	MULTI-ENGINE DAY	MULTI-ENGINE NIGHT	SINGLE ENGINE NIGHT	NUMBER CARRIER LDGS.	REMARKS
1	F9F-3	123029	2A1	1.3				1.3	✓					
2	"	123029	2A1	1.9				3.2	✓					1 C.L. 1 CAT
2	"	123064	2A6	1.7				4.9	✓					1 C.L. 1 CAT
3	"	123039	3A1	1.3				6.2	✓					1 C.L.
6	"	122582	1A6	2.0				8.2						1 CAT
7	"	123075	1A6	2.0				10.2						
7	"	123037	1A6	1.5				11.7						
8	"	123027	1A6	1.0				12.7						Lead Pilot
11	"	123024	1A1	1.6				14.3						X-C San Diego–El Paso
11	"	123024	1A1	1.7				[illegible]						X-C El Paso–San Diego
13	"	123032	1A6	1.3				17.3						
14	"	123026	1A6	1.4				18.7						
15	"	123037	1A6	1.1				19.8						
16	"	123037	1A6	1.6				21.4						
17	"	123040	1A6	1.0				22.4						
19	"	123040	3A1	1.5				23.9				✓		
19	"	123040	3A1	1.2				25.1				✓		
20	"	12307[illegible]	1A6	.9				26.0						Shot off Banner & Hit it
20	"	123032	1A6	.9				26.9						
21	"	123024	1A6	.7				27.6						

27.6 TOTAL—THIS PAGE
844.8 BROUGHT FWD
872.4 GRAND TOTAL

3 / 26 / 29

I certify that the foregoing flight record is correct.
C. B. Basye PILOT
APPROVED [illegible signature]

15—15516-1

Author's log book for March 1950—Note 3 carrier landings and 3 catapult takeoffs. Note that 20 March shows target banner shot loose and hit by aircraft.

Catapult take off of F9F Panther from USS Valley Forge

The following three photographs were taken as we operated on the Valley Forge in January 1950. The first photograph shows a Panther taking off from the left catapult while another Panther sits on the right one. Panthers had a length of 38 feet, so you can get an idea of the necessary acceleration required for a catapult take off. The plane goes from the speed of the ship to flying speed in the length of the catapult, about 120 feet. I recall that it seemed that I was a passenger as opposed to the pilot during the first jet fighter catapult launch. After a few launches, however, I felt I was in control of the jet as we shot down the catapult track.

F9F Panthers parked on forward part of Valley Forge flight deck

During one of the Valley Forge operations, I was the second pilot launched from the catapult. I was flying in the opposite direction of the ship on the port side of the ship, preparing to start a left turn to land. The other squadron pilot who took off before me, Jim McFadden, landed. His tail hook engaged a wire on the flight deck, as it was designed to do. Then the tail hook broke off and his plane crashed into the restraining barrier which was strung across the deck. Without the barrier, the plane would either have gone overboard or crashed into parked planes. Jim was uninjured this time. How-

VF-52 F9F Panther in flight with photograph taken from the ship. Pilot has likely been given "wave off" by the LSO—Note the tail hook beneath rear of plane.

ever, there was a mess on the deck and I was advised to return to San Diego and wait until the mess on the deck was cleaned up.

On another occasion, we conducted an exercise to determine how quickly an entire squadron of jets could be launched. The planes were supposedly ready. We were to wait in the ready room until the signal was sounded. Then we would run to our assigned planes and prepare for a hurry-up launch. As I ran around my assigned plane to give it a quick inspection, as a Navy pilot always does religiously, I gave the wing tip tanks the "watermelon thump test." One tip tank was full; the other was empty. When I did not get into the cockpit, the flight deck boss ran over. He ordered me to get in and go, three times. I refused, three times. I was the Commanding Officer of that airplane. If I considered it unsafe, I did not go. I explained that it was probably impossible to make a successful catapult launch with 1,000 pounds of fuel at the end of one wing and zero pounds at the end of the other. I said to either fill the empty tank or drain the full one. Ensigns are not supposed to refuse direct commands from Commanders. But I did refuse to obey his commands and I knew that I had done the correct thing.

I can recall one other incident involving a hurry-up takeoff. Jim Verdin was to take off from the left catapult and I from the right one. When we received the signal, we started the jets. Jim took off and I followed in a few seconds. We were airborne within a very few seconds of the starting of the engines. We went up through a solid cloud overcast at 1500 or 2000 feet. It was perhaps 2000 feet in depth. It is more comfortable if the engine has run a time so that the instruments can stabilize before going through clouds. We could not see each other and didn't consider our instruments completely reliable in the clouds. When we broke through the overcast, I joined up in formation with Jim and we proceeded to carry out our assignment.

On 3 October 1953, Jim set the world speed record while flying a Douglas XF4D-1 Skyray above the Salton Sea in Southern California. He was timed at 752.944 miles per hour. For the first time in history, a carrier-based aircraft held the world speed record. The engine in the Skyray was a Westinghouse J-40 engine equipped with an afterburner. I was an engineer at the Aviation Gas Turbine Division of Westinghouse at that time. I remember that the J-40 was intentionally run hotter than normal for this speed record attempt. The exhaust nozzle opening was closed a bit, so as to run the engine hotter, resulting in an increase in thrust. This was appropriate for an attempt at a record, but is of course detrimental to engine life.

Jim Verdin

Jim later left active duty in the Navy to become a test pilot for the Douglas Aircraft Company. He was killed on 21 January 1955, while flying a Douglas A4D Skyhawk. This plane was destined to become a long-serving and highly successful aircraft for the Navy and Marine Corps. Jim held the Navy Cross, the Distinguished Flying Cross, and several Air Medals for his World War II service.

Dude Brannen asked me to go to a party in San Diego with him one night. He had a date and said that another lady attendee would be there and I was to be her date. When we got to the party, I noticed that my date was wearing a wedding ring. I asked her if her husband was in the Navy. She replied that "He used to be." No further explanation. I stayed on my best behavior and later she and I were on the San Diego-Coronado ferry going to Coronado. She lived in Coronado and the Naval Air Station was also there. The high bridge linking San Diego and Coronado had not yet been built. The next thing I knew, a San Diego policeman, in uniform and wearing his sidearm, opened the driver's side door, pushed her toward me, and got in the car under the steering wheel. She said to me, "This is my husband." He had just gotten off duty and was on the ferry as a pedestrian when he recognized his car. He said to me, "I guess you want to go to the Air Station." I told him that was my first choice. Apparently, this was not the first time that something like this had happened in their relationship. He did not act surprised. I was also thinking how fortunate that I had passed the Navy AAA swimming test which included swimming a mile with clothes on. It was about a mile to Coronado if I had decided to go over the side of the ferry. That proved to be unnecessary and he was nice enough to drop me off at the gate of the Naval Air Station.

One landing on the Valley Forge is etched in my mind, even though it occurred more than sixty-two years ago. The Valley Forge was at sea, west of San Diego. We were assigned to take off from NAS San Diego, then land on the carrier. We waited several hours due to a reported lack of sufficient wind across the deck. Finally, about mid-afternoon, we got word to go. James (Jim) Davidson led the flight and I was on his right wing. Jim had the distinction of being the first U. S. Navy pilot in history to operate a jet from an aircraft carrier. We flew past the ship and Jim entered his approach to land. LSO Peterson gave Jim a wave-off and I started my 180 degree approach turn. The ship was headed into large swells. The bow and stern were moving up and down at least 100 feet. I would have a hard time believing it if I had not witnessed it. Peterson had to try to judge the position of the approaching plane relative to the extreme pitching of the ship. My job was to fly a reasonably constant altitude and trust Peterson to make the land or wave off decision. When I got to the position relative to the ship, Peterson decided that the ship pitching action was consistent with a landing attempt. He gave me the cut signal and I cut the engine to idle. It seemed that the ship was going down away from me and I was having one hell of a time trying to catch up with it. Finally, I got on the deck and caught a wire. The arresting wire was slowing the plane down but I was going to hit the crash barrier. The barrier operator on the catwalk actuated the barrier retractor and the barrier rotated down on the deck as I rolled across it. It was a successful landing, one I will never forget.

A short video is available through an Internet search under the description "USS Oriskany launches F9F Panther fighters during the Korean War." This film clip is an accurate portrayal of catapult launching of these early jet fighters as was the case on the Boxer and Valley Forge. Another short video "F9F Panther crash on USS Midway in 1951" illustrates a landing similar to Pawka'a first Boxer landing, except luckily Pawka was about three feet higher than the pilot in the video.

In addition to the gunnery and other flying activities, we practiced instrument flying. For this, it is necessary for the jet pilot to have his vision for things outside the cockpit blocked, but be able to see the instruments and controls inside the cockpit. The solution was to wear colored flight goggles with a hood attached to the pilot's head. The hood was a color which, when combined with the goggle color, blocked the pilot's vision. I was on an instrument training flight and one of my friends was to fly behind me and keep a lookout to prevent me from flying into another airplane, since I was blind outside the cockpit. After some 30 minutes or so, I decided to take a short break. I tilted my head back to look out for a minute and—holy Hell!!!!! Dead ahead and at the same altitude coming right at me was a Corsair or Skyraider. The Commanding Officer of one of the attack squadrons in our Air Group was also practicing on instruments. Neither of the lookout pilots saw what was happening. I was probably going 450 miles per hour and the approaching plane was probably at 200 miles per hour. That created a closing speed of about 950 feet per second. I pulled back on the stick and went right over the top of the other plane. The pilot did not see me, but he said "What in the Hell was that? Jets?" The air disturbance let him know that something had come in close and fast. His escort lookout pilot's answer included some advanced profanity. We were on the same radio frequency so I heard their comments. We were both riding a leg of the San Diego radio range at the same altitude of 15,000 feet.

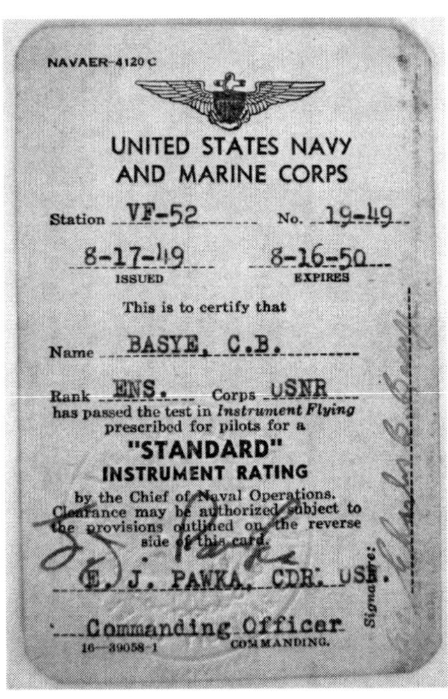

NAVAER-4120 C

UNITED STATES NAVY
AND MARINE CORPS

Station VF-52 No. 19-49

8-17-49 ISSUED 8-16-50 EXPIRES

This is to certify that

Name BASYE, C.B.

Rank ENS. Corps USNR

has passed the test in *Instrument Flying* prescribed for pilots for a

"STANDARD"
INSTRUMENT RATING

by the Chief of Naval Operations. Clearance may be authorized subject to the provisions outlined on the reverse side of this card.

E. J. PAWKA, CDR. USN.

Commanding Officer COMMANDING.

16—39058-1

Signature:

Author's Instrument Card

Instrument practice like I just described was part of the requirement for an Instrument Card.

Navy fighter pilots had a knee pad which was fastened to the right leg above the knee in such a manner that the he could read notes on it. A strap around the leg held the knee

Author's Knee Pad

pad in place.

The front page shown is the Standard Instrument Approach Procedures for the San Diego radio range station, which is typical of what would be on the knee pad if the pilot was on an instrument approach. I have had this one on my knee pad for over 60 years. The San Diego call number was SAN and the frequency was 224. The northeast and southwest quadrants would repetitively transmit the Morse code 'N', while the other two quadrants would transmit 'A'. The 'N' is a long signal followed by a short one, and the 'A' is short followed by long. When these signals meshed together in proper phase, the result was a continuous hum. All four legs of the range station would transmit this hum.

World War II planes used this method extensively. If you were tuned to this range station at its frequency (or another station at its appropriate frequency) and you heard a series of Morse Code 'N''s, you would know that you were either northeast or southwest of the station, but you would not know which. Other techniques would be necessary to assist in determining your position. Jet fighters and transports had an instrument with a needle which pointed to the source of the signal. This was

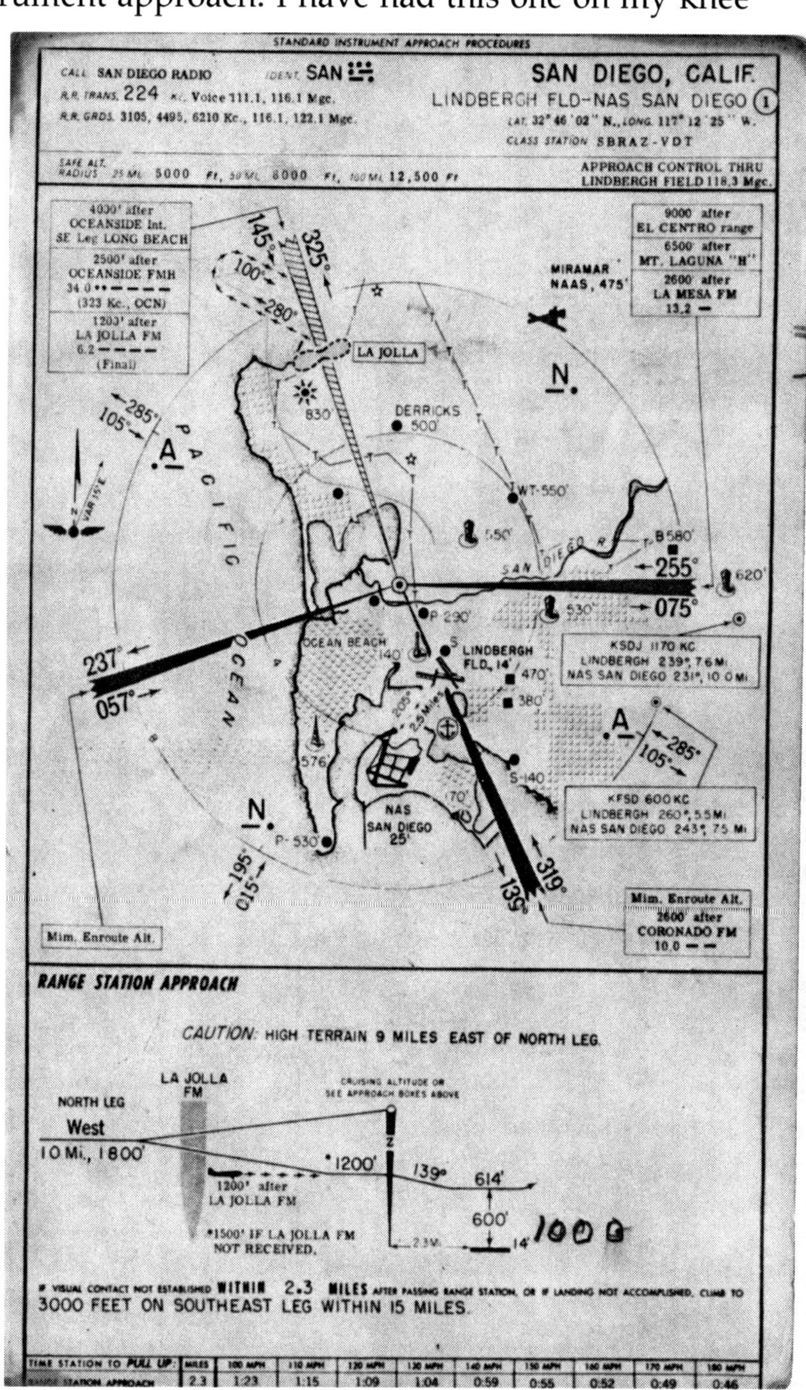

Standard Instrument Approach Procedures for the San Diego radio range station on Author's knee pad

a tremendous navigation aid. The earlier planes, such as the SNJ, F6F, and F4U had only the system briefly described above.

In March 1950, I received a letter from the Bureau of Naval Personnel (BUPERS) that said something like, "Due to budgetary limitations, we cannot retain you on flight status and pay you flight pay. You have two choices: (1.) Go to inactive duty in the reserves; or (2.) Remain on active duty without flight pay." I chose inactive duty. I had never applied to go the regular Navy route, although most of my contemporaries did. I fully expected to make the far-east tour aboard the Valley Forge, then to go to inactive duty. I was one of only a few pilots in the entire Pacific Fleet with jet experience on carriers. But BUPERS sometimes tended to lose sight of the details.

I took my last F9F flight as a member of VF-52 on 7 April 1950. It was hard to leave my good friends, knowing that they would soon be leaving for a projected six-month deployment to the Far East. One of the VF-52 pilots, Dave Tatum, was shot down on his seventh mission while flying ground support during the Korean War. A rescue ship pulled him out of the ocean. He completed that tour and later went back for a second tour. He was shot down on the seventh mission again, and again was rescued by helicopter after another emergency ocean landing. Three missions later he was shot down again and killed. Dave joined VF-52 after the photograph of the pilots was taken.

I also remember Jesse Brown, the first Negro pilot in the history of the U. S. Navy. He was a few months behind me as we made our way through the pilot training program. He was not a product of affirmative action nor was he a part of a Navy with such a hang-up on "diversity" that we see today. I sincerely believe that he would have considered himself to be a U. S. Navy pilot who happened to be a Negro, rather than an "African-American" who happened to be a U. S. Navy pilot. I never witnessed any treatment of Jesse that differed from that accorded to other cadets.

In early December 1950, our Army and Marine Corps infantry were tremendously outnumbered in heavy fighting at the Chosin Reservoir in North Korea. Jesse was flying ground support in a F4U Corsair, having taken off from the carrier USS Leyte. He was shot down by the Chinese. His wingman was Thomas Hudner, a Naval Academy graduate. Tom saw Jesse's mangled Corsair smoking and Jesse waving at him. Tom crash landed his Corsair close to Jesse's wrecked one. He could not extricate Jesse. Jesse died there and Tom was rescued by helicopter. Tom was awarded the Medal of Honor in the White House by President Truman. In 1973, the Navy named a guided missile frigate for Jesse. I did not know Tom Hudner but, as a tribute to him, I am including his picture here.

Jesse Brown

Tom Hudner

About a month prior to release from active duty I was transferred to a squadron identified as VR-32. VR-32 delivered airplanes from wherever they were to wherever they were supposed to be. I flew a Corsair from San Diego to Corpus Christi, and then delivered a twin engine SNB from Corpus Christi to Litchfield, just west of Phoenix. On 1 May 1950, the day my friends left for the western Pacific on the Valley Forge, I rode a Navy transport from San Diego to Corpus Christi, and on to Dallas. My assignment was to accept delivery of a new F4U-5N Corsair night fighter from the Chance Vought factory and deliver it to NAS Quonset Point, Rhode Island. I made a 30 minute acceptance test flight on 2 May and everything appeared satisfactory. This was analogous to Major Richard Bong's flight when he was killed at Lockheed, flying a production F-80.

I left Dallas and planned to make NAS Atlanta my next stop. However, before reaching Jackson, Mississippi, I heard noises like a large flock of geese. I had heard such noises before. The hydraulic system includes an element with a rubber diaphragm with compressed air on one side and hydraulic fluid on the other. If there is a leak resulting in low hydraulic pressure, this element makes those loud noises. I landed the Corsair at the Municipal Airport at Jackson. A Piper Cub mechanic assisted me in trying to find the leak. He was flattered to get close to the new Corsair. We detected hydraulic fluid beneath one wing and removed an access panel. It was apparent where the leak originated. At assembly, an o-ring had been cut by coupling fitting threads. The result was a slow leak. We located a new o-ring of the proper size and re-

F4U-5N Corsair Night Fighter

filled the hydraulic system. The entire episode took perhaps two hours.

Bad weather resulted in two nights at Spartanburg, South Carolina. After refueling at NAS Norfolk, I delivered the Corsair to Quonset Point on a Sunday morning. Two Navy Reserve pilots gave me a ride in an SNB to Bethpage, Long Island, home of the Grumman Aircraft Company. My next task was to accept delivery of a new jet from Grumman and deliver it to San Diego.

On Monday morning, 8 May 1950, I talked with a Grumman test pilot, then made the acceptance test flight. Everything appeared normal, so I signed the proper papers signifying that the new jet was the property of the U. S. Navy. I stopped briefly at NAS Patuxent River, Maryland and went on to Maxwell Air Force Base, in Montgomery, Alabama, to spend the night. Air Force personnel were directed to fill the jet with fuel and to check the engine oil. The next morning I left Maxwell AFB, intending to next land at Carswell AFB, at Ft. Worth. All appeared normal until I turned on the cockpit pressure system. The cockpit immediately filled with smoke. The smoke went away when I turned the pressure system off and returned when I turned the pressure system back on. By then I was closer to the Barksdale Air Force Base at Shreveport, Louisiana, than to Maxwell, so I landed there. It turned out that the Air Force service people at Maxwell had not only checked the engine oil, they had also poured oil in the engine until it reached the top of the dipstick. The solution was to find the proper drain plug and drain out the excess oil. Afterwards, there was no further smoke problem. I went on to Carswell AFB at Ft. Worth. Bad weather over west Texas meant a three-night stay there. I got acquainted with several B-36 pilots. The B-36 was made at the Convair factory at Ft. Worth. It was a very large bomber, with six propeller engines and four jet engines. The six propellers were behind the wings. I left Ft. Worth on 12 May and landed at San Diego later that day. I passed the slow B-36's at 30,000 feet altitude along the way.

MONTH MAY YEAR 1950

DAY	AIRCRAFT		CHARACTER OF FLIGHT	FLIGHT TIME AS				TO FLI TI
	MODEL	BUREAU NO.		PILOT	CO-PILOT	STUDENT	PASSENGER	
1	R4D-5	17212	1R2				3.7	3.
1	R4D-5	17212	1R2				3.7	7.
2	R4D-5	17212	1R2				2.5	9
2	F4U-5N	124461	1L	0.5				10
3	F4U-5N	124461	1J	1.9				[illegible]
3	F4U-5N	124461	1J	1.3				13
4	F4U-5N	124461	1J	0.8				14
4	F4U-5N	124461	1J	0.7				15
5	F4U-5N	124461	1J	1.6				16
7	F4U-5N	124461	1J	2.0				18
7	SNB-3	51130	1R2				1.0	1
8	F9F-2	123520	1L	0.5				2
8	F9F-2	123520	1J	0.7				2
8	F9F-2	123520	1J	1.9				22
9	F9F-2	123520	1J	1.3				2
9	F9F-2	123520	1J	0.5				2
12	F9F-2	123520	1J	1.4				2
12	F9F-2	123520	1J	1.9				2
TOTAL—THIS PAGE								2
BROUGHT FWD.								9
GRAND TOTAL								9

16—180

The May 1950 flig

While I was involved in the paperwork before leaving Grumman for the trip to San Diego, I got acquainted with a Navy pilot from VR-31, based at NAS Norfolk. I was attached to VR-32 at San Diego. He had similar duties to mine; that is to deliver airplanes as ordered. He was a LCDR, with much more experience than I, but I had the definite feeling that he was scared to death of the jet that he had been assigned to deliver to San Diego. We did not talk a long time but I had the impression that all of his experience was in propeller planes. He was still at Grumman when I left for NAS Patuxent River. This duty involved flying anything you were assigned to, whether you were familiar with it or not. To illustrate, I had never seen a F4U-5N or F9F-2, both of which I picked up at the factory and delivered on this trip. The F4U-5N was similar to the F4U-4 with which I was familiar, but did have a few differences. The F9F-2 had a Pratt-Whitney engine with slightly different engine controls from the situation with the F9F-3 with its Allison engine which we used in VF-52.

REMARKS
SAN DIEGO - EL PASO
EL PASO - CORPUS CHRISTI
CORPUS CHRISTI - DALLAS
TEST - CHANCE VOUGHT
DALLAS - JACKSON, MISS.
JACKSON - MONTGOMERY, ALA.
MONTGOMERY - ATLANTA
ATLANTA - SPARTANBURG, S.C.
SPARTANBURG - NORFOLK, VA.
NORFOLK, VA. - QUONSET PT, R.I.
QUONSET - BETHPAGE, N.Y.
TEST GRUMMAN
BETHPAGE - NAS PATUXENT, MD.
PATUXENT - MONTGOMERY, ALA.
MONTGOMERY - SHREVEPORT, LA.
SHREVEPORT - FT. WORTH, TEX.
FT. WORTH - EL PASO
EL PASO - SAN DIEGO

I certify that the foregoing flight record is correct.
R B Basyl PILOT
APPROVED

umented in my Navy log book

I had told my mother that I might fly over the farm in Missouri with the new jet fighter that I was delivering from the factory in New York to NAS San Diego. However, when I was ready to leave Grumman, the weather was much better over the southern part of the country than the Midwest. I therefore went south to Alabama and then west as described earlier. Another Navy pilot went into the bad weather and was killed on 11 May, when he crashed close to Scott AFB east of St. Louis. The plane was one of the new F9F-2's which was to have been delivered from Grumman to San Diego. I do not know if the deceased pilot was the LCDR I talked to at Grumman or someone else. News reports stated that a Navy jet crashed in Illinois, killing the pilot. I was not aware of this until later. Meanwhile, my frantic mother contacted the Navy and they would not tell her that the deceased pilot was not her son. That was disappointing, but his family had not been notified. I was at Carswell AFB in Ft. Worth waiting for better weather over west Texas when the Illinois crash occurred. The serial number of the F9F-2 which I delivered was 123520, while that of the plane in the Illinois crash was 123531. I found extensive statistics and information on the Internet regarding the Grumman F9F-2 Panther, including detailed accident records and crashes related to the Panther. I found an entry for 11 May 1950, and noted the information related to the fatal Illinois crash. F9F-2 serial number 123520, which I delivered from Grumman to NAS San Diego, was destroyed by a fire in Korea on 30 July 1951 at Marine location K-3 while assigned to Marine fighter squadron VMF-212. One reason that rules regarding weather were so stringent on these flights was the fact that in many cases the pilot was unfamiliar with the plane he was flying.

These accident statistics found on the Internet listed eight accidents of VF-51 and VF-52 Panther jet fighters on the Valley Forge between 21 May 1950 and 11 December 1950, when Air Group 5 was in combat in Korea. Six of the eight involved carrier take-off and/or landing accidents. The other two were on 19 September 1950, when Dave Tatum was shot down, and the fatal crash of a VF-51 pilot hit by AAA (anti-aircraft artillery) fire on 12 August 1950. Thus, on this combat cruise for the jet fighters of VF-51 and VF-52, 75% of the reported accidents and/or crashes were carrier take-off or landing accidents and 25% were due to enemy fire. The canted deck carrier innovation and more responsive jet engines made later carrier operation much safer and less exiting.

These same Panther accident statistics researched on the Internet also reveal that Ensign Neil Armstrong, as a VF-51 pilot, successfully ejected from a Panther that had been damaged by enemy fire in Korea on 3 September 1951. He became the first man to step on the moon. Also note that Boston Red Sox outfielder Ted Williams, while flying ground support on 16 February 1953, was hit by small arms fire and landed his Panther in flames. He was a Marine Reserve pilot recalled to active duty for the Korean conflict.

Vought F4U Corsair records, also found through Internet searches, reveal that Corsair accidents during World War II accounted for more losses than combat, totaling 922 due to accidents and 538 due to combat. This is somewhat similar to the Panther situation in Korea, as illustrated above.

United States Pacific Fleet
Air Force
Fighter Squadron Fifty-two

This is to Certify That ENS. CHARLES B. BASYE
has satisfactorily completed the prescribed course
of instruction in Jet Aircraft Transition.

30 March 1950

G. J. Pawka
Commander, USN
COMMANDING OFFICER

CDR Pawka issued these certificates to squadron pilots who completed the transition to jets.

Jet aircraft, as well as aircraft carriers, underwent considerable change in the decade following World War II. The early jet fighters were all underpowered by today's standards. The engines had a fixed area exhaust nozzle and no afterburner. The variable area exhaust nozzle permitted the pilot to increase power in a short time by making the nozzle smaller. The variable area was achieved by either electrical or hydraulic actuators. Had CDR Pawka had a variable area exhaust nozzle on his initial approach to land on the USS Boxer, he could have increased power in a fraction of a second instead of two or three seconds. The difference can be life or death, a good landing or a crash.

The afterburner was a large cylindrical addition to the rear of a jet engine. It provided a method of inserting large amounts of jet fuel for ignition by the hot jet exhaust. The result was a great, sudden increase in thrust. Afterburners were extremely inefficient, but were most helpful in certain take-off or emergency situations. The early engines had either a centrifugal flow or an axial flow compressor. The F-80 and Panther engines were centrifugal flow. This means that the incoming air was compressed by being directed outward, then being redirected toward the rear through combustion chambers. The F2H banshee engine was an axial flow design. I will discuss this engine extensively in Chapter 9.

The World War II Essex-class aircraft carriers, like the Boxer and Valley Forge, featured a rectangular flight deck. Often during landing operations, planes would be parked forward (on the front of the flight deck). When the pilot received the cut sign from the LSO, he immediately cut the engine to idle. One of three outcomes was certain: (1) a safe landing on the rear part of the flight deck; (2) a crash into the safety barrier or parked planes; or, (3) a trip over the side of the carrier. Number (1) was the only acceptable outcome, of course.

When the angled deck, or canted deck, aircraft carrier came along, it made carrier landings much less exciting and dangerous. Test operations began in January, 1953, on the Antietam, the first of the angled carriers. The pilot lands on the angled deck part of the flight deck, slightly offset to port (the left) from the fore and aft direction of the carrier. Nothing is ever parked in front of the landing aircraft during landing operations. The pilot can apply full power upon touchdown and either go around again if the hook does not catch a wire, or throttle back if it does catch one. The inertial force of the plane is much greater than the thrust load of the engine, so applying full power during landing does not overburden the landing system. The following photograph shows the USS Harry S. Truman. The angled landing part of the flight deck has some aircraft on it now but they will be removed before landing operations. This modern nuclear powered ship is much larger than the Essex-class carriers. It is easy to observe how very long the landing area of the deck really is. Contrast the situation on the Harry S. Truman with that of the Boxer in the other photograph. Note the planes parked on the front of the flight deck and observe that the landing part is only about the after third of the flight deck.

My friends in VF 52 were on the Valley Forge in Hong Kong when the North Koreans invaded South Korea on 25 June 1950. Eight days later, on 3 July 1950, they were flying ground support missions.

I have a few additional comments regarding military decorations awarded to some of the carrier-based Navy pilots referred to herein. As previously noted, Dick Bates, Bill Bauhof, and Jim Verdin all held the Navy Cross. Dick's citation stated that he "dauntlessly braved withering hostile antiaircraft fire to launch a smashing aerial torpedo attack against the enemy and by his relentless determination and indomitable courage, succeeded in scoring a devastating hit on a Japanese battleship." Bill's and Jim's citations were equally impressive. Babe Edmonston was awarded the Distinguished Flying Cross for leading a fighter strike against airports in the Tokyo area shortly before the Japanese surrender. Cliff Fanning's DFC citation read as follows. "Fanning, Clifford Earl, LCDR, United States Navy is awarded the Distinguished Flying Cross for heroism and extraordinary achievement while participating in an aerial flight against enemy forces on 20 June 1944. Leading an extremely hazardous, long-range mission against enemy surface forces between the Marianas and Philippine Islands when intercepted by a vastly superior number of enemy fighter airplanes which also had the altitude advantage, he nevertheless attacked without hesitation. Again and again he engaged enemy fighters in the midst of a fierce and protracted aerial action, definitely shooting down at least one enemy airplane before his own plane was seriously damaged by the opposing fire. Subsequently, although his damaged plane was almost out of control and he himself painfully wounded, he accomplished the return flight to a carrier base alone, without radio facilities and at night against great odds, effecting a carrier landing without further injury to himself or other personnel. His determination, courage, and skill were at all times inspiring and in keeping with the highest traditions of the United States Naval Service."

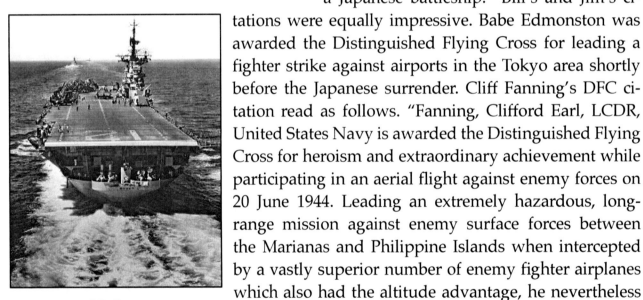

USS Harry S. Truman

USS Boxer

Chapter 7: Active/Ready Reserve, 1950-1987

I returned to Missouri in May, 1950, following release from active duty at NAS San Diego. Soon thereafter, I traveled to NAS St. Louis, Missouri, and applied for assignment to a Navy Reserve fighter squadron. I received orders to Reserve Fighter Squadron VF-923. I made my first flight, in a SNJ, on 15 October 1950, and my first flight in a Grumman F8F Bearcat on 11 November 1950. The F8F was an extremely high-performance fighter. It was powered by the same 2,000 horsepower Pratt-Whitney engine used in the Hellcat and Corsair, but it weighed only about two-thirds as much. It was Grumman's solution to the highly agile Japanese Zero. One Bearcat took off in 115 feet from a standing start. On 29 August 1952, I refueled a F8F Bearcat at the Wright-Patterson Air Force Base in Dayton, Ohio. The base featured a long runway, approximately 10,000 feet, as I recall. To show the Air Force people what the Bearcat was capable of, I applied full power and left it on until reaching the base of some clouds approximately 10,000 feet above the ground. Looking down, I could see that the end of the runway had not yet been reached.

The adjustment from life as a Navy fighter pilot to civilian life was most pronounced during the summer and fall of 1950. I recall definitely feeling out of place. I felt like a tightly wound spring which could suddenly and violently unwind.

Most reserve pilots had never flown a jet fighter. The Navy decided to have reserve pilots make a few flights in the McDonnell FH-1 Phantom and the McDonnell F2H Banshee. I took five Phantom flights during April and May, 1951, and the five Banshee flights in December, 1951 and January and March, 1952. These McDonnell planes carried Westinghouse jet engines, about which I later became most knowledgeable.

On Thursday night, 12 July 1951, I spent the evening with my parents on the farm. VF-923 was scheduled to be on active duty at St. Louis the following Saturday and Sunday. Vehicle headlights appeared out of the darkness and two of our neighbors, Walter Johnson and George Harper, arrived. George was the Rocheport mail carrier. He had received the telegram telling my parents that their youngest son, my brother George, had been fatally injured in a Navy aircraft accident that day. He could not deliver it by himself; he asked Walter to help him. Walter said to my mother, "Dorothy, we have some awful bad news." I took the telegram from him and read it aloud. As bad as it was for Dad and me, it was much worse for my mother. Words cannot describe her anguish. The telegram is below, as is the clipping that appeared in the Los Angeles Times on Friday, 13 July 1951.

I have also included a copy of a letter from VADM J. H. Cassady and a copy of a letter from George's Commanding Officer, LCDR John R. Strane. In addition, my parents received letters of condolence from the Secretary of the Navy and the Governor of Missouri.

LCDR Strane referred to "target fixation." When fighter pilots are practicing

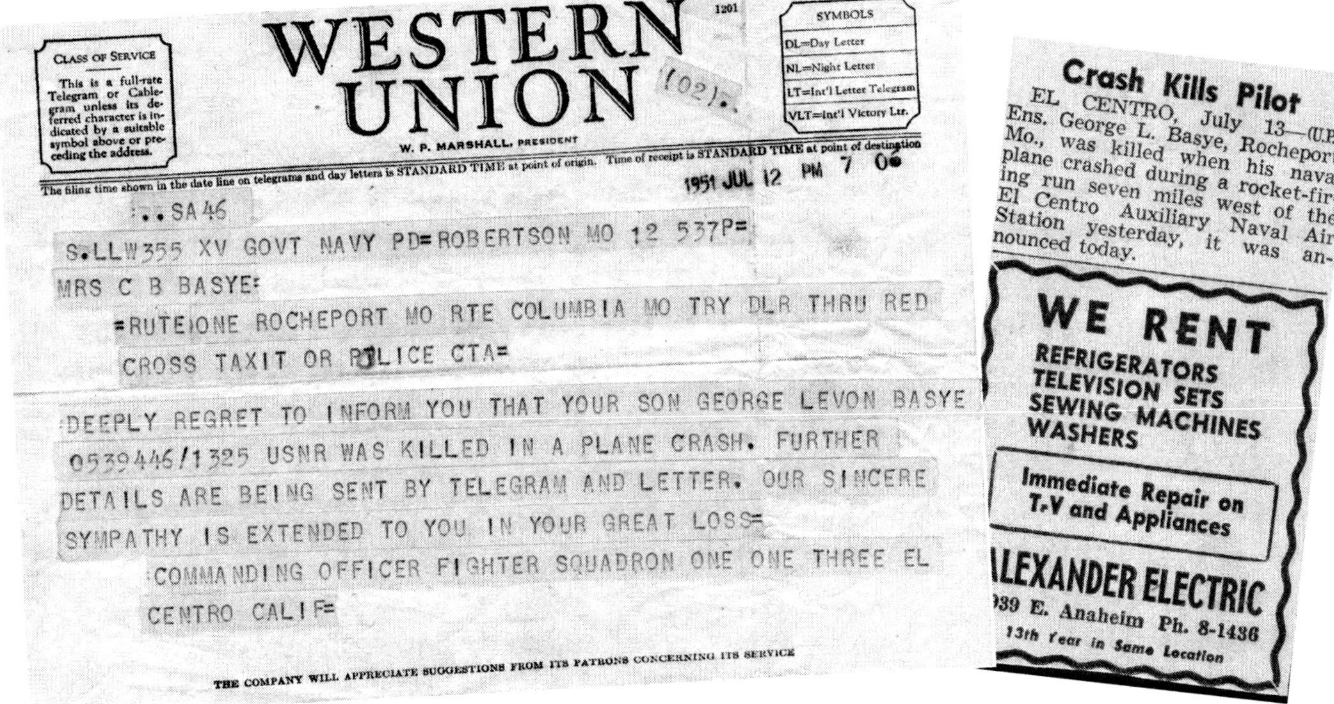

WESTERN UNION

W. P. MARSHALL, PRESIDENT

CLASS OF SERVICE — This is a full-rate Telegram or Cablegram unless its deferred character is indicated by a suitable symbol above or preceding the address.

SYMBOLS — DL=Day Letter; NL=Night Letter; LT=Int'l Letter Telegram; VLT=Int'l Victory Ltr.

The filing time shown in the date line on telegrams and day letters is STANDARD TIME at point of origin. Time of receipt is STANDARD TIME at point of destination

1951 JUL 12 PM 7 06

SA46

S.LLW355 XV GOVT NAVY PD=ROBERTSON MO 12 537P=

MRS C B BASYE=

=RUTE ONE ROCHEPORT MO RTE COLUMBIA MO TRY DLR THRU RED CROSS TAXIT OR POLICE CTA=

DEEPLY REGRET TO INFORM YOU THAT YOUR SON GEORGE LEVON BASYE 0539446/1325 USNR WAS KILLED IN A PLANE CRASH. FURTHER DETAILS ARE BEING SENT BY TELEGRAM AND LETTER. OUR SINCERE SYMPATHY IS EXTENDED TO YOU IN YOUR GREAT LOSS=

COMMANDING OFFICER FIGHTER SQUADRON ONE ONE THREE EL CENTRO CALIF=

THE COMPANY WILL APPRECIATE SUGGESTIONS FROM ITS PATRONS CONCERNING ITS SERVICE

Crash Kills Pilot

EL CENTRO, July 13—(U.P.). Ens. George L. Basye, Rocheport, Mo., was killed when his naval plane crashed during a rocket-firing run seven miles west of the El Centro Auxiliary Naval Air Station yesterday, it was announced today.

Telegram, Newspaper article

dive bombing or rocket firing in steep dives in propeller planes like the Hellcat or Corsair, the plane approaches the earth at high velocity—perhaps as fast as 400 feet per second. It is a demanding task to aim the plane so as to hit the target and go low for better accuracy but not too low to be able to pull out safely. Each second relates to several hundred feet of elevation difference. Many Navy pilots have lost their lives as a result of target fixation. Later Navy pilots had access to much advanced air-to-ground and air-to-air weapons. Methods utilized to assist in hitting the target included infrared sensing, radar, and lasers. Being able to fire from long distance with these more advanced weapons meant much more safety for the pilot, in both ground support and aerial firing missions.

Prior to 5 August 1950, Air Group 5 on the Valley Forge was the only Navy Air presence in the Korean War. The USS Philippine Sea, with Air Group 11 aboard arrived on 5 August. Fighter Squadron VF-113 was part of Air Group 11. George was assigned to VF-113 after they returned to San Diego in the spring of 1951. They were training for another tour in Korea at this time. Three of the VF-113 pilots involved in the combat before George joined the squadron were Ken Burrows, Ed

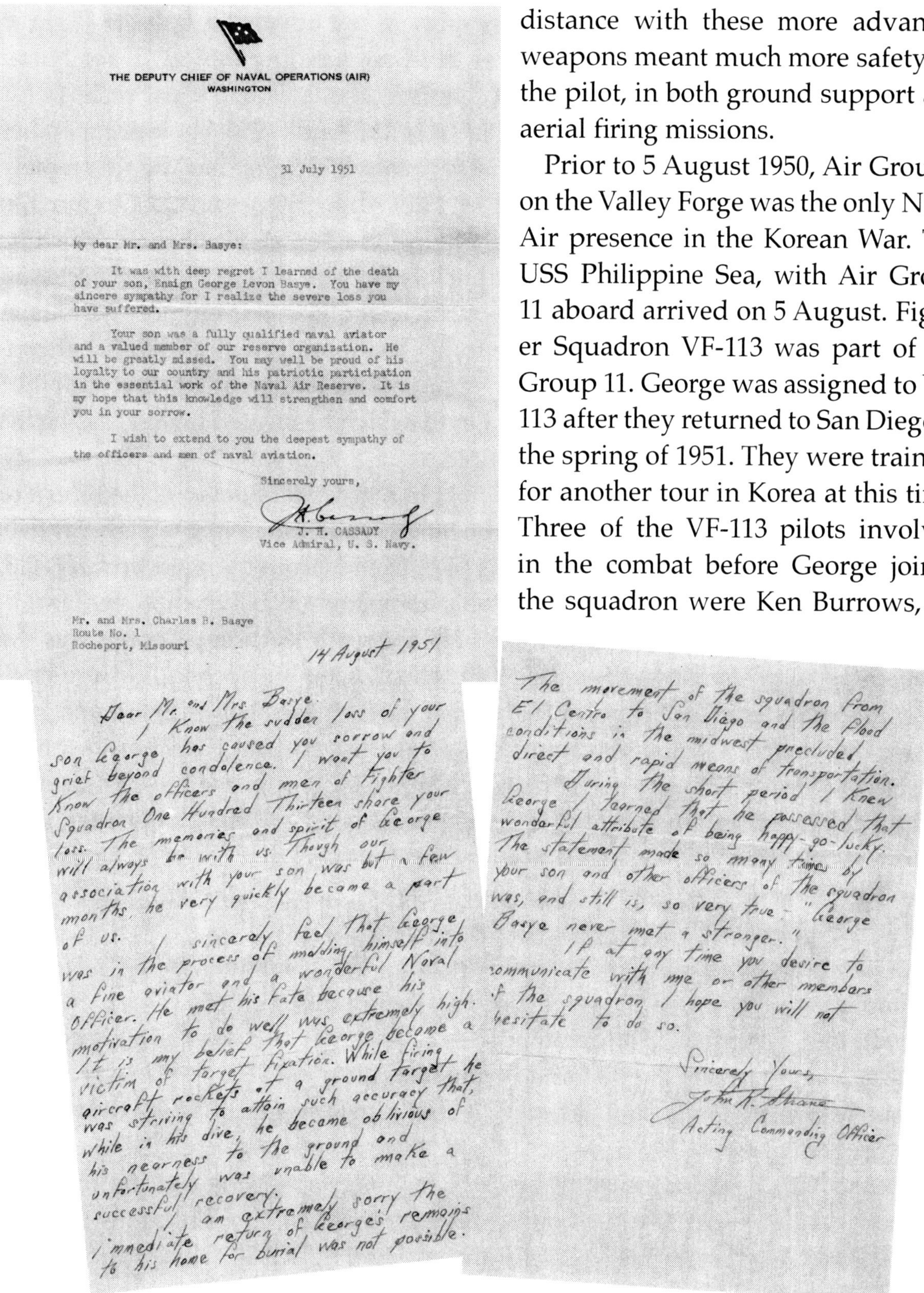

THE DEPUTY CHIEF OF NAVAL OPERATIONS (AIR)
WASHINGTON

31 July 1951

My dear Mr. and Mrs. Basye:

It was with deep regret I learned of the death of your son, Ensign George Levon Basye. You have my sincere sympathy for I realize the severe loss you have suffered.

Your son was a fully qualified naval aviator and a valued member of our reserve organization. He will be greatly missed. You may well be proud of his loyalty to our country and his patriotic participation in the essential work of the Naval Air Reserve. It is my hope that this knowledge will strengthen and comfort you in your sorrow.

I wish to extend to you the deepest sympathy of the officers and men of naval aviation.

Sincerely yours,

J. H. CASSADY
Vice Admiral, U. S. Navy.

Mr. and Mrs. Charles B. Basye
Route No. 1
Rocheport, Missouri

14 August 1951

Dear Mr. and Mrs Basye.

I know the sudden loss of your son George has caused you sorrow and grief beyond condolence. I want you to know the officers and men of Fighter Squadron One Hundred Thirteen share your loss. The memories and spirit of George will always be with us. Though our association with your son was but a few months, he very quickly became a part of us.

I sincerely feel that George was in the process of molding himself into a fine aviator and a wonderful Naval Officer. He met his fate because his motivation to do well was extremely high. It is my belief that George became a victim of target fixation. While firing aircraft rockets at a ground target he was striving to attain such accuracy that, while in his dive, he became oblivious of his nearness to the ground and unfortunately was unable to make a successful recovery.

I am extremely sorry the immediate return of George's remains to his home for burial was not possible. The movement of the squadron from El Centro to San Diego and the flood conditions in the midwest precluded direct and rapid means of transportation.

During the short period I knew George I learned that he possessed that wonderful attribute of being happy-go-lucky. The statement made so many times by your son and other officers of the squadron was, and still is, so very true: "George Basye never met a stranger."

If at any time you desire to communicate with me or other members of the squadron I hope you will not hesitate to do so.

Sincerely Yours,

John K. Strane
Acting Commanding Officer

Letters from Cassady and Strane

Klapka, and Sport Horton. Ken was a member of my advanced training flight at Jacksonville, so I knew him well. Ed was the Commanding Officer of the Naval and Marine Corps Reserve Center in St. Louis in the late 1970's just prior to his retirement. Sport and I were friends at Olathe in 1953 and 1954. He was a member of Hal Avants advanced training flight at Jacksonville. Sport had two extremely close calls in Korea on 21 and 27 November 1950 while flying ground support. On 21 November, the Chinese shot a large hole in the wing of his Corsair which he described as being the size of a bathtub. Luckily, he was able to make a successful landing on the Philippine Sea. The 27 November flight was even more serious. A Chinese bullet lodged in his chest close to his heart, and medical personnel concluded that it could not be successfully removed. In bad weather, low visibility, and in serious pain, Sport landed on the Leyte, which he located before finding his own carrier, the Philippine Sea. Sport retired as a Captain for TWA in Kansas City.

One of the most severe Midwestern floods in many years delayed the return of George's remains for the funeral and burial in Ashland Cemetery, on Highway 240, in Howard County. Bob Evans, one of his pilot friends from his squadron, VF-113, accompanied his remains to Missouri. Bob's home town was Lebanon, Indiana.

At graduation, only three months past his sixteenth birthday, George was the president of his senior class at Fayette High School. After high school, George studied to be a minister at the School of Religion at the University of Missouri and John Brown University in Arkansas. He preached at several rural churches in central Missouri before deciding to enter the Navy. When he was home for Christmas in 1950, he told me that if he lost his life during training or in Korea, he wanted Janie Carroll, his girlfriend in Pensacola, to attend his funeral. I met her in St. Louis. One of the Professors at the Missouri School of Religion, Gene Wetherell, preached his funeral at Big Spring Church in southeast Howard County.

This photo was taken when George was home for Christmas in 1950. He had received his Navy wings at Pensacola shortly before this picture.

I continued flying the F8F Bearcat in VF-923. We spent two weeks on active duty at NAS New Orleans in August and September 1951. We also flew one weekend per month from St. Louis. In August 1952, we did two weeks of active duty flying out of St. Louis.

In May, 1953, I graduated with the B. S. in Mechanical Engineering from the University of Missouri. Westinghouse offered—and I accepted—employment in Kansas City. Therefore, in July, 1953, I transferred out of NAS St. Louis and VF-923 into VF-884 at NAS Olathe, Kansas.

The Navy recalled VF-923 to active duty during the Korean War in fall, 1952. We

The author, left, and brother, George Levon Basye

were scheduled to report in late 1952, to stay at St. Louis for an indeterminate period, then to transfer to the west coast. However, shortly before the reporting date, the Navy decided that all of the pilots were not needed. Most of the pilots, all the other personnel, and the planes were to go. The pilots who had been off extended active duty the longest were chosen for the recall. In other words, those of us who had been on extended active duty recently, like me, were not recalled. Those who had been recalled were in training on the West Coast when the fighting ended in the spring of 1953. They were soon released from active duty.

Shortly after being recalled, several of the pilots began to express some frustration in the St. Louis Officers Club. Two of them, Cletus Oing from Indiana and Delmar Johansen from Illinois, decided to throw several whiskey glasses across the room and break them against the opposite wall. Cletus was summoned to the office of the Base Executive Officer the next day. The Exec told him that such behavior was unacceptable. As Cletus was leaving, the Exec said, "Tell that Hansen feller that I know that he was involved in it as well as you. I will be watching him." He did not realize that Johansen was the last name, as opposed to Hansen. Everyone had a good laugh over that one.

By that time, VF-884 was flying Corsairs at Olathe. In December 1953, three of us were on two weeks of informal active duty. The other two, Marvin Zimmerman and Banks, were TWA pilots. Banks's first name escapes me. Nothing formal was scheduled. We were expected to get flight hours without any accidents or the breaking of any rules. We decided to fly to Dallas, spend the night at the Naval Air Station, and return to Olathe the next day. One of them navigated down and I was to navigate back to Olathe. We went to a night club in Dallas where we could not get one drink, which was all that we wanted. They had a strange law that you had to buy a bottle, and then buy ice and water to mix it with.

On the return trip, I had the almost full bottle of whisky in my Navy issue cloth pilot suitcase in the Corsair cockpit. About halfway back to Olathe, I could see through peripheral vision that Marvin Zimmerman was in close formation on the right side of my Corsair. I did not look directly at him. I zipped open the suitcase and removed the quart of whisky. Holding it up where he could see it, I faked tak-

F9F-7 PILOT X-O LIST

PRE-START

1. Check Ejection Seat
2. Strap in/Perform Oxygen X
3. Speed brake T handle
4. Speed brake over-ride OFF
5. Emergency Flapperotte air bottle OFF(NOTE PRESSURE)
6. Flying tail OFF
7. Wing tank dump normal
8. Set totalizer
9. Cabin Pressurization OFF
10. Circuit Breakers IN
11. Fuel Master ON
12. Battery ON-Check Voltage
13. X low pressure fuel boost light
14. Cage & Un-cage Gyro
15. External Power-Start Engi[illegible]

STARTING

1. Aux Hydraulic pump [illegible]
2. Press to test lights
3. Set all tabs-Emergency & Normal
4. Ch Eng driven fuel boost
5. Test fuel gage & fire warning lights
6. Ch generator
7. Cycle start master
8. Ch Aux Hyd pump OFF
9. Test Flapperettes/Flaperon[illegible]
10. Radio On
11. Cycle Canopy & Seat
12. 80% Fuel Integrity X
13. Perform cockpit take-off check-off list

SHUT DOWN

1. 70% - X Tail pipe temp steady-shut down
2. Radios OFF
3. Fuel Dump Off
4. Battery OFF
5. Start Master OFF
6. Speed brake Override OFF
7. Oxygen OFF
8. Bleed Hyd system
9. Ch fire out
10. Fuel Master OFF-use batter[illegible] last flight only

FLAME OUT

1. Throttle CLOSED
2. Glide 185 kts toward field
3. Descend below 30,000
4. Cycle Start Master
5. RPM 10-16%
6. Throttle to Start-5 sec.
7. Throttle to IDLE
8. Advance Throttle after RPM Stabelizes.

BAIL OUT

1. Pre-ejection
2. Position Feet
3. Actuate Bail out O_2
4. Pull Face Curtain
5. Seperate from seat
6. Pull Rip Cord

DEAD STICK LANDING

Glide - 185 Kts Clean - 160 Kts(MIN)GEAR, FLAPS ON.

OPTIMUM ALTITUDES:	GEAR, FLAPS EXTENDED	GEAR EXTENDED
INITIAL POSITION	8000'	6000'
180° POSITION	4500'	2500'
90° POSITION	2500'	Lower Flaps as Needed

SHOOT FOR POSITION 1/3 UP RUNWAY

F9F-7 Pilot Check Off List.

ing the cap off and taking a long swig. Then I "replaced" the cap and put it away. After a period of time, I glanced at him. It was quite a reaction; TWA did not permit its pilots to pull such stunts, which he let me know. Navy pilots have always known how to have fun.

VF-884 started flying the F9F-7 Cougar jet fighter in June. 1954. The Cougar was the swept-wing version of the Panther, with which I was most familiar. I felt right at home since the cockpits were virtually identical. The Cougar was slightly faster than the Panther but handled almost the same. We spent two weeks in July on active duty at Olathe flying the Cougar.

We had a check-off list for the F9F-7 Cougar. This list was kept on the pilot's knee pad which was discussed earlier. A copy of this check-off list is shown. Note that there are fifteen things to do or to check prior to starting. Thirteen items are involved in starting the jet engine. Items to do, or to be aware of for shutdown, in case of a flameout, such as I experienced over the Pacific, and for bailing out of the plane, are also on the sheet. Helpful information in case one makes a dead stick (engine not operating) landing is also on the card. I was given a similar sheet which applied to the F9F-2 when I accepted that aircraft from Grumman in May of 1950. I still have that sheet on my knee pad.

Author in flight gear prior to F9F-7 Cougar flight; NAS Olathe, Kansas in July, 1954

The following photograph, taken in 1954, shows me in my flight suit and helmet before a flight in the F9F-7 Cougar. An oxygen mask would be attached to the four metal buttons on the inner cloth helmet. The oxygen mask included a radio microphone. We wore the oxygen mask at all times when flying the jets because most flights were above 10,000 feet altitude. Most flights in the

F9F Cougar on USS Essex

TO GIVE PRECISION FLYING DEMONSTRATION— These five pilots, members of an organized reserve jet team at the Olathe naval air station, will demonstrate precision flying and aerial gunnery to the public at 5 o'clock Sunday at the station. They are (from top down) Lieut. Comdr. Henry H. Shimer, 3417 Arlington street, Intercity district, Lieut. James R. Hansen, Jamestown, Kas., Lieut. Aaron L. Hall, Powhattan, Kas., Lieut. Charles Basye, Fayette, Mo., and Lieut. Comdr. W. L. Bauman, Mission.

News article and photograph in Kansas City Star, July, 1954

Corsair or Hellcat were below 10,000 feet, so oxygen was not required. The inner flight suit, with the heavy zippers below my neck, was a 'G' suit. It was close fitting and air pockets in the suit functioned to exert pressure on the torso and legs when pulling high 'G's in tight turns. The purpose of the 'G' suit was to keep blood in the head and prevent pilot blackout.

The Navy decided to have an open house on Sunday, 18 July, and to stage an air show. This would be the last day of our two weeks of active duty. In an advertisement for the air show, the Kansas City Star ran a picture of the five of us pilots who were to participate. LCDR Hank Shimer, the Commanding Officer of VF-884, asked me if I would do some aerobatics. He knew I was the only pilot with experience in jets. He said that he and the three other pilots would make passes over the Air Station in different formations and I was to entertain the spectators with aerobatics while the other four were preparing for the next pass.

The four pilots participating in the air show formations were Shimer, Lee Hall, Jim Hansen, and Bill Bauman. Lee was the pilot who made the unauthorized parachute jump discussed earlier. Jim was a student in law school at the University of Kan-

JET FLIERS GIVE DEMONSTRATION AT 600 MILES AN HOUR

Mrs. Charles Basye, Mrs. Kenneth Earl, and David and Jimmy K. Wiswall attended the jet plane demonstration at the Olathe (Kan.) Naval Air Station Sunday afternoon in which Mrs. Basye's son, Lt. Charles Benjamin Basye, was one of the five men of Reserve Squadron 884 who participated.

The show portrayed planes taking off from a carrier, with the hangar representing the ship. After four pilots who flew in formation took off, they were followed by Lt. Basye who flew alone. All went to Wichita, Kan., and the four returned in several different formations, each time followed by Lt. Basye who entertained with some aerial action. One time as he passed he made four rolls, another time five, going at a speed of more than 600 miles per hour, as was reported by the announcer in the tower.

During the final pass he emptied his surplus fuel in the air, which made an interesting sight This maneuver showed how planes returning to their ships get rid of surplus fuel, thus lessening fire hazard to the carriers.

The air was rough Sunday and the four pilots flying in formation did not reach their accustomed speed .

Mrs. Basye said she had quite a thrill in watching the show but doesn't care to see it repeated.

News article in Fayette paper

sas. Jim, Lee, and I were the only unmarried pilots In VF-884. We always had a good time at the Officers Club bar after duty hours on our drill Saturdays. Hank Shimer was married, but he spent a lot of time with us. On one occasion, I recall that we had a hot sausage eating contest to decide whether Basye or Shimer had to buy the next round of beer. I fully expected to win because Hall and Hansen were eating part of mine. All went well until Shimer caught Hall and Hansen eating the sausages. Hank Shimer was a World War II pilot and Jim Hansen flew in Korea. Political correctness with its diversity and feminization mania apparently was the excuse to abolish Officers Clubs and various enlisted clubs.

I did not tell my parents about the air show. I was not convinced that the aerobatic demonstration was something that my mother should witness. However, since the Kansas City Star ran the story, people in Fayette knew about it. One of our neighbors, David Wiswall, volunteered to bring my mother, his young son, and his mother-in-law to see the show. Mother and the other lady, Mabel Earl, brought a nice picnic lunch and I joined them. Mother had prepared things she knew to be my favorite foods. However, I did not eat a bite. I thought it best in light of the aerobatics I would be performing in about two hours, especially since it was an extremely hot Kansas July day. Mother was disappointed that I did not eat, but I am sure that she understood after witnessing the show. She said she enjoyed the show but did not care to see it repeated. Mabel Earl had played the piano for George's funeral in 1951 and her two daughters, Mary and Martha sang duets. I still remember that one of the beautiful comforting songs they sang was "Life is Like a Mountain Railway." Following the air show, I flew the Cougar only five more times, on drill weekends in August, October, and November, 1954, and January, 1955. My Dad asked me "How much better off are you?" (from doing the aerobatic show) the next time I saw him after the show. It was apparent that my continued Navy flying was extremely stressful on my parents.

Joanne Brown

In early summer 1954, I went into a store in Fayette to say hello to an old friend from Fayette High School who worked there. He was not in, but I came face to face with a girl who also worked in the store. She was only 19 years old. I later asked my friend Roy Werner, who I had gone to see in the store, who she was. She was Joanne Brown. Her senior class picture is shown. I thought that she was about the prettiest girl I had ever seen.

At Roy's urging, Joanne wrote a letter wishing me good luck in the air show. After that we were together every weekend, except when I was flying the Cougar, until our marriage in December 1954. Roy was a gunner on a B-17 Flying Fortress in Europe during World War II and had been a prisoner of war after being shot down. He was the best man at our wedding and told me that "A good lawyer can still get you out of this" as we were preparing to enter the church for the wedding.

My friends at Westinghouse decided to go all out for a so-called "bachelor party." I should have been more suspicious. They rented a private room upstairs in the Hillside Tavern in Kansas City. Their scheme was to have me drink an excessive amount of whisky and pass out, then wake up with a cast on the right leg, supposedly to hold a broken knee in place. They had an x-ray of a broken knee with my name and the date of the event already on it. One of them had a brother who was an M. D. who just happened to be on duty at a convenient hospital. I had previously met him. To further their dastardly deed, they assigned my boss, Harry Card, and another friend, Al Cucco, to take turns trying to get me to consume large amounts of whisky. Harry was a World War II P 47 Thunderbolt pilot and Al was a Navy PBY pilot. What they did not know was that I did not drink the whisky. I purposely spilled almost all of mine while Harry and Al drank theirs. When it was time to leave the Hillside Tavern, Harry was lying in the gravel by the front door, unable to get up. He pointed at me and said, "He ain't going down, he just ain't going down." Al spent the night in the Kansas City jail. When the Kansas City police stopped him, he was wearing the lining of my ten gallon hat, which one of them had stomped until it came out. It was a hat that I had been most fond of.

They kept telling me that I had hurt my knee. I kept telling them that I had not. They kept telling me that I had fallen, which was true. Almost everyone there fell at least once. The floor was slick and was covered with whisky, among other things. To keep grown men from crying, I consented to let Dick, the M. D., take a look at the knee. When Dr. Dick showed me the previously prepared x-rays with my name and the date on them, what was I to conclude? I gave Dick permission to put a cast on the leg. He seemed to take great pleasure in the entire situation. At least, they did not ask me to pay for the hospital visit. They confessed the next day and took the cast off.

I recall that Joe Pimentel, from the Westinghouse Sales Department, attended the party. Joe had a nice, expensive suede sport coat that he was very proud of and careful with. Later, after hearing that his coat took some punishment, I said to him "Joe, I heard that your sport coat got hit by a flying greasy steak bone." Joe said "Several times."

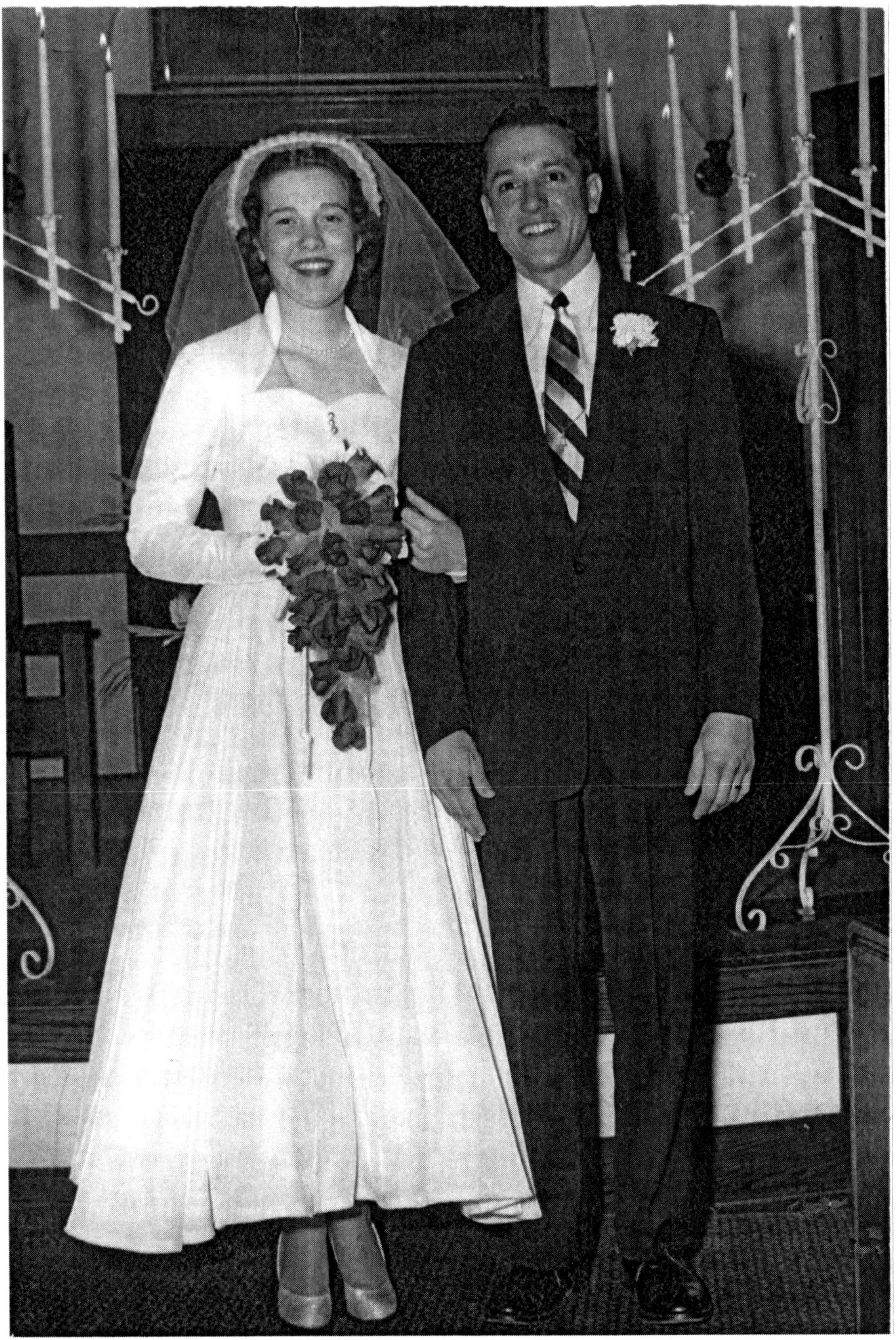

Joanne Brown and Ben Basye wedding, 12 December 1954.
First Christian Church, Fayette, MO

Later the day after the party, the Saturday before our wedding on the Sunday of the following week, I went to Fayette and told Joanne some of the details of the previous night's debauchery. A neighbor lady, Mrs. Wallace Hammond, heard the story and advised Joanne to call the wedding off. "If he carries on like that, you had better stay away from him" was her advice. I had grown up on a farm only some two miles from her home.

During our wedding, about the only guest that I can remember quite clearly was Mrs. D. C. Rogers. She was in the front row of spectators and I had the feeling that she was not too happy about it all. She was extremely fond of Joanne and probably thought that an individual who flies a jet upside down at 600 miles per hour over the Court House steeple should be avoided at all costs. I had done that several times, I suppose for the same reason that Major Richard Bong flew down Market Street in San Francisco. Fighter pilots do these things at times. Two of Mrs. Rogers's children were my friends in Fayette High School.

In early 1955, I knew that my 20 year old wife and I would soon be parents. I also knew that my continued Navy flying was difficult for my parents. Their two daughters now resided in Ohio and California, and did not have the opportunity to visit often. Since George's fatal Navy accident, I was the only one of their children they saw with any frequency. I recognized that any parent who has lost a child suffers immensely, and my parents possibly even more so since their loss was due to military service. It was also a fact as established by the F9F Panther history in Korea and by the F4U Corsair history in WWII that flying Navy fighters was an extremely dangerous undertaking, even when no combat was involved. The loss of friends and acquaintances to accidents in daily routines was accepted as part of the situation. Even though I had numerous close calls, some of which are described in this book, I felt it was time to stop tempting fate. I could perform a valuable service for the Navy as a maintenance officer. Neither Joanne nor my parents asked me to stop flying, but taking all things under consideration, I decided that nine years of flying Navy fighters was enough. On 20 March 1955, I wrote a letter to BUPERS, the Navy's Bureau of Personnel. The Navy permitted me to remain active in aircraft maintenance in the same squadron, so I still associated with my Navy friends. We performed two weeks of active duty at Olathe in both 1955 and 1956. I ran the flight line with the assistance of thirty or forty young American men. They were outstanding, hard-working maintenance crewmen.

After about ten of the fourteen days of our scheduled duty in 1956 had passed, our Commanding Officer, CDR Ron Puckett, decided to reward the hard-working crew. We had worked day and night and had excellent results, with no accidents.

Ron decided to take the entire squadron to Las Vegas for a night. One of our pilots, B. D. Mills, was a Captain for Braniff Airlines. There, he flew the same Douglas airplane that our squadron used as a Navy transport. When B. D. took the required permission slip necessary for us to use the transport, the Commander in charge of the airplanes, CDR Oleson, declared; "Hell no, you are not going to use that airplane. No damn fighter squadron is taking one of my transports to Las Vegas. You sons-a-bitches will get that airplane over my dead body." B. D. reported the situation to Ron. Ron took the permission slip to the station Commanding Officer and told him why we wanted to make the trip. He did not tell the CO about the previous rejection of permission. The CO said it sounded like a good idea and signed the paper giving us permission to use the plane. We were gone the next morning before CDR Oleson arrived on the Air Station.

The men helping me run the flight line at NAS Olathe worked extremely hard when a flight was going out or coming in. There were always several planes needing attention at the same time. A starting generator mounted on a jeep-like vehicle was plugged into the jet to furnish electrical power to start the engine. One day, the starting Jeep was plugged into one of the outgoing planes but the pilot was not ready to start his engine. One of my ground crewmen told the pilot that they were going to start an adjacent plane, which was ready. They would then come back and start him. The pilot raised hell with the crewmen and let them know that they were to stay there until he released them. After the flight had departed, the ground crew told me how much his unreasonable chewing out bothered them. I told them that I would report the incident to the CO, Ron Puckett, since the pilot was a higher rank than I. Ron said to tell them that as they travel down the long pathway of life, they would encounter some horse's asses. Tell them they met one today, and to not let it bother them. They were so elated that he would say this about one of his senior officers that they laughed profusely and worked even harder. It made their day.

Ron Puckett

One of the young men in my ground crew complained continuously for several months about the hard work. He said he could not wait for his enlistment to be up. He kept talking about which month would be his last one. That month passed and he was still with us. I asked him why he was still with us after his enlistment had expired. He said "Mr. Lillibridge told me that I was needed here and if I did not reenlist I would be a chickenshit. I did not want to be one of those. So I reenlisted." Bob Lillibridge was our Ordnance Officer and did not have much to do. But he knew how to accomplish this reenlistment.

Ron Puckett, a well-known test pilot, had served in both World War II and Korea. He came in in second place in the 1949 Thompson Trophy Race at Cleveland. His F2G Super Corsair had a speed of 393.527 for the closed course, All three top finishers were Super Corsairs powered by 3000 horsepower Pratt-Whitney engines. The P-51 Mustangs in the race choked in the dust from the Super Corsairs.

Ron was not impressed with my decision to leave Westinghouse and go to graduate school. He told me that I would have more education than sense if I received a Ph. D.

Ron and I decided that, as opposed to a more traditional delegation of authority to the Chief Petty Officers, I was to have continuous first-hand knowledge of the status of each plane. I had a clipboard with detailed notes relative to each plane and its status. One summer afternoon, a severe Kansas thunderstorm suddenly descended on the Air Station as several of our jets were landing. We got the planes secured, or so we thought. I looked out from the hangar and saw that one of the Cougars was not adequately tied down. It was rolling to-

F8F Bearcats fly past the USS Valley Forge on 28 April 1948

F2H Banshee approaching the USS Oriskany for landing on 8 February 1955. Note the tail hook and the planes parked on the front of the ship.

F2H Banshee over Wonsan, North Korea.

McDonnell FH-1 Phantom taking off from the USS Franklin D. Roosevelt on 21 July 1946. LCDR James Davidson was the pilot for this historic event. He was later a pilot in VF-52 with the author.

ward the hangar as it was being pushed by the wind. I recall throwing my clipboard down and running to the Cougar. I climbed up on the rolling Cougar and was opening the cockpit canopy. Luckily, I just had time to get the canopy open, get in the cockpit, and get the brakes on before the wind pushed the Cougar into the hangar. About 10 of the men got in front of each wing and pushed the plane back to where we could securely tie it down to the concrete.

Ron was a test pilot for Westinghouse flying the Chance Vought F7U Cutlass. The Cutlass was powered by two Westinghouse J-46 jet engines with afterburners. As noted earlier, Hal Avants was killed later while flying in a two-plane Cutlass formation with Ron.

In the following letter, 1315 designates pilot, and 1355 designates aircraft maintenance. The Navy approved my reluctant request and I made my last flight as a U. S. Navy fighter pilot on 22 January 1955. My pilot friends were perplexed by my decision to stop the flying we all enjoyed so much. However, more than three

20 March 1955

From: LT Charles Benjamin BASYE, 514556/1315 USNR-R
To: Chief, Bureau of Naval Personnel
Via: (1) Commanding Officer NRA VF Squadron 884, NAS Olathe, Kansas
(2) Commanding Officer NAS Olathe, Kansas
(3) Chief of Naval Air Reserve Training

Subj: Transfer to 1355 classification; request for

1. It is hereby requested that I be reclassified from 1315 to 1355 designation in the Naval Air Reserve.

2. I very much desire to continue to participate in the Naval Air Reserve Program in a non-flying status. My civilian occupation is as a mechanical engineer with the aviation Gas Turbine Division of the Westinghouse Electric Corporation. My duties at Westinghouse are with field problems of Navy Jet Engines, as well as participating in test programs and general engineering on present and future engines.

3. My primary reason for this request is the anxiety felt by my family towards my continued flying since the fatal accident of my only brother, Ensign George Levon BASYE, VF 113 in an F4U Corsair at NAS El Centro, California on 12 July, 1951.

4. This request is made with extreme reluctance, but with the sincere belief that I can be of service to the Naval Air Reserve as a non-flying officer in a Maintenance or some similar billet, in view of my civilian experience with Jet Engines.

Charles Benjamin BASYE

BUPERS Letter

decades of maintenance and engineering work, many years of it for no pay, lay ahead for me as a member of the U. S. Navy Reserve.

VF-884 spent two weeks at NAS Alameda, California, in the summer of 1957. I was extremely busy as squadron maintenance officer during this time. It was my last two weeks of active duty as a member of the Navy aviation community. I had been classified as an Aircraft Maintenance Officer (in training) since early 1955, but was formally designated an Aircraft Maintenance Officer on 19 April 1958.

After we moved from Kansas City to Ames, Iowa, in August, 1958, I had to make

U. S. NAVAL AIR STATION
OLATHE, KANSAS

P16-3/4

18 APR 1958

From: Commanding Officer, USNAS, Olathe, Kansas
To: LT Charles B. BASYE, USNR-R, 514556/1355

Subj: Aircraft Maintenance Officer; designation as

Ref: (a) CNARESTRA Instruction 3550.32

1. Having met the requirements of qualification as outlined in enclosure (3) of reference (a), and having been recommended by the Ground Officer Examining Board, you are hereby designated as a Aircraft Maintenance Officer.

2. A copy of this designation should be placed in your Official Record (NAVPERS 3021). You are reminded that information concerning your completion of this course of instruction should be entered in Block 16 of your next Officer's Annual Qualification Questionaire (NAVPERS 319).

F. M. Slater
F. M. SLATER

Copy to:
CO, NRA VF 884
GOEB, Station Snr Mbr
Res Pers

Acceptance letter from Naval BUPERS

a decision about future Naval Reserve participation. I knew I would be extremely busy, not only with teaching engineering to University students, but with taking graduate courses as well. It did not seem to be a wise use of time to drive to Olathe one weekend per month to continue the aircraft maintenance activity. I settled on the option of getting involved in the "Naval Reserve Officers School."

The Naval Reserve Officers School (NROS) met one night per week on the Iowa State University campus. I was a NROS student for five years and an Instructor for two of the seven years at Ames. I also participated in NROS several years later in St. Louis. NROS Courses included Military Planning, National Strategy, NBC Defense, Logistics, Economics of National Security, Command at Sea, and International Relations. A disadvantage of the NROS program for me was that NROS was not highly regarded from a promotion standpoint as participation in aviation squadrons.

I completed three two-week active duty tours while at Iowa State, in 1961, 1962, and 1963. Respectively, they took place at NAS Grosse Isle, Michigan, William Jewell College, in Liberty, Missouri, and the U.S. Naval Oceanographic Office, then in Maryland.

After receiving the Ph. D. in 1965, I took a position at the University of Missouri at Rolla. As far as the Navy was concerned, I was inactive for the two years at Rolla, except for a two-week assignment on the aircraft carrier USS Intrepid. It was tied up at the Brooklyn Navy Yard at that time. It was later moved to the west side of Manhattan and is now a tourist attraction.

Emerson Electric Company in St. Louis offered me a position as Senior Staff Engineer in the Electronics and Space Division in the summer of 1967. The University permitted me a leave of absence, so we moved to St. Charles, Missouri, a suburb of St. Louis. This move made possible a more active participation in the Naval Reserve. I had missed out on promotion. While I was still considered part of the Navy aviation community, I had only been involved in the NROS program, and not in aviation. This meant that the only participation available in the Naval Reserve was as a non-pay officer. I therefore joined a Navy reserve ordnance unit which met at the Naval Reserve Center at Lambert Field, in St. Louis. I devoted one weekend each month to this activity. Non-pay means just what it says.

Beginning in 1968, I completed a two week active duty tour for each year through 1980. They are briefly summarized below.

1. 1968 Naval Ordnance Laboratory; White Oak, MD
2. 1969 West Coast Weapons Course NAS; Alameda, CA
3. 1970 Naval Ordnance Systems Command Headquarters; Washington, D. C.
4. 1971 Naval Civil Engineering Laboratory; Pt. Hueneme, CA
5. 1972 Naval Ordnance Systems Command Headquarters; Washington, D. C.
6. 1973 Navy Technical Office, McDonnell-Douglas; St. Louis, MO
7. 1974 Naval Ordnance Station; Louisville, KY
8. 1974 West Coast System Management Seminar; San Diego, CA
9. 1975 Undersea Warfare Seminar; Newport, R. I.
10. 1976 Naval Ocean Systems Center; San Diego, CA
11. 1977 Naval Ship Weapon System Engineering Station; Pt. Hueneme, CA
12. 1978 Naval Ship Weapon System Engineering Station; Pt. Hueneme, CA
13. 1979 Naval Sea Systems Command Headquarters; Washington, D. C.
14. 1980 Naval Ocean Systems Center; San Diego, CA

The activities in 1, 2, 8, and 9 were educational, or seminar-type programs. The other ten were consulting engineering assignments. I typically received an outline of the problem upon reporting to the duty station. I had complete freedom to do anything reasonable, interview any personnel I wished to, visit any parts of the activity, and review past and present plans. I presented a report, usually written, to the designated officer at the end of the assignment.

The Navy uses an evaluation form called a "fitness report" for officers. One of these was submitted to the Bureau of Naval Personnel at the completion of each duty tour. Fitness reports have significant influence regarding promotion decisions. As illustrations, copies of these reports for the duty periods in 3, 5, and 13, above, are included herein. In addition to the systems covered in these three duty periods, the Tomahawk missile and Harpoon missile were among the systems I worked with in other active duty periods.

On reporting to the Naval Ship Weapon System Engineering Station at Pt. Hueneme, CA in 1977, the Project Officer I was to assist said I was to tell him what I thought he needed to know, as opposed to what his civil service engineers wanted me to tell him. He was aware that I was an engineering professor with significant education and consulting experience in vibrations and dynamics. I reported to him on my last day there. He was so busy that we talked as he was eating his lunch, a glass of milk and a lunchmeat sandwich, at his desk. The issue was how to proceed with extremely complicated, time consuming, and expensive vibration and mechanical shock tests of large missile components. My advice was much different from that of his civil service engineers. Officers with responsibility for managing large complicated weapon development programs, such as the man I reported to at Port Hueneme, carry a heavy load. Their responsibilities include budget, personnel, performance, and timely task completion. Engineers are the best problem solvers in these situations, which is why the service academies have traditionally and successfully trained future military officers as engineers. Unfortunately for America, that is no longer the case. In the politically correct and feminized 'new military', many future military officers study trivial things with much less substance than engineering.

In addition to the two-week active duty activities discussed above, I was involved in several Navy reserve units at St. Louis. I was promoted from Lieutenant Commander (LCDR) to Commander (CDR) in 1971, which restored me to eligibility for pay status. I had previously been promoted to Lieutenant Junior Grade (LTJG) after three years as an Ensign (ENS), and to Lieutenant (LT) after three years as a LTJG. Promotion to Lieutenant Commander followed four years as a Lieutenant. I was the Commanding Officer of three different organizations, all of which were related to Navy ordnance. They were identified as Naval Reserve Ordnance Division 9-2s, Weapons Laboratory 312, and a unit identified as a part of the Naval Ship Weapon System Engineering Station at Pt. Hueneme, California. One member of the Pt. Hueneme unit was Chief Petty Officer Kern Etter. Kern and his wife had lived in my mother- and father-in-laws' house in Fayette when Kern attended Central College after World War II. This was before I knew my in-laws, Harry and Ethel Brown. My designator was still 1355, (aircraft maintenance), as shown on the 1970 Fitness Report, even though I had been away from that for twelve years. The 1972 Fitness Report shows my designator as 1705, which means Ordnance Engineering. By the time of the 1979 report, my designator was 1415, which means shipboard engineering, as I recall. I was selected for promotion to the rank of Captain in 1979. The letter of congratulations from Vice Admiral C. R. Bryan is enclosed.

The 200th birthday of the U. S. Navy occurred while I was the Commanding Officer of Weapons Laboratory 312. All members of the unit received a copy of a certificate acknowledging that 200th birthday.

Official Navy photograph
C. Ben Basye
November 1963

It is unusual for an officer to be promoted after remaining in one rank as long as I had. I was a Lieutenant Commander from 1958 until 1971, primarily due to being considered an aircraft maintenance officer while not at all being involved in aircraft maintenance. The primary factor in beating the odds, so to speak, was the fact that the Navy was quite pleased with my two-week active duty engineering contributions.

There was no pay billet available after the promotion to Captain, so it was non-pay again until transfer to the Retired Reserve on my 60th birthday, in 1987. All told, the non-pay years probably totaled eighteen or more.

Before closing this chapter, I would like to commend Rear Admiral Wayne E. Meyer, the "Father of AEGIS." AEGIS was the fleet defense weapon system I worked on during my 1970 active duty at the Naval Ordnance Systems Command. It is the primary system that revolutionized air defense. Today it is installed

SEP - 9 1970 X
AUG 1 7 1970 D

0100
NAVPERS 1611/1 (Rev. 12-69)

REPORT ON THE FITNESS OF OFFICERS

F

(Refer to BUPERSINST 1611 Series)

1. NAME (Last, first, middle)	2. GRADE	3. DESIGNATOR	4. SSAN	5. FILE NUMBER
Basye Charles Benjamin	LCdr	1355	511-22-4189	514556

6. SHIP OR STATION (at which duty evaluated was performed): Naval Ordnance Systems Command Headquarters

7. DATE REPORTED THIS DUTY STATION: 24 May 1970

8. OCCASION FOR REPORT: ☐ PERIODIC ☐ DETACHMENT OF REPORTING SENIOR ☒ DETACHMENT OF OFFICER

9. TYPE OF REPORT: ☒ REGULAR ☐ CONCURRENT ☐ SPECIAL

10. PERIOD OF REPORT: FROM 24 May 1970 TO 6 June 1970

11. DUTIES: (Identify PRIMARY and principal COLLATERAL duties assigned, indicating number of months assigned each during period of report - list Primary duties first. For reports based on other than "Close Observation" indicate after Primary duty the number of months duties were performed physically separated from the reporting senior, if applicable. (e.g. 6/4). Indicate inclusive date of periods of non-availability due to hospitalization, temporary additional duty, leave and travel between duty stations. Describe the demands, qualifications necessary, responsibilities, and conditions peculiar to any billet of an unusual nature and not understood by naval officers in general - append supplemental sheet for this purpose if space is inadequate.)

Annual Active Duty for Training (½) Attached to Advanced Surface Missile Systems (AEGIS) Program, Surface Missile Systems Directorate

12. EMPLOYMENT OF COMMAND (DEPARTMENT/DIVISION/UNIT) DURING PERIOD OF THIS REPORT: (The setting in which officer displayed his abilities - Do NOT use code, names, unusual or extreme abbreviations)

Technical and Logistic Support of the Operating Forces (Naval Ordnance Systems Command Headquarters)

13. GENERAL INSTRUCTIONS

(a) ALL EVALUATIONS MADE IN THIS REPORT SHALL BE IN COMPARISON WITH OFFICERS OF THE SAME GRADE, COMPETITIVE CATEGORY (I.E., UNRESTRICTED LINE WITH UNRESTRICTED LINE, SUPPLY CORPS WITH SUPPLY CORPS, ETC.), AND APPROXIMATE TIME IN GRADE WHOM YOU HAVE KNOWN.

(b) A MARK IN THE ... MARKING BOX OF SECTION 18(a) CONSTITUTES A NOMINATION FOR ACCELERATED PROMOTION AHEAD OF YEAR GROUP. SUCH A REPORT, IF NOT COMPLETED BY A FLAG OFFICER, MUST BE FORWARDED VIA THE NEXT SENIOR IN THE CHAIN OF COMMAND FOR REVIEW AND ENDORSEMENT ON SUPPLEMENTAL FORM NAVPERS 1611/5 (REV. 12-69).

(c) REPORTS ON CERTAIN CAPTAINS, IF NOT COMPLETED BY A FLAG OR GENERAL OFFICER, MUST BE FORWARDED VIA THE FIRST FLAG OR GENERAL OFFICER IN THE CHAIN OF COMMAND, FOR ENDORSEMENT AND COMMENT REGARDING FLAG POTENTIAL ... NAVPERS 1611/5, (REV. 12-69).

14. Entries on this report are based on which one of the following relationships?
☐ Close Observation ☒ Frequent Observation ☐ Infrequent Observation ☐ Records and Reports Only

15. PERFORMANCE OF DUTIES: (Indicate evaluation by "X" in appropriate marking column for each item and provide supporting comments in Section 21)

(Details of duties noted in Section 11)	NOT OBS OR N.A.	Outstanding performance.	Excellent performance. Frequently demonstrates outstanding performance.	Very good performance. Frequently demonstrates excellent performance.	Satisfactory performance. Basically qualified.	Inadequate performance. He is not qualified. (Adverse)
(a) EVALUATION OF OVERALL PERFORMANCE OF ALL DUTIES ASSIGNED		X				
(b) SPECIFIC ASPECTS OF DUTIES (1) SHIPHANDLING AND SEAMANSHIP	X					
(2) AIRMANSHIP	X					
(3) SUBSPECIALTY/SPECIALTY (IDENTIFY):	X					
(4) MANAGEMENT	X					
(5) AS WATCH/DUTY OFFICER	X					

16. DESIRABILITY: Indicate your attitude toward having this officer under your command in the following categories of assignment:

CATEGORIES	NOT OBS	Particularly desire	Prefer to most	Pleased to have	Satisfied to have	Prefer not to have (Adverse)
(a) COMMAND		X LHS				
(b) OPERATIONAL	X					
(c) STAFF	X					
(d) JOINT/OSD	X					
(e) FOREIGN SHORE	X					

17. FUTURE ASSIGNMENT: Based on your observation of this officer's capacity for accepting increased responsibilities, for what type of duty do you consider him best qualified for future assignment - sea and shore? (Including employment in a subspecialty for which best fitted)

(a) SEA: Type Commander Staff
(b) SHORE: R&D - NRL NWC China Lake

Comment, if appropriate

18. OVERALL EVALUATION:

(a) BASED ON YOUR OBSERVATION OF THIS OFFICER'S PERFORMANCE AND CONSIDERING EVERYTHING THAT YOU KNOW ABOUT HIM, HOW WOULD YOU DESIGNATE HIM?	NOT OBS	NOMINATE HIM FOR ACCELERATED PROMOTION	One of the top few	An excellent officer of great value to the service	A fine and typically effective officer	Entirely satisfactory in present grade	Unsatisfactory (Adverse)
				X			

*If you designate more than one in this category, you must indicate this officer's standing in relation to the others (e.g., 1 of 3, 2 of 3, 3 of 3, etc.)

(b) In order to assist report users in making comparison among reports submitted by different seniors with varying standards of evaluation, a reasonably large sampling of the overall evaluations given other officers at this time is required. Accordingly, for reports submitted on this occasion indicate here how many officers of his grade (including all categories or designators and time in grade) you have marked in each category of (a). Indicate line/staff corps breakdowns within each summary figure. (e.g., 5(3L/2S), 11(9L/2S), etc.) The reporting of no breakdown will indicate that all are the same general category.

0	0	0	1L	0	0	0	0

19. NAME, GRADE, FILE NUMBER, DESIGNATOR, AND TITLE OF REPORTING SENIOR

Leslie H. Sell, RADM.,USN, 165625/1100 Vice Commander, Naval Ordnance Systems Command
Authority: CHNAVPERS ltr PERS E23 VWK-cah Ser E23/1039 of 31 Mar 1970

Fitness report on LCDR Basye for two weeks duty at Naval Ordnance Systems Command Headquarters in 1970.

NAVPERS 1611/1 (Rev. 12-69) (BACK)

20. PERSONAL CHARACTERISTICS: *To what degree has this officer exhibited the following qualities?*

0101

MARKING INSTRUCTIONS

Assign a mark of "X" in the appropriate column for each quality.

	NOT OBSERVED	IS NOT EXCEEDED	ONE OF THE TOP FEW	ABOVE THE MAJORITY	EQUAL TO THE MAJORITY	BELOW THE MAJORITY	BARELY SATISFACTORY	UNSATISFACTORY (ADVERSE)
(a) PROFESSIONAL KNOWLEDGE *(Comprehension of all aspects of the profession)*			X					
(b) MORAL COURAGE *(To do what he ought to do regardless of consequences to himself)*	X							
(c) LOYALTY *(His faithfulness and allegiance to his shipmates, his command, the service and the nation)*			X					
(d) FORCE *(The positive and enthusiastic manner with which he fulfills his responsibilities)*			X					
(e) INITIATIVE *(His willingness to seek out and accept responsibilities)*			X					
(f) INDUSTRY *(The zeal exhibited and energy applied in the performance of his duties)*			X					
(g) IMAGINATION *(Resourcefulness, creativeness, and capacity to plan constructively)*		X						
(h) JUDGMENT *(His ability to develop correct and logical conclusions)*		X						
(i) ANALYTICAL ABILITY *(Logical incisiveness which discriminates between assumption, fact, and hypothesis)*		X						
(j) DECISIVENESS *(The ability to act rationally and with dispatch within limits of authority assigned or delegated)*			X					
(k) RELIABILITY *(The dependability and thoroughness exhibited in meeting responsibilities)*	X							
(l) COOPERATION *(His ability and willingness to work in harmony with others)*			X					
(m) PERSONAL BEHAVIOR *(His demeanor, disposition, sociability and sobriety)*	X							
(n) MILITARY BEARING *(His military carriage, correctness of uniform, smartness of appearance and physical fitness)*			X					
(o) SELF-EXPRESSION *(ORAL) (His ability to express himself orally)*		X						
(p) SELF-EXPRESSION *(WRITTEN) (His ability to express himself in writing)*		X						

21. COMMENTS: Make specific comments consistent with marks in other sections. Mention strengths, special accomplishments, or weaknesses. Emphasize displayed potential for professional development and leadership ability and potential for assuming greater responsibilities and promotion. Support nominations for accelerated promotion fully. Comment upon degree of attainment of objectives for which subordinate was accountable. When applicable: comment upon efforts and effectiveness in retention/reenlistment of quality personnel; upon economy displayed by effective use of manpower/material; attention to and use of good material maintenance procedures and engineering practices. Comment on performance in, and contribution to, subspecialty, if appropriate. Mention attainment of specific qualifications (e.g., OOD Underway, plane commander, submarine or destroyer command, etc.). (THIS SPACE MUST NOT BE LEFT BLANK)

LCdr Basye served his two weeks training duty in the AEGIS Weapon System Management Office. AEGIS is an advanced anti-air warfare system for surface combatant ships. The AEGIS program has just begun engineering development. Because of his extensive background in structures design and analysis, LCDR Basye was assigned the task of investigating the structural interface between the AEGIS deckhouse and the rest of the DLGN-38 ship. In carrying out this assignment LCdr. Basye showed himself to be highly industrious and conscientious. His experience in this field was obvious as was his great intelligence. His technical analysis and report of AEGIS deckhouse s structure was excellent, showing an orderly approach to the problems. It will be quite useful to the Weapon System Management Office. LCdr. Basye welcomes responsibilities and has a high degree of initiative. His exceptional ability of being able to analyze problems effectively, and his methodology in their accomplishment have been of great value to this Office. In his two weeks training duty he has made a significant contribution to the better definition of the AEGIS/DLGN-38 interface design. He is highly recommended for promotion.

22. ADMINISTRATIVE ACTIONS (Each question in this section MUST be answered)

(a) Significant weaknesses should be discussed with the officer-- Has this been done? ☐ YES ☐ NO *(Explain in Section 21)* ☒ NO SIGNIFICANT WEAKNESSES NOTED

(b) What has been the trend of his performance since your last report? ☒ FIRST REPORT ☐ IMPROVING ☐ CONSISTENT ☐ DECLINING *(Must discuss with officer)*

(c) Has the officer seen this report? ☐ YES ☒ NO

In the interest of maintaining effective communications with subordinates, reporting seniors are encouraged to discuss this report with the officer, but not necessarily show it to him. Has this been done? ☐ YES ☒ NO

(d) Communications which are a direct reflection of this officer's performance should be considered in making comments in Section 21. Such communications may be forwarded separately for file in his Selection Board Jacket. Exception: A copy of a letter of censure (including appeal and denial) must be appended to the first fitness report submitted after it becomes final.

(e) Reports containing matter of an adverse nature (in marks or comments or appended) must be referred for statement pursuant to Navy Regulations. Statement of officer must be endorsed and attached to this report.

23. DATE FORWARDED: 4 August 1970

SIGNATURE OF REPORTING SENIOR: L H Sell

24. DATE NOTED AND FORWARDED

SIGNATURE OF REGULAR REPORTING SENIOR ON CONCURRENT OR SPECIAL REPORT

Concurrent and special reports must be forwarded via the officer's regular reporting senior. To avoid possible loss or misrouting of a concurrent or special report, the receipt form must be mailed direct to BuPers as the concurrent or special report is forwarded to the regular reporting senior.

26 AUG 1970

GPO 863-730

A-14001

Page 2: Engineering study of AEGIS deckhouse-ship interface. Report signed by RADM L. H. Sell.

0114
NAVPERS 1611/1 (Rev. 12-69)

REPORT ON THE FITNESS OF OFFICERS

(Refer to BUPERSINST 1611 Series)

1. NAME (Last, first, middle)			2. GRADE	3. DESIGNATOR	4. SSN	
BASYE	Charles	Benjamin	LCDR	1705	511-22-4189	514556

6. SHIP OR STATION (at which duty evaluated was performed): Naval Ordnance Systems Command, Department of the Navy

7. DATE REPORTED THIS DUTY STATION: 7 May 1972

8. OCCASION FOR REPORT: [X] Detachment of officer

9. TYPE OF REPORT: [X] Regular

10. PERIOD OF REPORT: From 7 May 1972 to 20 May 1972

11. DUTIES:

Active Duty Training (1/2)
SAMID (Ships Anti-Missile Integrated Defense) Weapon System, Surface Missile Systems Project

12. EMPLOYMENT OF COMMAND: Technical and logistic support of the operating forces. (Naval Ordnance Systems Command Headquarters)

13. GENERAL INSTRUCTIONS

14. Entries on this report are based on which one of the following relationships?
[X] Close Observation [ ] Frequent Observation [ ] Infrequent Observation [ ] Records and Reports Only

15. PERFORMANCE OF DUTIES:

(Details of duties noted in Section 11)	Not obs or N.A.	Outstanding performance		Excellent performance		Very good performance		Satisfactory performance		Inadequate performance (Adverse)
(a) Evaluation of overall performance of all duties assigned			X							
(1) Shiphandling and seamanship	X									
(2) Airmanship	X									
(3) Subspecialty (identify): OEDO			X							
(4) Management	X									
(5) As watch/duty officer	X									

16. DESIRABILITY:

Categories	Not obs.	Particularly desire		Prefer to most		Pleased to have		Satisfied to have		Prefer not to have (Adverse)
(a) Command	X									
(b) Operational	X									
(c) Staff		X								
(d) Joint/OSD			X							
(e) Foreign shore			X							

17. FUTURE ASSIGNMENT:
(a) Sea: Not Observed
(b) Shore: Material Command (NAVORDSYSCOM)

18. OVERALL EVALUATION:

(a) Based on your observation...	Not obs.		One of the top few	An excellent officer	A fine and typically effective officer	Entirely satisfactory in present grade	Unsatisfactory (Adverse)
			X				
(b)		1 of 2	21				

17 AUG 1972

19. NAME, GRADE, FILE NUMBER, DESIGNATOR, AND TITLE OF REPORTING SENIOR

T.J. Christman, RADM,USN, 263-60-7347/1700, Vice Commander, Naval Ordnance Systems Command
(Authority: CHNAVPERS ltr Pers E23-VWK-cah Ser E23/1112 of 14 Feb 1972)

Page 1: Fitness report on LCDR Basye for two weeks duty at Naval Ordnance Systems Command Headquarters in 1972.

NAVPERS 1611/1 (Rev. 12-69) (BACK)

20. PERSONAL CHARACTERISTICS. To what degree has this officer exhibited the following qualities?

0115

MARKING INSTRUCTIONS

Assign a mark of "X" in the appropriate column for each quality.

Quality	NOT OBSERVED	EXCEPTIONAL	ONE OF THE TOP FEW	ABOVE THE MAJORITY	EQUAL TO THE MAJORITY	BELOW THE MAJORITY	BARELY SATISFACTORY	UNSATISFACTORY (ADVERSE)
(a) PROFESSIONAL KNOWLEDGE (Comprehension of all aspects of the profession)			X					
(b) MORAL COURAGE (To do what he ought to do regardless of consequences to himself)	X							
(c) LOYALTY (His faithfulness and allegiance to his shipmates, his command, the service and the nation)		X						
(d) ATTITUDE (The positive and enthusiastic manner with which he fulfills his responsibilities)			X					
(e) INITIATIVE (His willingness to seek out and accept responsibilities)			X					
(f) INDUSTRY (The zeal exhibited and energy applied in the performance of his duties)			X					
(g) IMAGINATION (Resourcefulness, creativeness, and capacity to plan constructively)			X					
(h) JUDGMENT (His ability to develop correct and logical conclusions)			X					
(i) ANALYTICAL ABILITY (Logical incisiveness which discriminates between assumption, fact, and hypothesis)			X					
(j) [illegible] (The ability to act rationally and with dispatch within limits of authority assigned or delegated)	X							
(k) RELIABILITY (The dependability and thoroughness exhibited in meeting responsibilities)			X					
(l) COOPERATION (His ability and willingness to work in harmony with others)		X						
(m) PERSONAL BEHAVIOR (His demeanor, disposition, sociability and sobriety)		X						
(n) MILITARY BEARING (His military carriage, correctness of uniform, smartness of appearance and physical fitness)			X					
(o) SELF-EXPRESSION (ORAL) (His ability to express himself orally)		X						
(p) SELF-EXPRESSION (WRITTEN) (His ability to express himself in writing)		X						

21. COMMENTS. Make specific comments consistent with marks in other sections. Mention strengths, special accomplishments, or weaknesses. Emphasize displayed potential for professional development and leadership ability and potential for assuming greater responsibilities and promotion. Support nominations for accelerated promotion fully. Comment upon degree of attainment of objectives for which subordinate was accountable. When applicable: comment upon efforts and effectiveness in retention/reenlistment of quality personnel; upon economy displayed by effective use of manpower material; attention to and use of good material maintenance procedures and engineering practices. Comment on performance in, and contribution to, subspecialty, if appropriate. Mention attainment of specific qualifications (e.g., OOD Underway, plane commander, submarine or destroyer command, etc.). (THIS SPACE MUST NOT BE LEFT BLANK)

LCDR Basye is extremely intelligent and highly motivated. He exhibited intense interest in his assigned tasks and responsibilities during this training period. These traits facilitated more efficient indoctrination and training. LCDR Basye has an outstanding background in mechanical/metallurgic engineering. He quickly adapted to his assignment in the Surface Missile Systems Project Office in the shipboard radar area. In fact during the two-week training period he contributed significantly in efforts to find solutions to the continuing vibration and corrosion problems in shipboard radar antennas. LCDR Basye is an outstanding officer with high potential to contribute significantly when mobilized into a Naval Material Command billet. He is strongly recommended for promotion.

22. ADMINISTRATIVE ACTIONS. (Each question in this section MUST be answered)

(a) Significant weaknesses should be discussed with the officer. Has this been done? ☐ YES ☐ NO (Explain in Section 21) ☒ NO SIGNIFICANT WEAKNESSES NOTED

(b) What has been the trend of his performance since your last report? ☒ FIRST REPORT ☐ IMPROVING ☐ CONSISTENT ☐ DECLINING (Must discuss with officer)

(c) Has the officer seen this report? ☐ YES ☒ NO

In the interest of maintaining effective communications with subordinates, reporting seniors are encouraged to discuss this report with the officer, but not necessarily show it to him. Has this been done? ☐ YES ☒ NO

(d) Communications which are a direct reflection of this officer's performance should be considered in making comments in Section 21. Such communications may be forwarded separately for file in his Selection Board Jacket. Exception: A copy of a letter of censure (including appeal and denial) must be appended to the first fitness report submitted after it becomes final.

(e) Reports containing matter of an adverse nature (in marks or comments or appended) must be referred for statement pursuant to Navy Regulations. Statement of officer must be endorsed and attached to this report.

23. DATE FORWARDED: 15 AUG 1972

SIGNATURE OF REPORTING SENIOR: Thomas J Christman

Concurrent and special reports must be forwarded via the officer's regular reporting senior. To avoid possible loss or misrouting of a concurrent or special report, ... to BuPers as the concurrent or special report is forwarded to the regular reporting senior.

Page 2: Engineering study of shipboard radar antennas. Report signed by RADM T. J. Christman.

BUPERS USE ONLY

086

JUN 12 1979

BUPERS USE ONLY

03

REPORT ON THE FITNESS OF OFFICERS

1. NAME (LAST, FIRST, MIDDLE)	2. GRADE	3. DESIG.	4. SSN
BASYE, CHARLES BENJAMIN	CDR	1415	511-22-4189

5. ACDUTRA/TEMAC	6. UIC	7. SHIP/STATION	8. DATE REPORTED
X	00024	NAVAL SEA SYSTEMS COMMAND	79MAY14

OCCASION FOR REPORT: 9. PERIODIC [ ] 10. DETACHMENT OF REPORTING SENIOR [ ] 11. DETACHMENT OF OFFICER [X]

PERIOD OF REPORT: 12. FROM 79MAY14 13. TO 79MAY25

TYPE OF REPORT: 14. REGULAR [X] 15. CONCURRENT [ ] 16. SPECIAL [ ] 17. OPS. CDR [ ]

BASIS FOR OBSERVATION: 18. CLOSE [X] 19. FREQUENT [ ] 20. INFREQUENT [ ]

21. EMPLOYMENT OF COMMAND (CONTINUED ON REVERSE SIDE OF RECORD COPY)
TECHNICAL AND LOGISTIC SUPPORT FOR SHIPS, CRAFT, SHIP-

22. DAYS OF COMBAT: N

23. REPORTING SENIOR (LAST NAME, FI, MI)	24. TITLE	25. GRADE	26. DESIG.	27. SSN
LISANBY, J W	DEPCOM	RDML	1440	[redacted]

28. DUTIES ASSIGNED (CONTINUED ON REVERSE SIDE OF RECORD COPY)
ACDUTRA-ACTIVE DUTY FOR TRAINING (1/2)

SPECIFIC ASPECTS OF PERFORMANCE (TYPE IN OCR CODE LETTER FROM WORK SHEET)

29. GOAL SETTING & ACHIEVEMENT	30. SUBORDINATE MANAGEMENT & DEVELOPMENT	31. WORKING RELATIONS	32. EQUIP & MATERIAL MANAGE	33. NAVY OPGAN SUPPORT
A	N	A	N	A

34. RESPONSE IN STRESSFUL SITUATIONS	35. EQUAL OPPORTUNITY	36. SPEAKING ABILITY	37. WRITING ABILITY
A	N	A	A

WARFARE SPECIALTY SKILLS (FROM OCR WORK SHEET)

38. SEAMANSHIP	39. AIRMANSHIP	40. WATCH STANDING	41.	42.	43.
N	N	N			

44. SUBSPECIALTY CODE — REQUIRED BY BILLET: 45. YES [ ] 46. NO [ ] — UTILIZATION: 47. FREQUENT [ ] 48. INFREQUENT [ ] 49. NONE [ ] — (WORK SHEET CODE) 50. PERFORMANCE: N

MISSION CONTRIBUTION	NOT OBS.	HIGH				MID			LOW	MARG.	UNSAT
51. EVALUATION		X									
52. SUMMARY	0	1	0	0	0	0	0	0	0	0	

TREND OF PERFORMANCE: 53. FIRST REPORT [X] 54. CONSISTENT [ ] 55. IMPROVING [ ] 56. DECLINING [ ]

DESIRABILITY (TYPE IN OCR CODE FROM WORK SHEET)

57. COMMAND	58. OPERATIONAL	59. STAFF	60. JOINT/OSD	61. FOREIGN SHORE
N	N	A	N	N

RECOMMENDATION FOR PROMOTION: 62. EARLY [X] 63. REGULAR [ ] 64. NO [ ]

RANKING FOR EARLY PROMOTION: 65. NUMBER RECOMMENDED 1 66. RANKING 1

PERSONAL TRAITS (TYPE IN OCR CODE FROM WORK SHEET)

67. JUDGMENT	68. IMAGINATION	69. ANALYTIC ABILITY	70. PERSONAL BEHAVIOR	71. FORCEFULNESS	72. MILITARY BEARING
A	A	A	A	A	A

73. [ ] 74. [ ] 75. [ ] 76. [ ]

WEAKNESSES DISCUSSED?: 77. NONE NOTED [X] 78. YES [ ] 79. NO [ ]

STATEMENT: 80. NOT DESIRED N 81. ATTACHED N

82. SIGNATURE OF OFFICER EVALUATED (IAW BUPERS INST. 1611.12 SERIES): "I ACKNOWLEDGE THAT I HAVE SEEN THIS REPORT, HAVE BEEN APPRISED OF MY PERFORMANCE AND RIGHT TO MAKE A STATEMENT."

COPY FORWARDED

A

B

C

D

E

F

83. FORWARDED: JUN28 84. [ ]

85. SIGNATURE OF REPORTING SENIOR

86. DATE FORWARDED

87. SIGNATURE OF REGULAR REPORTING SENIOR ON CONCURRENT AND CONCURRENT/SPECIAL REPORT

RECORD COPY

NAVPERS 1611/1 (REV. 5-77) S/N 0106-LF-016-1100

U.S. GOVERNMENT PRINTING OFFICE: 1977 — 240-618/013

Page 1: Fitness report on CDR Basye for two weeks duty at Naval Sea Systems Command Headquarters in 1979.

BOARD WEAPONS SYSTEMS, GUIDED MISSILES, MINES AND TORPEDOES; ENCOMPASSING THE LIFE CYCLE OF THESE SYSTEMS THROUGH RESEARCH, ENGINEERING, ACQUISITION, MAINTENANCE AND FLEET SUPPORT.

087

28. DUTIES ASSIGNED (Continued)

88. COMMENTS. Particularly comment upon the officer's overall leadership ability, personal traits not listed on the reverse side, and estimated or actual performance in combat. Include comments pertaining to unique skills and distinctions that may be important to career development and future assignment. A mark in boxes with an asterisk (*) indicates adversity and supporting comments are required.

CDR BASYE, WITH A VERY MINIMUM OF POLICY GUIDANCE DEVELOPED A DETAILED, TECHNICALLY SUPERIOR REVISION AND MODERNIZATION OF A NAVY SPONSORED GRADUATE LEVEL TRAINING COURSE FOR ENGINEERS. HIS WORK IN THIS PERIOD WILL SERVE AS THE BASIS FOR FUTURE ACTIONS BY THIS COMMAND IN PROVIDING SPECIALIZED TRAINING IN THE TECHNICAL SUB SPECIALITY OF SHOCK ANALYSIS FOR SHIP SURVIVABILITY AND HARDENING. IN DEVELOPING THE TRAINING COURSE, CDR BASYE WAS EXCEEDINGLY EFFECTIVE IN HIS ABILITY TO QUICKLY ASSIMILATE A LARGE AMOUNT OF INFORMATION ON THE NAVY'S CRITERIA, STANDARDS, AND TECHNOLOGY ON SHOCK HARDENING. THEN USING HIS OUTSTANDING KNOWLEDGE IN HIS TECHNICAL FIELD, DESIGNED A TRAINING COURSE WHICH SHOULD BE HIGHLY EFFECTIVE IN EDUCATING ENGINEERS IN NAVY POLICY AND IN THE MOST UP-TO-DATE DESIGN TECHNIQUES. CDR BASYE IS HIGHLY RECOMMENDED FOR EARLY PROMOTION.

FORWARDING ADDRESS:
RADM J. W. LISANBY, USN
DEPUTY COMMANDER FOR SHIP SYSTEMS
NAVAL SEA SYSTEMS COMMAND
WASHINGTON, DC 20362

Page 2: Development of graduate level engineering training course.
Report signed by RADM J. W. Lisanby.

COMMANDER NAVAL SEA SYSTEMS COMMAND
WASHINGTON, D. C. 20362

14 March 1979

Commander Charles B. Basye, USNR
3100 Mockingbird Drive
St. Charles, MO 63301

Dear Commander Basye:

It is with great pleasure that I extend my sincere congratulations to you on your recent selection for promotion to the rank of Captain in the U. S. Naval Reserve,

You may feel justly proud of your selection as I am quite certain that it is not only a reward for your past performance but also a recognition of the potential for future contributions to the Navy. I am sure that your selection will be an inspiration for Reserve Engineering Duty Officers throughout the country.

Your past affiliation and support of the Naval Sea Systems Command Reserve Program is commendable and I am confident you will continue your performance in the future. Your assistance in improving the vitality of our reserve forces is solicited and will be appreciated.

Sincerely yours,

C R Bryan

C. R. Bryan
Vice Admiral, USN

Letter of Congratulations on being selected for promotion to rank of Captain.

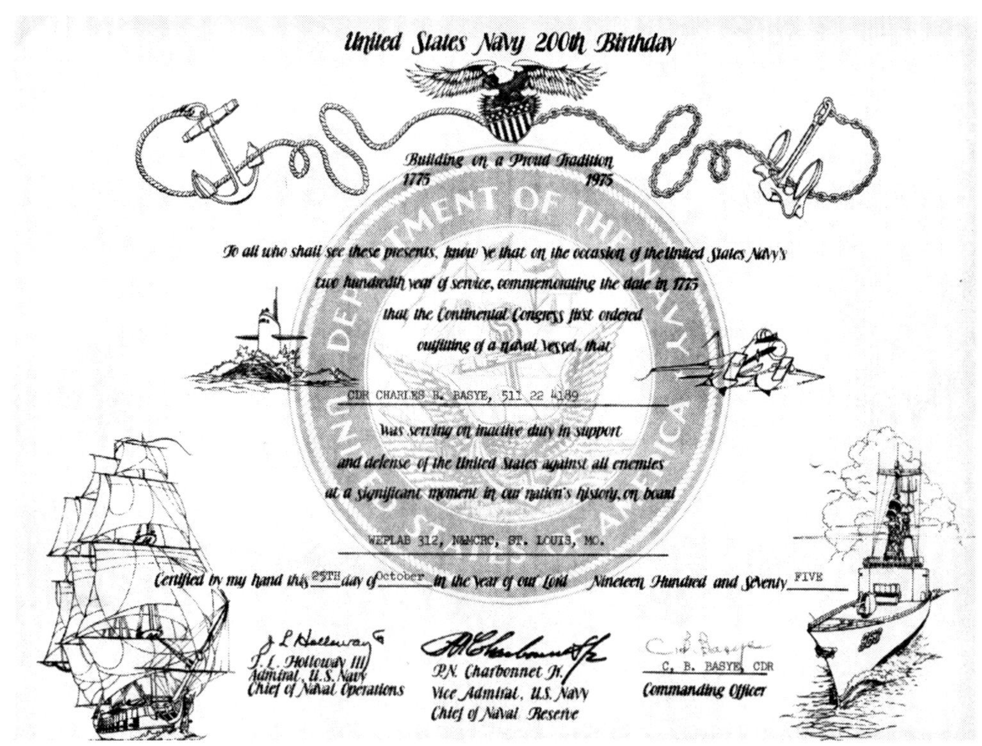

United States Navy 200th Birthday

Building on a Proud Tradition
1775 1975

To all who shall see these presents, know ye that on the occasion of the United States Navy's
two hundredth year of service, commemorating the date in 1775
that the Continental Congress first ordered
outfitting of a naval vessel, that

CDR CHARLES B. BASYE, 511 22 4189

was serving on inactive duty in support
and defense of the United States against all enemies
at a significant moment in our nation's history, on board

WEPLAB 312, N&MCRC, ST. LOUIS, MO.

Certified by my hand this 25TH day of October in the year of our Lord Nineteen Hundred and Seventy FIVE

J. L. Holloway III
Admiral, U.S. Navy
Chief of Naval Operations

P.N. Charbonnet Jr.
Vice Admiral, U.S. Navy
Chief of Naval Reserve

C. B. BASYE, CDR
Commanding Officer

Certificate acknowledging the 200th Birthday of the U. S. Navy.

State of Missouri
World War II Veteran
Award For Patriotic Service
CAPT CHARLES B. BASYE
United States Navy
Awarded in recognition of your bravery and selfless sacrifice to the State of Missouri and United States of America during World War II. Thanks to you, Americans today enjoy unprecedented freedom and prosperity.

Governor of Missouri

Secretary of State

State of Missouri award for World War II service.

on seventy-six destroyers and cruisers. Once, most Navy people considered AEGIS too expensive and complicated. Fortunately, Admiral Meyer's vision and perseverance prevailed. He was a small-town Missouri farm boy from Brunswick. He was born on 21 April 1926 and died on 1 September 2009. He attended a one-room country school and was in the Navy V-12 program at the University of Kansas. It would be difficult to overstate the importance of Wayne Meyer's contribution to the defense of his country.

I transferred into the Retired Reserve of the United States Navy on my 60th birthday, 10 June 1987. The Navy included my Army service and the few days between

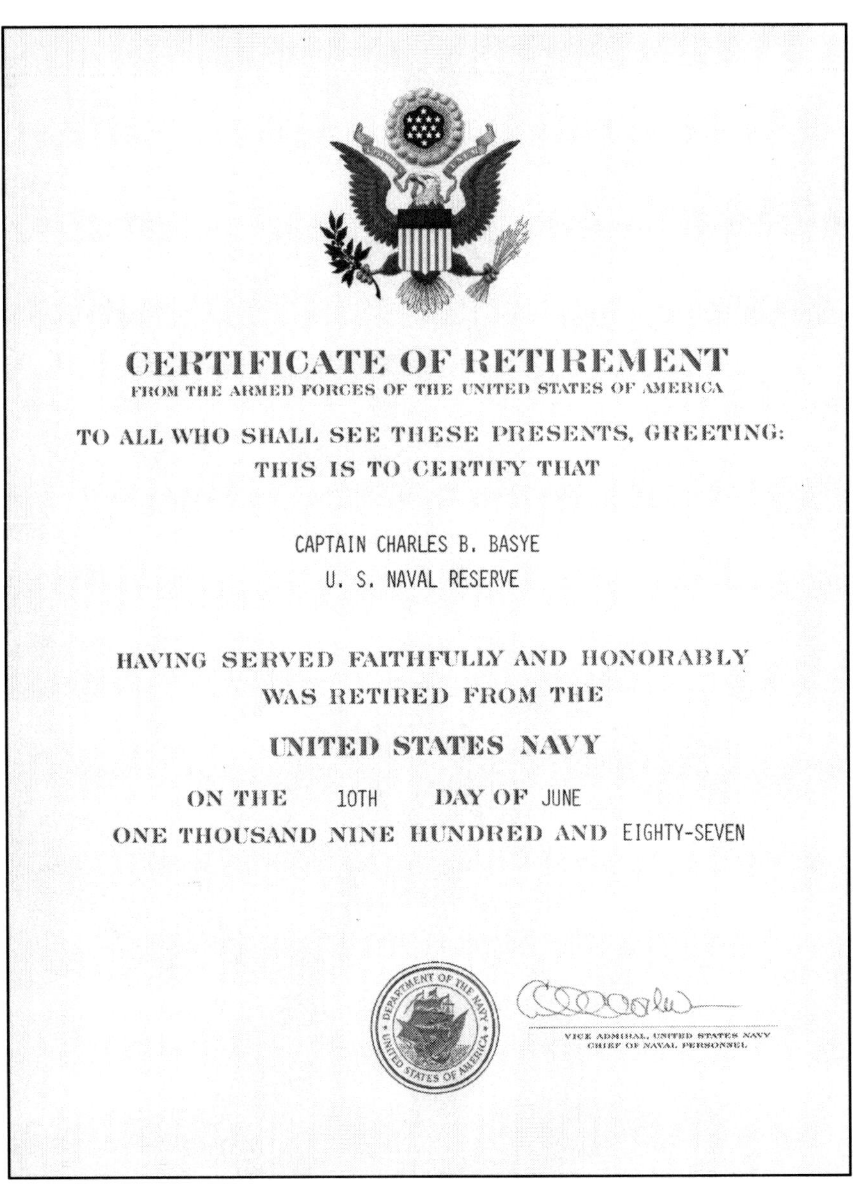

CERTIFICATE OF RETIREMENT
FROM THE ARMED FORCES OF THE UNITED STATES OF AMERICA

TO ALL WHO SHALL SEE THESE PRESENTS, GREETING:
THIS IS TO CERTIFY THAT

CAPTAIN CHARLES B. BASYE
U. S. NAVAL RESERVE

HAVING SERVED FAITHFULLY AND HONORABLY
WAS RETIRED FROM THE
UNITED STATES NAVY
ON THE 10TH DAY OF JUNE
ONE THOUSAND NINE HUNDRED AND EIGHTY-SEVEN

DEPARTMENT OF THE NAVY • UNITED STATES OF AMERICA

VICE ADMIRAL, UNITED STATES NAVY
CHIEF OF NAVAL PERSONNEL

My Certificate of Retirement

the Army discharge and entry into Navy active duty in 1945 in calculating my pay entry base date as 4 October 1944. Thus, my total military service extended from 4 October 1944 to 10 June 1987, or forty-two years, eight months, and six days.

My only regret in this long military journey was that—because of a Navy decision—I could not accompany my VF-52 shipmates on the deployment in 1950. It was a bittersweet regret. As documented herein, we trained rigorously for a year for the deployment and I felt like I belonged with my friends in VF-52. Being one of the select group of young American men to wear the Navy "Wings of Gold" has to be the highlight of a lifetime. Navy engineering endeavors, lasting for so many years, were challenging, enjoyable, and extremely important, but not nearly as colorful being a Navy fighter pilot.

Retirement plaque from my friends at the
St. Louis Naval and Marine Corps Reserve Center

PART 3. Education and Industry

Iowa State University
of Science and Technology
hereby confers upon
Charles Benjamin Basye
the degree
Doctor of Philosophy

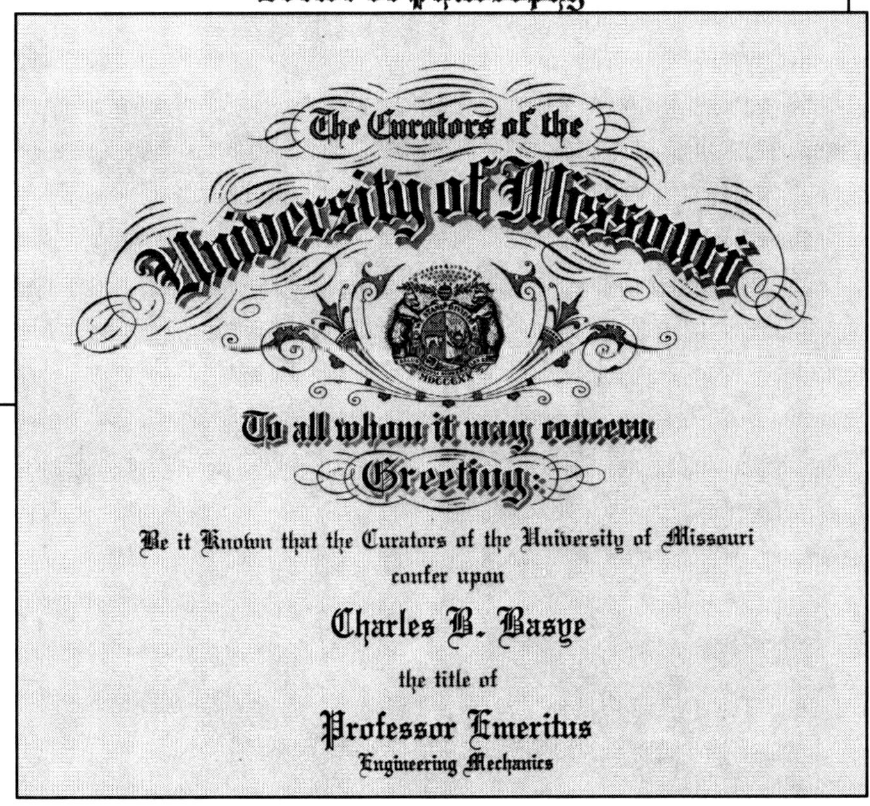

The Curators of the
University of Missouri
To all whom it may concern
Greeting:
Be it Known that the Curators of the University of Missouri
confer upon
Charles B. Basye
the title of
Professor Emeritus
Engineering Mechanics

Chapter 8: Engineering School, University of Missouri, 1950-1953

In the early summer of 1950, shortly after returning to Missouri, I visited the Mechanical Engineering Building on the campus of the University of Missouri, in Columbia. No classes were underway. Dean of Engineering Huber Croft was the only person I encountered that day. He was most gracious and spent perhaps an hour with me. He looked at the records from my time at the Universities of Nebraska and Wyoming, as well as Central Missouri State University and Brown University. He advised me of what I needed to do to apply for entry into the Mechanical Engineering program that fall.

Dean Croft's entire office staff was miniscule compared to the bloated administrative staffs of today. A few years ago, the present Dean of Engineering at the University of Missouri-Columbia had six full-time people in development alone. "Development" is a term that describes people whose function it is to try to get productive citizens and government agencies to donate money to the University.

I received G. I. Bill educational benefits to attend the University. And the Navy paid me to fly Navy fighter planes one weekend per month, and two weeks each year. This provided enough money for a single man to live on. Because Columbia was only about 15 miles from our family farm, I visited the folks often. I also helped my Dad in the summers.

I enrolled in a thermodynamics course, taught by Professor Milo Bolstad, in the summer session of 1951. I missed about three weeks of the eight-week course when the Flood of 1951 caused havoc as we tried to get my brother's remains home following his Navy plane accident. Another student did some of the work for me. I should have repeated this course since subsequent courses required mastery of its content.

This was a time for forming some lifelong friendships. Darrell Kirkendall was an Air Force veteran who, after graduation, spent his entire career with General Electric. Don Williams was from Kansas City. He and his two brothers ended up in the banking business, among other things. Owen Hornkohl had previously been a cadet in Navy flight training, but that career came to an end when he rode an SNJ over the side of a training aircraft carrier in the Gulf of Mexico. The four of us spent much time together while at the University.

St. Patrick's Week in 1953 was especially memorable. Owen Hornkohl painted the front door of the Law School a St. Patrick's green color one night. He then painted the prize buck sheep of the Agriculture School the same green. Later, there was a St. Patrick's parade going east on Broadway in downtown Columbia. We in the ASME (American Society of Mechanical Engineers) mounted a cardboard replica of a locomotive on a jeep, and had the jeep pull two trailers. The second trailer, a flat-bed one, was labeled as the club car. Owen, Don, and I rode on the front of the Club Car, each drinking a bottle of beer. I was wearing my prized ten gallon hat that was later destroyed by being stomped during the bachelor party in Kansas City as discussed earlier. Recall that Al Cucco wore the lining of this hat to the Kansas City jail that night when the Kansas City police gave him free lodging.

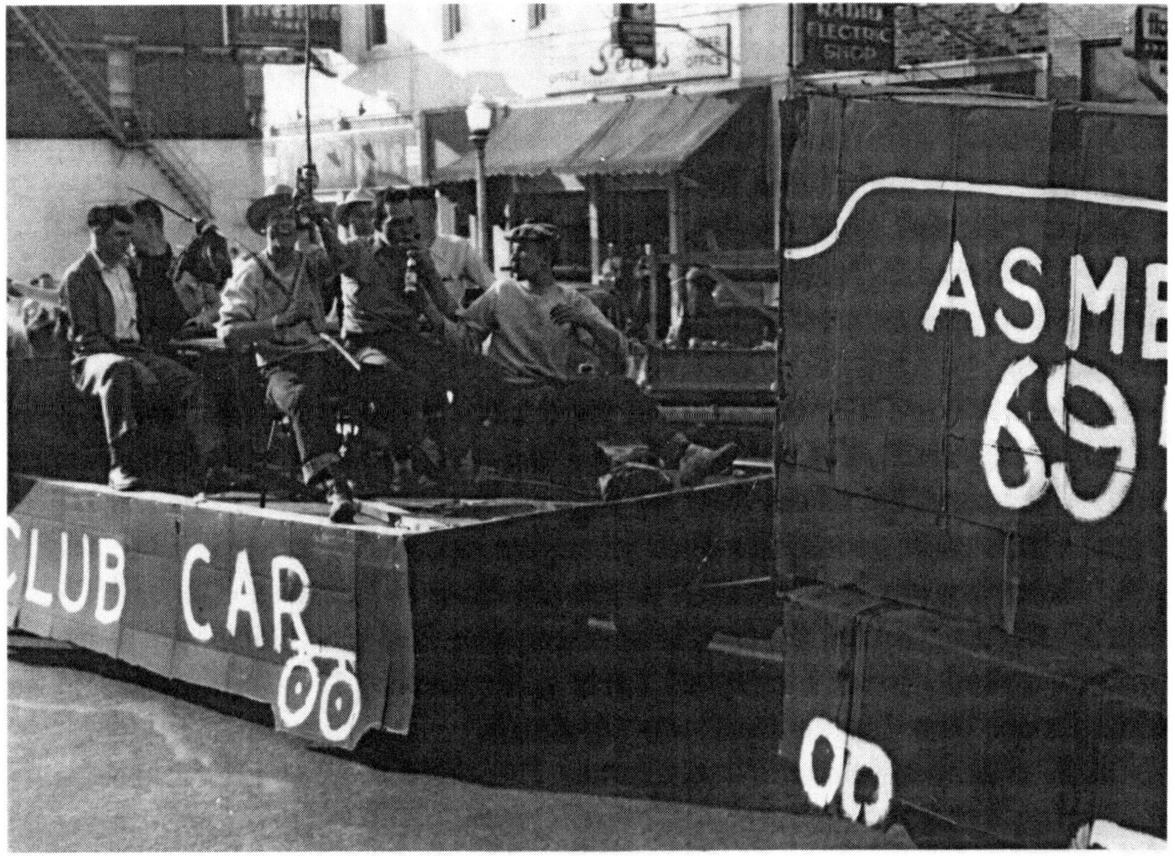

St. Patrick's Parade on Broadway in Columbia, MO, March, 1953.
Front row, the Author, Don Williams, Owen Hornkohl

Perhaps the producer of the "Animal House" movie got some ideas from this.

I was successful as far as grades were concerned. I became a member of Tau Beta Pi, Pi Mu Epsilon, and Pi Tau Sigma. They were an engineering honorary society, a mathematics honorary fraternity, and a mechanical engineering honorary fraternity, respectively. I was also active in the student chapter of the ASME and became Chapter President my senior year. Professor Alan Pringle served as our faculty adviser.

On a senior trip to St. Louis during the spring of 1953, we visited several local plants. Someone had a one-inch long hard rubber worm, which looked like the real thing. Granite City Steel was kind enough to furnish us a nice meal in the company dining hall. Professor Pringle was at the end of the table with company people. Darrell and I got everyone's attention at the opposite end of the table, while Don slipped the worm in Pringle's salad. After we sat down, Pringle put the worm in his mouth without detecting it, then had quite a reaction. He got the worm out on the tablecloth and punched it with his fork. By then, our hosts were extremely embarrassed. Pringle told me several years later that there had never been another bunch like us.

The University of Missouri was a most pleasant experience. The faculty consisted of Professors Pringle, Love, Sneed, Bolstad, and Scorah. Dr. Scorah was the Department Chairman. Unlike today, the faculty members were not pressured to do "research." Research, for the most part, means trying to get federal money, large parts of which can be used to support overhead and non-teaching administrative bureaucrats.

Westinghouse and General Electric were among the companies interviewing potential graduates in the spring of 1953. I had accepted a job offer from Westinghouse in Kansas City, where their jet engine plant was located. General Electric offered a little more money for their jet engine operation, either in Cincinnati or Lynn, Massachusetts but I wanted to remain close to Missouri. General Electric wrote a letter and invited the people to whom they had made job offers to be their guests for a steak dinner. I accepted. Later in the evening I told them I would be a Westinghouse man. But the steak was top notch.

In 1958, after five years at Westinghouse, I decided to go to graduate school in engineering. I visited Dr. Scorah in Columbia and told him my intentions. He said "You can come here if you wish, but you should go to a University that does more graduate education." What excellent advice that was. I entered Iowa State University, one of the finest engineering schools in the nation that fall.

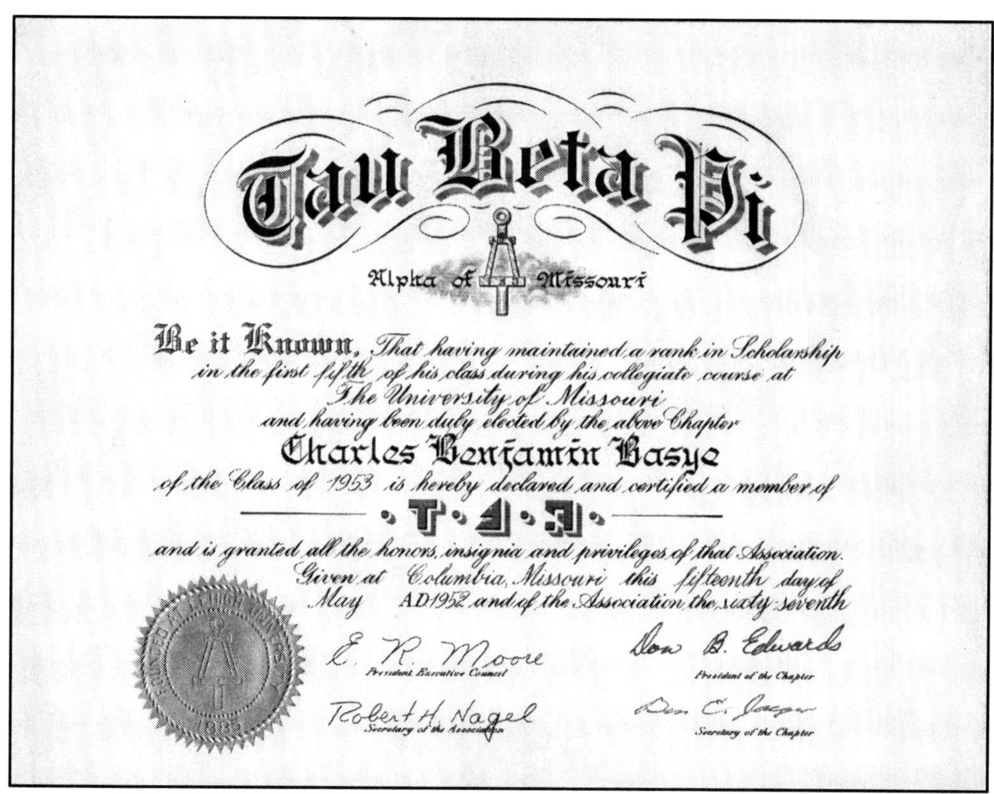

Tau Beta Pi

Alpha of Missouri

Be it Known, That having maintained a rank in Scholarship in the first fifth of his class during his collegiate course at The University of Missouri and having been duly elected by the above Chapter

Charles Benjamin Basye

of the Class of 1953 is hereby declared and certified a member of

T B Π

and is granted all the honors, insignia and privileges of that Association. Given at Columbia, Missouri this fifteenth day of May AD 1952 and of the Association the sixty-seventh

E. R. Moore, President Executive Council

Don B. Edwards, President of the Chapter

Robert H. Nagel, Secretary of the Association

Secretary of the Chapter

Certificate of Membership in Tau Beta Pi, the Honorary Engineering Society.

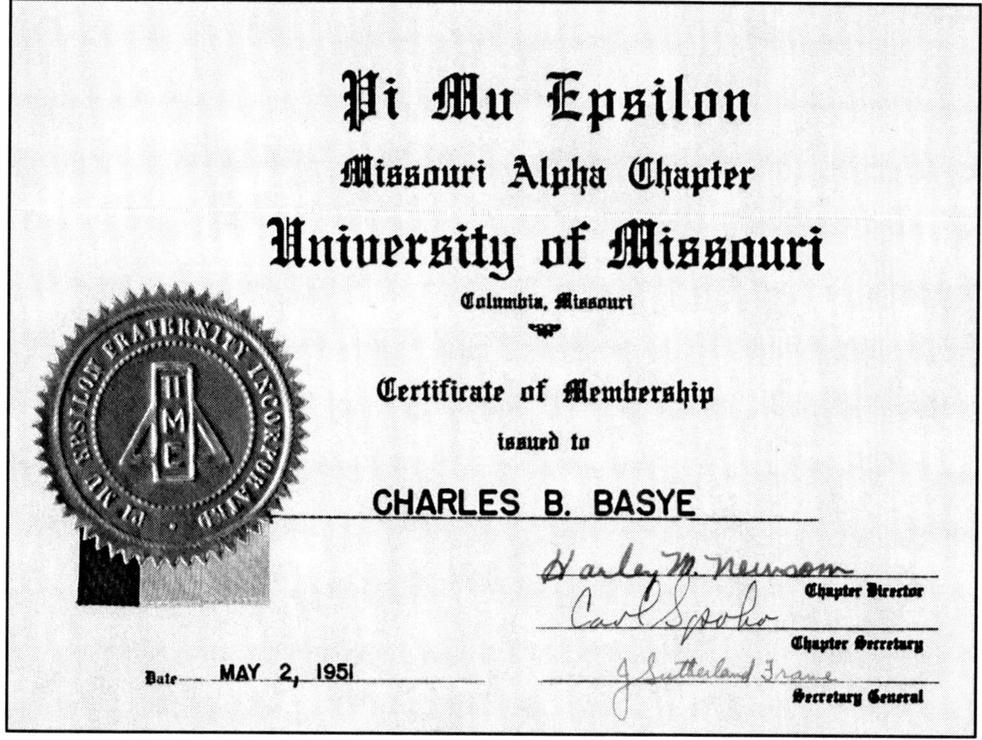

Pi Mu Epsilon

Missouri Alpha Chapter

University of Missouri

Columbia, Missouri

Certificate of Membership

issued to

CHARLES B. BASYE

Harley M. Newsom, Chapter Director

Chapter Secretary

Date MAY 2, 1951

J Sutherland Frame, Secretary General

Certificate of Membership in Pi Mu Epsilon, Honorary Mathematics Fraternity.

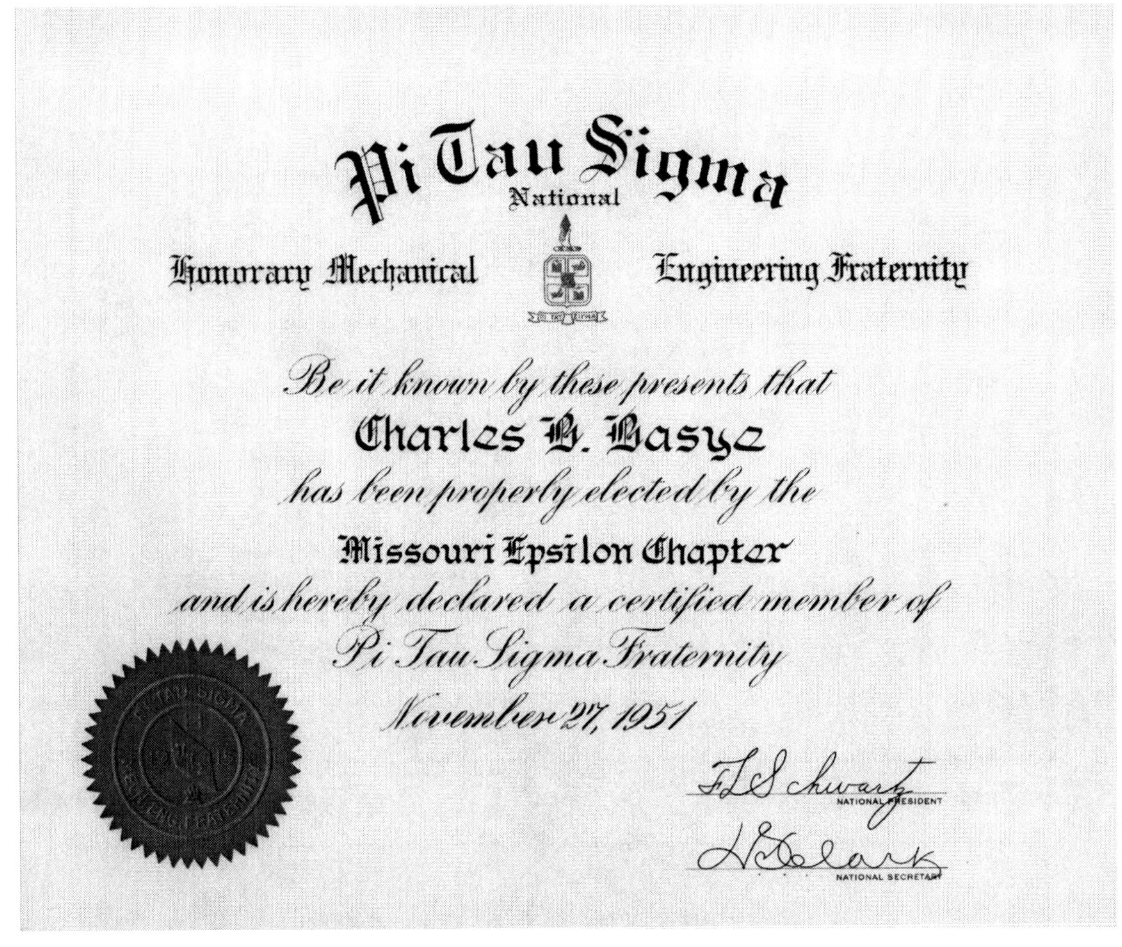

Pi Tau Sigma
National
Honorary Mechanical Engineering Fraternity

Be it known by these presents that
Charles B. Basye
has been properly elected by the
Missouri Epsilon Chapter
and is hereby declared a certified member of
Pi Tau Sigma Fraternity
November 27, 1951

NATIONAL PRESIDENT

NATIONAL SECRETARY

Certificate of Membership in Pi Tau Sigma,
Honorary Mechanical Engineering Fraternity.

Chapter 9: Westinghouse Electric, Kansas City, MO, 1953-1958

I began working in the jet engine division of Westinghouse Electric Corporation shortly after graduating from the University of Missouri in 1953. Westinghouse called this unit the Aviation Gas Turbine Division. Westinghouse and General Electric had been involved in steam turbine manufacturing for many years. Both steam and gas turbines are high rotational speed machines. It was a natural move for both companies to become involved in jet engine work. At this time there were five companies deeply involved in the jet engine business in the United States. In addition to Westinghouse and GE, the major players were Wright Aeronautical, Pratt-Whitney, and Allison. The latter three had an extensive background in piston aircraft engines. The Westinghouse plant in Kansas City was at 95th and Troost. Pratt-Whitney had manufactured piston engines for the U. S. military in the same plant during World War II.

I was assigned to a group called "Field Liaison Engineering." We coordinated closely with the users of our engines, which for the most part was the U. S. Navy. I was given responsibility for the J-34 engine. Both the McDonnell F2H Banshee and the Douglas F3D Skynight were powered by two J-34's. Westinghouse also had two newer engines, the J-46 and the J-40, both of which were more complicated than the J-34. They had afterburners and variable area exhaust nozzles. The J-46 was the engine for the twin engine Chance Vought F7U Cutlass. The larger J-40 powered the McDonnell F3H and the Douglas F4D. This was a time of rapid development in the jet engine business. Our searches for better fuel consumption characteristics and lighter weight were highly demanding.

Westinghouse assigned numerous service representatives covering operating squadrons, maintenance activities, and overhaul bases. The Service Department had a file on each engine, by serial number. The service representatives reported all problems and failures, so we had a good handle on which parts were causing problems.

Figure 1. Cut-away view of Westinghouse J-34 Jet Engine
Engine components are laid out on display tables in the background.

Figure 1. is a cutaway of a J-34-WE-34 engine. The front of the engine is to the left and the electric starter is in the center of the inlet. Incoming air flows around the starter. The air is then compressed by the eleven-stage axial flow compressor. The compressor incorporates a ten-stage aluminum forging and a steel eleventh stage. The reason for the steel is because the temperature at this part of the engine is too high for aluminum. Although not shown in the cutaway, fixed airfoil guide vanes direct the air in the proper direction between each rotating stage of the compressor. The rotating compressor blades are attached to the eleven-stage disk. The air next enters the combustion chamber. Fuel is inserted by sixty nozzles in two concentric circular rings. The outer ring has thirty-six nozzles and the inner ring has twenty-four. The fuel-air mixture is ignited and there is continuous burning.

A two-stage turbine absorbs some of the energy from the hot gas and powers the compressor by a shaft which connects the compressor and turbine. The turbine has two rotating stages and two sets of stationary guide vanes. The hot exhaust gas then exits the engine through the fixed area exhaust nozzle, passing around the fixed exhaust cone. The thrust that pushes the plane forward results from the fact that incoming air is accelerated and expelled out the exhaust at high velocity. The magnitude of the thrust is dependent on the product of mass (weight) of air and increase in velocity of the air. This is a simplified—but I hope useful—explanation of the operation of a jet engine.

The J-34 incorporated three bearings. The two rearmost were roller bearings, and the front one was a ball bearing, to absorb the thrust load from the rotating parts.

The J-34 rotated 12,500 revolutions per minute at top speed, more than 200 revolutions every second. This resulted in extremely high centrifugal forces on the rotating blade attachment mechanism.

These details apply to the J-34, but the principles apply universally. In some designs, part of the entering air does not go through the combustion process. In all turbo jet engines, however, a turbine drives a compressor with part of the available energy from the hot gas.

The requirement for the J-34 was for a 150-hour life. It was quite successful, and many engines had upwards of 750 hours. There were problems, however. Many turbine blade fatigue failures occurred. Some of these failures were in the airfoil part of the blade and some were in the root attachment. Luckily, the debris would almost always go out the exhaust nozzle, not seriously damaging the aircraft. Both the F2H Banshee and the F3D Skynight could successfully fly and land on the remaining engine. That was the only reason so many turbine blade fatigue failures were tolerated. Recall that a turbine blade failure in the single engine F-80 caused Tony LeVier's serious accident, discussed in an earlier chapter.

While turbine blade failures were tolerated in the J-34, compressor blade or compressor disk failures could not be. The housing surrounding the compressor was made of light, brittle aluminum or magnesium. These housings would not contain debris from a failure. The cylindrical housing surrounding the hot turbine was of a tough material which contained the failed parts which went out the exhaust nozzle.

Based upon close attention to failure records, we knew which parts would tend to fail and how serious such a failure would be. On one of my regular trips through the Marine Corps overhaul facility at Cherry Point, N. C., I made a shocking discovery. I spotted a fatigue failure of a compressor disk in the eighth stage of the eleven-stage compressor. This was a first, and a cause for concern. Such a failure could easily cause loss of the airplane. The debris would be slung outward and could go through fuel tanks or other critical areas. In the next few months, a few more of these eighth-stage disk fatigue failures occurred. Aluminum and magnesium have a behavior characteristic that causes them to have lower fatigue resistance as they are subjected to more and more operating hours. As stated previously, some of the engines had around 750 hours of usage. I sounded the alarm but could not get Westinghouse management to aggressively address the problem.

Our division received a report that an F2H Banshee had suffered a problem after taking off from NAS Miramar. The Navy pilot was killed trying to return and land. To investigate this crash, I traveled to NAS San Diego, where the wrecked parts had been taken. I determined that the cause of the fatal accident was fatigue failure in the eighth-stage compressor disk. The pilot was J. B. Morris, a fellow flyer in VF-211 in Seattle a few years earlier. He is in the group photos on pages 43 and 48. I had lunch with a Commander who was the Power Plants Officer for all aircraft in the Pacific Fleet. He reported to the Admiral who was in charge of Navy air operations for the Pacific Fleet. I explained the situation to him on a Friday. Upon reaching the Westinghouse plant Monday morning, a telegram from Navy Headquarters was already there. Because of this telegram, the action I had been trying to get started for several months now got underway at maximum effort. I have always regretted that I was not successful in getting meaningful action on the eighth stage compressor fatigue problem earlier. I certainly tried to get that action. J. B. Morris might not have had that fatal accident had I been more successful.

Inspection techniques and capabilities are continually being improved. We received word that one of the three overhaul locations had discovered cracks in the outer diameter of a turbine disk. The three locations that overhauled the J-34 were NAS San Diego, NAS Quonset Point, and MCAS Cherry Point. The Cherry Point facility had recently begun using an improved "Zyglo" crack detection system. It was more sensitive than the previous Zyglo system, capable of detecting cracks that the old system had missed. The cracks were on the outer surface of the turbine disk. The inspectors re-inspected a group of 25 disks with the improved system. While the old system had not detected cracks in any of the twenty-five, the new system detected cracks in sixteen of them. We investigated rigorously. It turned out that we had been flying with cracked disks without realizing it. As the Westinghouse engineering representative, I recommended to the Navy Bureau of Aeronautics that nothing be done other than continue monitoring the situation. The Bureau accepted my recommendation. My background as a Navy fighter pilot did not hurt my credibility in their eyes. The reason for the disk cracking was the fact that the outer part of the turbine disk heats up quickly when the jet engine starts, while the larger, bulkier part of the disk is still much cooler. The outer part heats up and expands so much that it cracks slightly. Luckily, none of the cracks grew large enough to cause a rupture.

I visited all three overhaul activities, other maintenance facilities, and occasionally an operating location, with some frequency. The Navy Bureau of Aeronautics in Washington held regular meetings. Having records on all of the several thousand engines, we knew which parts had caused problems. I asked Navy maintenance people about a certain part I knew had had some failures. They were adamant that the part in question had not caused a problem in their organization, and would never cause one.

Among the parts driven by the gearbox below the front of the J-34 shown in Figure 2 were the Holley fuel control and the oil pump. The Holley Company par-

Figure 2. Cut-away view of Westinghouse J-34
in manufacturing plant in Kansas City, Missouri

ticipated in some of the meetings at the Bureau of Aeronautics. One of the Navy officers assigned to conduct these meetings, Carl Cox, was a "mustang," an officer who had come up through the enlisted ranks. He used language I cannot repeat here to describe failed parts. He could, and did, render a meeting of twenty or so people speechless with his descriptions. He was especially abusive in describing the shortcomings of the Navy Aviation Supply Office (ASO), in Philadelphia.

We received a message that one of the J-34's had failed shortly after take-off in one of the twin engine Navy fighters. The oil pump drive shaft was sheared in two. The engine was returned to the plant in Kansas City. I observed the disassembly of the engine. A small steel washer was found in the close fitting oil pump gears. The washer prevented the oil pump from rotating and resulted in subsequent shearing of the drive shaft. This was soon followed by rotor bearing failure, due to oil starvation. The washer had apparently been dropped in the oil pump, and not retrieved, by military maintenance personnel.

During the Westinghouse years I became a family man. Westinghouse friends participated in the dastardly deeds at the so-called bachelor party at the Hillside Tavern. I also decided to retire from being a fighter pilot. Financially, Westinghouse had treated me extremely well. However, in 1958, after five years there, I decided to pursue graduate work in engineering.

One of my friends in the Naval Reserve at Olathe, John Smith, lived in Ames, Iowa. He had a Ph. D. in Physics from Iowa State University and was employed at the Ames Laboratory doing nuclear work. I traveled to Ames one Saturday and visited the campus. In the course of a conversation with Professor Steve Chamberlain about my interest in Graduate School, I mentioned that I was going to visit my friend John Smith. Later that day, Dr. Glenn Murphy called me at John's residence. Professor Chamberlain had contacted him. We set up a weekday visit, during which Dr. Murphy offered me a teaching position. Accepting that position never became a cause for regret. The job paid $4500.00 for nine months. I was leaving a situation in Kansas City with an income of about $11,000.00 per year.

Chapter 10: Graduate School, Iowa State University, 1958-1965

Westinghouse granted me a leave of absence to pursue graduate education in engineering. Before finally deciding upon Iowa State at Ames, I considered the possibility of moving to St. Louis to attend Washington University. McDonnell Aircraft offered me an engineering position which would have entailed a certain amount of travel. The Iowa State move appeared to be the best choice.

We placed our house in Kansas City up for sale and signed a contract to buy a house in Ames. It was close to the Iowa State campus and had a nice yard for the boys to play in. It was about 900 square feet with a full basement the same size. The back yard contained a large cottonwood tree.

Our three oldest boys were three years, two years, and two months old when we moved from Kansas City to Ames in August 1958. Joanne's parents moved the boys and her in their car. I hauled our belongings in a rented moving truck. A teenage boy from Kansas City assisted. I drove the truck back to Kansas City the next day and returned to Ames with our car.

Many engineers do not use books to a large degree in their work. That was true in my case at Westinghouse. The mental discipline associated with engineering education is utilized, but actual engineering calculations are not. Therefore, my initial undergraduate teaching, which was all books, was a tremendous adjustment. Many other engineers use books and calculations almost exclusively.

I taught in the Department of Theoretical and Applied Mechanics, abbreviated as T & AM. Engineering professors in other departments referred to it as Torture and Applied Misery. We taught statics, dynamics, mechanics of materials, materials laboratory, fluid mechanics, and fluid mechanics laboratory. In many other engineering schools, some of this content is taught by the departments of civil or mechanical engineering. This subject matter is indeed the foundation of basic engineering. A thorough knowledge of it is crucial for design and/or structural engineers.

The Professors at Iowa State had a system that almost guaranteed that any student who could pass these courses would learn the material. Before any individual taught any lesson in any of these courses, he or she attended a seminar on that lesson that emphasized important concepts. Each instructor approved any examination which students in that instructor's class were to take. The class roll was called each day. Each student answered with the number of assigned problems he or she could place on the board if asked to do so. One third of the student's grade was based on previously unannounced examinations. This rigorous approach meant that a student either learned the valuable material, or failed the course. It probably also meant that students could not devote as much time to other courses as they otherwise might have.

One of my friends from the University of Missouri was a design engineer for Caterpillar in Peoria, Illinois. He had been one of the top students at Missouri during our time there. He came to Ames one weekend to visit. He said that he could not believe how Iowa State graduates at Caterpillar were so proficient in basic engineering topics. His boss at Caterpillar was an Iowa State graduate, younger than he. That proficiency was a result of the Iowa State system.

As noted previously, in addition to teaching and graduate study, I was active in the Naval Reserve Officer School courses. Also, I got involved in a YMCA program called Y-Indian Guides. A father and one son became members of an Indian Guide tribe. This ensured that a son had the Dad's undivided attention during these meetings. It was indeed a busy time.

The T&AM Department was notoriously frugal. The faculty kept the paper that students turned homework in on and used the reverse side, which saved the cost of buying new paper for the faculty.

Dr. Glenn Murphy was one of the most accomplished engineering educators in the United States. He had written seven books covering a variety of subjects, including: mechanics of materials; advanced mechanics of materials; properties of engineering materials; similitude in engineering; fluid mechanics; a materials laboratory manual (co-authored); and, a nuclear engineering textbook. He had served as the national president of an organization of engineering educators. He was the Chairman of two departments—Nuclear Engineering and T&AM. Following a re-organization, he remained Chairman of Nuclear Engineering and started a program in Engineering Science.

The Mechanics work became a separate department and I taught there with a different boss. Dr. Murphy asked me to devote some of my time to serve as faculty advisor for the approximately 40 students majoring in Engineering Science. Thus

I had two bosses: Dr. Murphy and the Chairman of the Mechanics Department.

I received the Master of Science in Engineering in 1960, and the Ph.D. in Engineering, with a minor in Applied Mathematics, in 1965. I had tenure in the Mechanics Department and could have remained. In addition, Dr. Murphy wanted me to stay and be a member of the Engineering Science Department. However, I thought it best to move on. When I told Dr. Murphy that I was returning to Missouri to join the faculty at Rolla, he stated; "Well, you are leaving, so before it is all over with, I will make you glad that you are leaving."

He was on my Ph. D. Graduate Committee. The last obstacle to receipt of the Ph.D. was the oral examination. The examiners included Dr. Murphy, the thesis advisor Dr. Young, Dr. Serovy from mechanical engineering, Dr. Davis, and my Navy friend and mathematics Professor Dr. Maple. It was something like a boot camp ritual. It seemed as if a major objective was to see how much the candidate would put up with. After they put me through the wringer for about three and a half hours, Dr. Young asked Dr. Murphy if he had any more questions for the candidate. Dr. Murphy, who enjoyed insulting Missouri, said, "You being from Missouri and being an expert on pool balls and lipstick mirrors, I want your definition of an ideal fluid." I should have given him the engineering definition which was a fluid that cannot be compressed and has zero viscosity. However, I had taken enough and had decided that it was time to strike back. I told him that Admiral Halsey said that he never trusted a man who did not cuss and drink, so we know what Admiral Halsey's ideal fluid was and that mine was the same. Dr. Maple, my Navy friend, was almost on the floor from laughing so hard. No one ever talked back to Dr. Murphy.

The reason he had included the part about pool balls and lipstick mirrors in his insult was because my research was a small amplitude vibration study. I mounted one of Joanne's lipstick mirrors on the vibrating system. The mirror was covered with black tape except for a few thousandths of an inch. With the application of a travelling microscope, the amplitude of vibration could be measured within a thousandth of an inch. The vibrating system had a sphere vibrating in a viscous fluid. The sphere was a pool ball. They made me cool my heels in the hall for a while before they called me back in to say that I was now a Ph. D.

I remember other Ph. D. candidates getting Dr. Murphy's treatment during their final oral examination. One of them was from India. He came out of the room where Dr. Murphy had been grilling him and was muttering in mixed languages. Sometimes the same sentence would be part English and part Hindi. Another man came out and said that Dr. Murphy asked him his name and he said "I could not give him my name." Another of my friends was a candidate for a Ph. D. in electrical engineering. He wanted to minor in nuclear engineering, which was managed by Dr. Murphy. He said that every time he faced Dr. Murphy across his desk, "I felt like a freight train was bearing down on me." Dr. Murphy was small in stature and the electrical engineer was at least twice his size.

Richard Klammer was a graduate student in Nuclear Engineering. He was a large man who looked like a tackle for the Chicago Bears. He was teaching a class that included one of the Engineering Science students. Klammer told me that the student argued with him about technical details of problems. The same student was in a follow-on class with me. Dr. Murphy wanted me to keep him informed about the relatively few Engineering Science students. I told him about Klammer's problem with this student, and said that I had no such problem. Murphy's immediate response was; "It is one thing for him (the student) to take on all that beef, but to take on a man with wit is something else."

I remember two other student problems during the Iowa State years. One involved a female student in Engineering Science. I was her faculty advisor. She could not pass the hard physics courses. Her aptitude tests indicated that her strong points were what she was doing. In other words, her aptitude tests indicated that her strong points were in things like physics, which she could not master. Her father in New Jersey was an Iowa State graduate and wanted her to attend his school. I was at my wit's end in trying to help her. We had her to our house for supper once or twice. I did everything I could to help her.

The other situation involved a Captain the Army sent to Iowa State to get an M. S. in Nuclear Engineering. He did not have an undergraduate engineering degree, so he had to take the basic courses. He was a minority person and one of the most pleasant people imaginable. He was in my statics class, which is the beginning course. I have never tried any harder to help someone. He was good at some things, but not at technical concepts. As badly as I wanted to, I could not pass him. I absolutely had to fail him. The faculty did something for him that we had never done, and would never do again. We arranged from him to be in Fred Graham's class when he repeated the statics course. Fred was my friend and the only Negro in our department. Fred tried as hard as I had, but he also had to fail the student.

Fred lived only one block over from us in Ames. Our fourth child was due in June, 1964, and I had a Navy meeting in Des Moines. I asked Fred if he would take Joanne to the hospital if she had to go while I was in Des Moines. His wife later told Joanne that he slept in his clothes that night in case he was called for taxi duty.

Our youngest son, Scott, was indeed born in June 1964. When we moved to Rolla in August 1965, our family was complete.

Our boys, from the left: Chuck, Randy, Scott, and George, 1965

Iowa State University
of Science and Technology

hereby confers upon

Charles Benjamin Basye

the degree

Doctor of Philosophy

with all the Honors and Distinctions belonging to this Degree in consideration of the satisfactory completion of the Course of Study prescribed in

The Graduate College

Given at Ames, Iowa, on the twenty-ninth day of May, in the year of our Lord one thousand nine hundred and sixty-five.

President of the State Board of Regents

President of the University

Copy of Ph. D. Certificate received on 29 May 1965

Chapter 11: University of Missouri-Rolla (UMR), 1965-1967

We rented a moving truck to haul our belongings from Ames to Rolla in early August 1965. My nephew, Ben Ballard, was tremendously helpful. His parents lived in Cincinnati, and he had been spending his summers at the farm helping my Dad, his grandfather. As a matter of interest, one of Ben's son's, Jake Ballard, is a tight end for the New York Giants professional football team. Again we called on Joanne's parents, Harry and Ethel Brown, to take our family to the new home in Rolla.

The real estate agent selling our Ames house was kind enough to pay the down payment on the Rolla house. We repaid him when the Ames house sale was finalized.

Shortly after we got to Rolla, I left for New York City for two weeks Navy duty on the USS Intrepid, an Essex-class aircraft carrier tied up in the Brooklyn Navy Yard.

The engineering mechanics courses at Rolla covered the same topic areas as those at Iowa State, except that at Rolla fluid mechanics was taught in the Mechanical Engineering department. Since the procedures at Iowa State were so successful for so many decades, I announced to my first class that we would conduct the class as I had done at Ames. As soon as they were dismissed, five Indian students went at high speed to the office of Professor Fred Davidson, the department chairman. They told him, "That man is mean. We cannot pass that course and we want to transfer out." The Rolla system was based on a curve. If a student was as good as the other students, it meant a passing situation. There was too much inertia associated with the Rolla system to easily effect a change to the much superior Iowa State system. I at least tried to improve the situation.

I spent the summer of 1966 in Connecticut as part of a summer faculty program with Pratt-Whitney Aircraft. Also, I was inducted into Sigma Xi, a scientific research society in 1966.

I was scheduled to teach summer school at Rolla for the summer of 1967 for extra income. The night before classes were to start, I was told that no money was available. I would have to do something else. I went to St. Louis to look into a summer job, with the intention of returning to Rolla in the fall. Emerson Electric offered me a full-time position as Senior Staff Engineer. After thinking about it, I decided to accept Emerson's offer and return to industry for a time. While discussing the situation with Professor Davidson, he said "Why don't you go on leave instead of resigning?" That sounded like a good idea, so I did just that. I was able to work for Emerson and to continue teaching classes for Rolla, at night, through the Rolla Graduate Engineering Center in St. Louis.

Our house sold almost as soon as we listed it, so we left our Rolla friends and moved to St. Charles. It was a much easier move this time, since Emerson paid a professional mover to handle everything.

Jake Ballard: tight end for the New York Giants

Chapter 12: Pratt-Whitney, East Hartford, CT, 1966

Pratt-Whitney Aircraft, of East Hartford, CT operated what they labeled a "Summer Faculty Program." They arranged for engineering professors to spend the summer there. There were perhaps twenty-five of us in the summer of 1966, representing universities from all sections of the United States. I became friends with professors from the University of Illinois and from Brigham Young University. The Illinois professor and I were assigned to a group deeply involved in fatigue of jet engine turbine blades. The Brigham Young professor said that Missouri was the prettiest state he drove through as he traveled from Provo, Utah to Hartford. Pratt-Whitney engineers worked extremely hard and did not take coffee breaks. The Illinois professor and I took short breaks in mid-morning and mid-afternoon at a coffee shop just outside the front door of the facility.

Joanne and I had our four sons with us so we needed a sizeable living space. An English teacher with a nice house in West Hartford took his family to stay on their farm in Vermont every summer. He permitted Pratt-Whitney to recommend families to live in the West Hartford home. We were lucky to be recommended in 1966. The house was close to a swimming pool and a nice park. The boys enjoyed the summer.

The specific area of my engineering project was what is identified as "low-cycle fatigue." Historically, fatigue usually is associated with initiation and propagation of cracks in structures. That was the case with the numerous fatigue failures in the J-34 turbine blades. In traditional fatigue tests, engineering studies have related other factors to the number of cycles, where a cycle would correspond to a cycle of vibration or fluctuating load of some kind. The analysis method in low-cycle fatigue is much different. A cycle might mean starting the jet engine and bringing it up to the high temperatures, going to high altitude, returning to ground level, stopping the engine, and letting parts cool down to ambient temperature.

The low-cycle approach has also been used in analyzing temperature cycling associated with nuclear reactors, among other things. This low-cycle fatigue analysis approach is more appropriate where it is applied.

The specific engineering low-cycle fatigue approach was to relate the total engineering strain to a sum of elastic and plastic components. Strain relates to change in dimension whereas stress relates to change in load. Stress is used more in traditional fatigue studies, while strain is used more in the low-cycle fatigue. These descriptions are not rigorously correct, but do provide an accurate description of the problem.

A continuing goal in engineering is to build engines that weigh less and less, and that run hotter. Lower fuel consumption is always a priority. Better airfoil performance in turbine blades might be associated with sharper leading and trailing edges. These sharper edges are probably more prone to cracking problems. Trade-offs regarding weight, temperature, and other design parameters are central to the engineering process.

Chapter 13: Emerson Electric, St. Louis, Mo, 1967-1969

At Emerson, I was involved in a variety of engineering endeavors. I was in a group headed by Jack Lewis, who flew C-47 Army transports during World War II. The following list enumerates some of the things I did at Emerson:

1. Ten-month research project into Computer-Aided-Design,
2. Manager and chief lecturer for internal engineering education program,
3. Planned and analyzed helicopter flight tests,
4. Performed vibration analysis of armament system components, and
5. Served as consultant to electronic and radar groups for vibration problems.

Even though I was on leave from the University, I taught one graduate class each semester at the Graduate Engineering Center in St. Louis. Several internal publications resulted from some of the work. Among my publications were:

1. MOTARDES Flight Test, Final Report.
2. Cheyenne Vibration Testing.
3. Mini-Tat/OH-58 Structural Analysis.

In Vietnam, the Army used a small, unarmed observation helicopter. The Mini/Tat was a retractable turret, utilizing a rotating six-barrel machine gun, designed to allow the pilot to defend himself. The weapon could be retracted between the landing skids when on the ground and be rotated down for firing when the helicopter was airborne. The Missouri Society of Professional Engineers (MSPE) held a contest for engineering achievements one year. We entered the Mini/Tat, which was nominated for a prize. However, some influential civil engineers in the MSPE objected to a prize being awarded for a weapon. As a result, they gave the prize to Emerson for a run-of-the-mill office building.

The ANSSR rocket was another interesting project. Emerson had been awarded a development contract by the U. S. Army for some test rockets. The initials stood for Aerodynamically Neutral Spin Stabilized Rocket. The rocket had no stabilizing fins and instead was stabilized by a high spin rate. It was about five feet long and eight inches in diameter. The ANSSR incorporated two separate rocket motors. Exhaust gas from the first motor exited through four tangential nozzles and brought the ANSSR to a rotational speed of 12,000 revolutions per minute in a fraction of a second. This is hard to believe, but it is true. Then the main rocket is fired resulting in launch of the ANSSR.

Two outstanding dynamics/vibration engineers, Dave Utterbeck and Bob Scheller, assisted me in the dynamics studies. Dave conducted a dynamics analysis of the ANSSR design before it was built. He used the blueprints to make a mathematical model, consisting of elastic spring elements connecting masses. This was utilized to set up equations of motion for computer solution. His results predicted a fundamental frequency of flexural vibration of 200 cycles per second. The rotational speed of 12,000 RPM corresponds to 200 revolutions per second, the same as the predicted natural frequency.

Dave wrote a memo to the decision makers and told them that if his analysis was correct regarding the 200 cps natural frequency, trouble should be expected. The spin rate should not coincide with the natural frequency. The Army and Emerson management ignored his cautionary alert. Emerson delivered the first ANSSR to the Army facility at Huntsville, Alabama, for launch testing. An extremely high speed camera recorded the test. The ANSSR came up to rotational speed as expected and immediately came out of the launcher. After nine revolutions, it destroyed itself. The second ANSSR also destroyed itself after nine revolutions.

We took several steps. First, the spin rate was lowered to well under 12,000 RPM, which was still adequate to stabilize the rocket. The natural frequency and spin rate no longer coincided. Secondly, we beefed up the structure at the failure location. Even though I had not personally assisted Dave with his analysis, I was his boss and was told to go to a meeting with Army people at Huntsville to discuss the situation. Four of us, including the department manager, made the trip. We left the airport at St. Louis early one morning without breakfast. There was no discussion of lunch. We had nothing to eat or drink until preparing to fly back to St. Louis late that afternoon. We did get a sack of peanuts and a drink of whisky before getting on the plane to return to St. Louis. That was not, and is not, my idea of fun. That manager had a strange mode of operations.

Lockheed was developing a new helicopter, called the Cheyenne, for the military. Emerson had the contract for three weapon systems in the Cheyenne, a 30-millimeter cannon, a 40-millimeter grenade launcher, and a nose turret incorporating a rotating six-barrel 7.62-millimeter machine gun. The firing rate could be as high as 6,000 shots per minute for the machine gun. The ammunition was stored in a large drum container some twenty feet back from the gun. The gun had the ability to swing plus or minus 120 degrees in azimuth, 18 degrees in elevation, and 70 degrees in depression. Getting the conveyor to deliver the ammunition with these requirements was an extremely challenging task. I set up equations of motion for this system and Bob Scheller had the computer solve them. I reported on the results of this study at a meeting of the Department of Defense Shock and Vibration Information Center in Langley, VA. The title of the study was "Dynamic Analysis of a High-Speed Linkless Ammunition Conveyor System."

At the end of the two year leave of absence from the University, I requested to be permanently assigned to the Graduate Engineering Center in St. Louis instead of returning to Rolla. The University approved this request. For the next 25 years, I stayed busy with graduate teaching in St. Louis. In addition, I continued to assist Emerson occasionally on a consulting basis.

Chapter 14: UMR Graduate Engineering Center, 1969-1995

The University of Missouri-Rolla Graduate Engineering Center—hereafter GEC—was located on the campus of the University of Missouri-St. Louis. The University of Missouri-Rolla (UMR) established the GEC in the early 1960s, as a means of offering Master of Science degrees in metallurgy and engineering mechanics to interested engineers in the St. Louis area. The GEC later became much larger in scope, offering M. S. degrees in engineering management, mechanical engineering, civil engineering, electrical engineering, aerospace engineering, and computer science. The original two areas of metallurgy and mechanics remained as well. At one time, full-time resident faculty at the GEC, in addition to myself, included two faculty members in mechanical and aerospace, one in civil, two in electrical, four in management, and one each in mathematics and computer science. The GEC also employed a full-time director and secretarial staff. At one time, there were about 1,000 graduate students enrolled in the various programs, making the GEC a large educational undertaking.

I became the full-time resident professor for the engineering mechanics program after returning to the University from the two years at Emerson. Due to the wide selection of graduate courses offered, the resident faculty taught a variety of courses. This is in contrast to the situation at most universities, where faculty members usually teach a relatively small number of graduate engineering courses. It appealed to me. I taught a total of eighteen different graduate courses at the GEC. They included continuum mechanics, advanced mechanics of materials, advanced dynamics, fracture mechanics, fatigue analysis, Vibrations I, Vibrations II, energy methods, theory of elasticity, theory of elastic stability, theory of plates, engineering aspects of product liability, feedback control theory, and others. I had not taken most of these courses before teaching them. It was helpful that the mathematics were similar in many courses. In most cases, the M. S. degree requirements called for eleven three-hour graduate courses, with no thesis. Two of the eleven courses had to be from a different department. A few students chose the thesis route, which required nine courses.

I recall a meeting with a former UMR Chancellor at the GEC. He had had some health problems. After recovery, his total assignment was to teach one beginning course in engineering management at the GEC. I explained to him that I taught ten different technical graduate engineering courses each twenty-four months. He shook his head and said that he did not see how that could be done. His one elementary management course was proving to be a challenge.

The freedom to select my texts and pretty well be my own boss was a bonus of the situation. The GEC Director, Dr. Anton Brasunas, told me one day that he had received a report that I had released one of my classes early. I told him that maybe he should look upon my services at the GEC like those of a bull. Don't worry about how long I am on the job, but just consider whether or not I got the job done. He never brought the subject up again. Before they could graduate, my students were required to pass examinations prepared by resident Rolla professors. And they did. I must have gotten the job done.

In addition to the teaching, serving as faculty advisor was an important duty. Another duty required managing the final examinations. The two faculty members in mechanical and aerospace engineering later left for other pursuits and I took over faculty advising in mechanical and aerospace engineering in addition to engineering mechanics. I served as faculty advisor to over 400 graduate students while at the GEC.

One of the professors who left was thinking of applying for a dean's position. He asked several of us what kind of a dean we thought he would make. The mathematics professor told him that he would be no worse than the rest of them.

Most of my graduate students were employed by McDonnell-Douglas Aircraft. They were outstanding engineers or McDonnell would not have hired them. Teaching them was most rewarding. The graduate students appreciated the fact that someone was available to answer questions regarding procedures and requirements, and to keep their interests in mind. The relationship with them was a professional one, but it was also a friendly one.

One of the students was named Callihan. He was not a shy person. He kept one of his friends laughing, even in class. One night, I publicly told the friend to be careful so as to keep Dirty Harry from getting him in trouble. After they graduated, when I got to my office at the University one morning, there was a case of 24 bottles of Budweiser beer on my desk from them and one of my other advisees.

I still have one of the bottles, unopened, with the card from Dirty Harry and the other two. I will never open the bottle. The card says; "Dr. Basye, Thanks for all your help. From Tim "Dirty Harry" Callihan, Joe Caligur, and Chuck Kaiser."

A girl who was a graduate of the University of Kansas was another advisee. She was working toward a M. S. degree in engineering mechanics. She decided to switch to engineering management and did not consult me about it. I pretended to be offended that she had not consulted me, but really was not. She called me one day to ask what I was going to require on her final examination. Even though her major was not in my area, she still had to take an exam I had prepared. I told her that she had to be prepared to answer any question asked regarding the poem "The Cremation of Sam McGee." There was complete silence for about 30 seconds. Then she could not stop laughing. Several years after she graduated, she wrote me a note and said that she still remembered the Robert W. Service poem she had memorized.

Some of the classes were quite large for the graduate level. When Rolla Chancellor Martin Jischke visited the GEC, he asked each of us about our activities. I told him that I had fifty-three students in a graduate engineering vibrations course. He just about fainted to learn of that large an enrollment in a graduate engineering course. A number like that is unheard of in resident on-campus engineering programs. Jischke later became the President of Iowa State University and still later, the President of Purdue.

On one of his visits Jischke said something to the effect that all engineering knowledge becomes obsolete in a reasonably short time. I took issue with him on that point. Much of the theory of structural analysis is based on things developed decades and centuries ago. I have a textbook written in 1941 which says that if you design an axle shaft a certain way, it will fail. One of the world's largest automobile companies designed axle shafts that way, and they failed. Euclid wrote a geometry book that was still used as a text in the early 1900's. Euclid lived before Jesus Christ. We ignore or pay insufficient attention to the lessons of history at our peril.

We had another visitor at the GEC at a time when UMR was searching for a Dean. This man, a prominent UMR graduate and supporter, expressed dismay that more faculty had not applied for the job as dean. He said, "Don't they think that they are qualified to be a dean"? I told him that I would only speak for myself, and that I felt completely qualified to be a dean. However, I prefer to be a professor teaching and using engineering. I consider it more satisfying and much more important. That ended the conversation.

There was always the effort on the part of some administrative bureaucrats to force faculty to do "research." Although they never acknowledged it, to them, research meant getting money from well-meaning alumni or the federal government to support institutional overhead or more bureaucracy. In my opinion, the engineering professor who knows his subject, keeps up to date, and succeeds in imparting that knowledge should be considered much more valuable than most of the researchers. It took a significant amount of research to successfully teach the extensive variety of graduate courses I offered.

Although graduate teaching and student advising were my primary responsibilities, I became extensively involved in some other things while at the GEC. They included:

1. Continued involvement in the U. S. Naval Reserve
2. Active involvement with the University of Missouri-St. Louis Speakers Bureau
3. Professional involvement with the American Society of Mechanical Engineers
4. Elective school board membership
5. Directing and teaching review courses for engineers taking state examinations
6. Consulting.

I discussed my Naval Reserve activities extensively in Chapter 7. I devoted one weekend per month to the Navy. Reserve meetings were usually held at the Naval Reserve Center at Lambert Field in St. Louis, which was convenient both to our home in St. Charles and to my office at the University. I regularly drove to the Naval Ordnance Station in Louisville, KY and met with the Commanding Officer there.

I was the Commanding Officer of an ordnance unit at St. Louis. Several of my officers had expertise in computer applications. We set up an agreement that authorized my reserve unit to establish a computerized system to manage preventive maintenance on the many manufacturing and overhaul machines of the Ordnance Station. The Station C. O. told me that we accomplished more on a weekend than his civil service people did in months. Larry Neill was the officer who supervised this work and he did a fabulous job. Larry is the owner of Larry's Honda, a large motorcycle and ATV dealership in Jefferson City. Those weekend trips to Louisville were always enjoyable.

The University of Missouri-St. Louis Speakers Bureau published a list of faculty who had agreed to speak on specified topics if requested to do so. Through this program, I made numerous presentations to service clubs and other groups. Information on the next three pages lists some of these presentations.

University of Missouri - Rolla

UMR GRADUATE ENGINEERING CENTER OF ST. LOUIS

8001 Natural Bridge Road
St. Louis, Missouri 63121

Telephone
314 453-5431

15 Oct 1973	Brentwood, Mo., Kiwanis Club	"Assault on the American Free Enterprise System"
13 Nov 1973	McKelvey School PTA, St. Louis County, MO.	"Some Trends in Public Elementary and Secondary Education-Progress or Regression?"
16 Nov 1973	Naval Ordnance Station, Louisville, Ky.	"Fatigue and Failure of Navy Structural Hardware"
13 Dec 1973	Kirkwood, MO, High-Twelve Masonic Club	"Assault on the American Free Enterprise System"
14 Jan 1974	Emerson Electric Engineers Club St. Louis, MO	"Our American Free Enterprise System - Where Do We Go From Here?"
28 Jan 1974 4 Feb 1974	Naval Reserve Officers School, NROS 9-7(M), St. Louis, MO	"Engineering Aspects of Product Liability"
16 Feb 1974	Boy Scout Blue and Gold Banquet St. Charles, MO	"U. S. Naval Aviation"
13 Mar 1974	First Capitol Kiwanis Club St. Charles, MO	"It's Time for More Americans to 'Speak Up' for Uncle Sam"
18 Apr 1974	C.I.D.E. (Distributive Education) High School Teachers, St. Louis, MO	"It's Time for More Americans to 'Speak Up' for Uncle Sam"
30 Apr 1974	American Association of Cost Engineers, St. Louis, MO	"Engineering Education for the Future"
22-24 May 1974	Naval Ordnance Station, Louisville, Kentucky	"Fracture Mechanics"
1 Oct 1974	Laclede Gas Company Management Club, St. Louis, MO	"Attack on the American Free Enterprise System"
6 Nov 1974	St. Louis Area High School Guidance Counselors	"Our Responsibilities as Educators and United States Citizens"
12 Feb 1975	Bellefontaine Business and Professional Women's Club	"It's Time for More Americans to 'Speak Up' for Uncle Sam"
21 Mar 1975	First Baptist Church Deacons' Meeting, St. Charles, MO	"It's Time for More Americans to 'Speak Up' for Uncle Sam"
3 May 1975	Jefferson City, MO, Loyalty Day Speech, State Capitol Rotunda	"It's Time for More Americans to 'Speak Up' for Uncle Sam"
22 July 1975	Northrop Aircraft, Hawthorne, California	"Use of Vibration Isolators for F-5 Radar Installation"
28 Feb 1976	Illinois Trial Lawyers Association Seminar, Fairview Hts, Ill	"Use of Engineers in Product Failure Cases"
1 Apr 1976	St. Peters, Mo. Kiwanis Club	"It's Time for More Americans to 'Speak Up' for Uncle Sam"
29 June 1976	University City, Mo. Kiwanis Club	"The 200th Birthday of the U. S. Navy"
8 July 1976	St. Charles, Mo. Rotary Club	"The Energy Crisis - An Engineering Viewpoint"
16 Feb 1977	Military Order of the World Wars, St. Louis, Missouri	"The Shifting Balance of Military Power"
30 Mar 1977	Ferguson-Florissant School District Advisory Council	"Some Trends in Public Elementary and Secondary Education-Progress or Regression?"

A partial list of speeches given by the author

THE KIWANICASTE

WEEKLY PUBLICATION OF ST. CHARLES MISSOURI KIWANIS

CHARTERED
OCTOBER 15, 1935

WESTERN LOUNGE
2310 WEST CLAY
TUESDAYS 12:05

Vol. 43, No. 32 May 10, 1977

1976 - 77 OFFICERS

GLEN GOELLNER
PRESIDENT
JOE DAUES
PRESIDENT-ELECT
RON WILLIAMS
VICE PRESIDENT
GIL LAUER
TREASURER
ART SCHNEIDER
SECRETARY

DIRECTORS
DEAN GRIGSBY
WAYNE HOFFMAN
BILL HUTCHINS
W. KARRENBROCK
JIM LONNING
LES PRINSTER
JOHN WARREN
BOB JACOBS

NEW MEMBERS
(Goal 30)

ED BAUMGARTH
LARRY BROWNING
BOB CLARK
RALPH KSITER
ANDY McCOLLOCH
LARRY NESSLAGE
MICK SANDERS
AL SHOEMAKER
CRANE SMILEY
DAROLD THORNE
JIM VAN DYNE
VINCE WOOD
MIKE McKEE

43%

On To Dallas . . . .

Among this week's guests at the Western Lounge luncheon meeting was Lt. Governor Ross Reagan who, following his introduction by Brownie Dawkins, delivered a highly interesting preview of this year's Kiwanis International convention slated for Dallas July 26 through 29.

It's the second such conclave to meet in Dallas, Ross said. Back in 1959, when Kiwanians met there...of a total membership of some 255,000 in two countries (The U.S. and Canada), 13,000 were in attendance. This year's convention will find delegates from 57 countries on hand, and of our current membership of 286,000 a crowd considerably larger than last year's 20,000 San Diego attendees is expected.

Noting that there's nothing to match the thrill of the International Convention, Reagan pointed out that this is the place to *really* see Kiwanians in action. He went on to stimulate interest in attendance by presenting this year's program highlights.

Among the notables on the program are Senator John Tower of Texas whose timely subject is to be "Social Security...Any Left for Me?" Others include "Doc" Severinsen of the Johnny Carson Show, who with Norm Crosby will present an evening of musical entertainment on Wednesday; humorist Art Buchwald; Roy Rogers and Dale Evans, who will be honored for their good works; Edie Adams, Polly Bergen, and plenty of pageantry and musical numbers sprinkled throughout the three days.

Goal for attendance from our district is 500, Reagan says, and it's important that we meet it in order to help elect former Mo-Ark District Governor Ray Lansford as an International Trustee. So...See you at the Dupont Plaza Hotel in Dallas...that's headquarters for the Mo-Ark District.

Guests. . .

Members extended a welcome to Tuesday guests Lee Hammerschmidt of Crest Mobile Homes and Alex Marshall, Banner-News circulation manager, who is a member of the Frontier Club.

Follies Tickets Request . . .

A reminder to each of us from Tom Boschert that the time is growing short before the Showtime Follies, scheduled for May 21 at the Duchesne HI Gymnasium. He's looking for $20 from all "volunteer" ticket sellers...not ticket returns.

• • •

Les Prinster promises an evening of entertainment for all who attend the Community Council Installation Dinner on May 19. Dr. Spencer of The Lindenwood Colleges is the speaker...see Les for additional details.

They're off!. . .

An even shorter time remains to firm up reservations for the Kiwanis "Night at the Races" set for June 10, as a deadline of May 17 has been set for reservations. Only 40 persons can be accommodated...and just $12.50 each covers bus transportation, gourmet dinner and clubhouse seats. Get your funds in to Henry Elmendorf right away to insure the success of this event.

Basye Speaks For U.S.

It has often been said, and continues to be proved, that the very best programs presented at our club are those of the "home grown" variety. Tuesday's meeting was no exception. Omar Osiek introduced our own Dr. Ben Basye, distinguished college professor, naval officer and school board member, whose talk was titled, "It's Time For More Of Us to Speak Up For Uncle Sam."

Ben made it clear in the beginning that he was ***not*** speaking in behalf of his college, the U. S. Navy nor the school board, but as a vitally interested individual. His fast-paced slide show presentation offered plenty of provocative material...with food for thought and concern on the part of his listeners.

For example, the section on "The Shifting Balance of Military Power" brought home vividly that the Soviet Union now has a decisive edge on the U.S. on both land and sea. He quoted one military leader as saying the Soviets could take all of Western Europe in two weeks.

Basye went on to describe our dependence on such vital imports as chromium....100 percent of which comes from South Africa, the USSR and Turkey. With Russia moving into a dominant position in South Africa, not only are these imports, but the very sea lanes upon which many of our other needs...including oil...threatened.

Dr. Basye drew a wry laugh from his audience when, in discussing the growth of bureaucracy in this country, he said that if OSHA had existed in 1927, Charles Lindberg would have never been allowed to make his famed trans-Atlantic flight.

Finally, he addressed the decline in the quality of our education system. "No wonder," he said, "so many of our young people have contempt for the American way of life as we once knew it, when they are being taught that socialism is better than free enterprise...and when American history has taken a back seat to something called 'social studies.'"

Next Week,The Needle

You've read about, perhaps wondered about it, next week come to the meeting and hear first hand about it...the ancient Oriental art of acupuncture. Omar Bizelli tells us that program co-chairman Tom Pillow will present a program on this pointed subject.

OUR LT. GOVERNORS

Lloyd Harmon	'44
Elmer Kolkmeier	'56
Arlie Greiwe	'60
Art Schneider	'64
Wm. Walsh	'65
John Warren	'68
Ray Luetkenhaus	'71
J. B. Dawkins	'74

Committee Assignments, Luncheon, Board and Special Events on Reverse Side

DIVISION 6

Monday, 7 P.M., Callaway Bldg., Main St., Elsberry
Tuesday, 6:45 A.M., Fischbach Hotel, St. Charles Frontier
Tuesday, 7 A.M., Howard Johnsons, 611 N. Lindbergh, Creve Coeur
Tuesday, 6:30 P.M., Prudential Bldg., Troy

MAKEUP MEETINGS

Wednesday, 6:30 P.M., Western Lounge, St. Charles 1st Capitol
Thursday, 6:30 A.M., Sambo's, Int. 70, St. Peters
Thursday, 12:05 P.M., Texoman Supper Club, O'Fallon

St. Charles, Missouri Kiwanis Club Newsletter, 10 May 1977 The author was a member of this club.

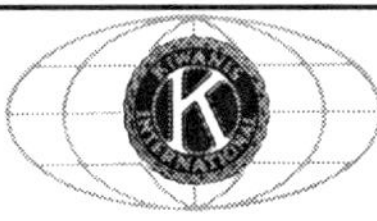

Certificate of Appreciation

Presented to DR. BEN BASYE

in recognition of your address before the

KIWANIS CLUB OF JENNINGS / NORTH ST. LOUIS

Your contribution to our club is deeply appreciated.

We hope this certificate will serve as a lasting memento

of this pleasant occasion.

President | Program chairman | 9-16-81 Date

illinois trial lawyers association

THE BOARD OF MANAGERS of the Illinois Trial Lawyers Association takes pleasure in awarding this

Certificate of Appreciation

C. Ben Basye, Ph.D.

Speaker-Revolutionary Seminar
Saturday, February 28, 1976
Fairview Heights, Illinois

In recognition of your Educational contribution to this Association which is "Dedicated to the Improvement of the Administration of Justice"

PRESIDENT

DATE 1976

EXECUTIVE DIRECTOR

Certificates of Appreciation from North St. Louis Kiwanis Club and Illinois Trial Lawyers Association

From about 1969 to the early 1980s I was active on a national level with the American Society of Mechanical Engineers. With Professor Don Young, of Iowa State, I co-authored a technical paper reporting the results of my Ph. D. thesis research and presented it at the ASME Winter Annual meeting in New York in 1966. We titled it "Oscillations of a Sphere in a Cylindrical Tube Containing a Viscous Liquid." I served as Vice-Chairman and technical papers reviewer for the Coupled Fluid-Mechanical Vibration Sub-Committee at a Vibrations Conference in Philadelphia in 1969. The next large vibrations conference took place in 1971 in Toronto. There, I was Chairman of the Sub-Committee on Structural Vibrations.

Also at the Toronto conference, I was appointed Chairman of the 1973 Vibrations Conference to be held in Cincinnati, OH. This was a large time-consuming job. The University was considerate enough to reduce my

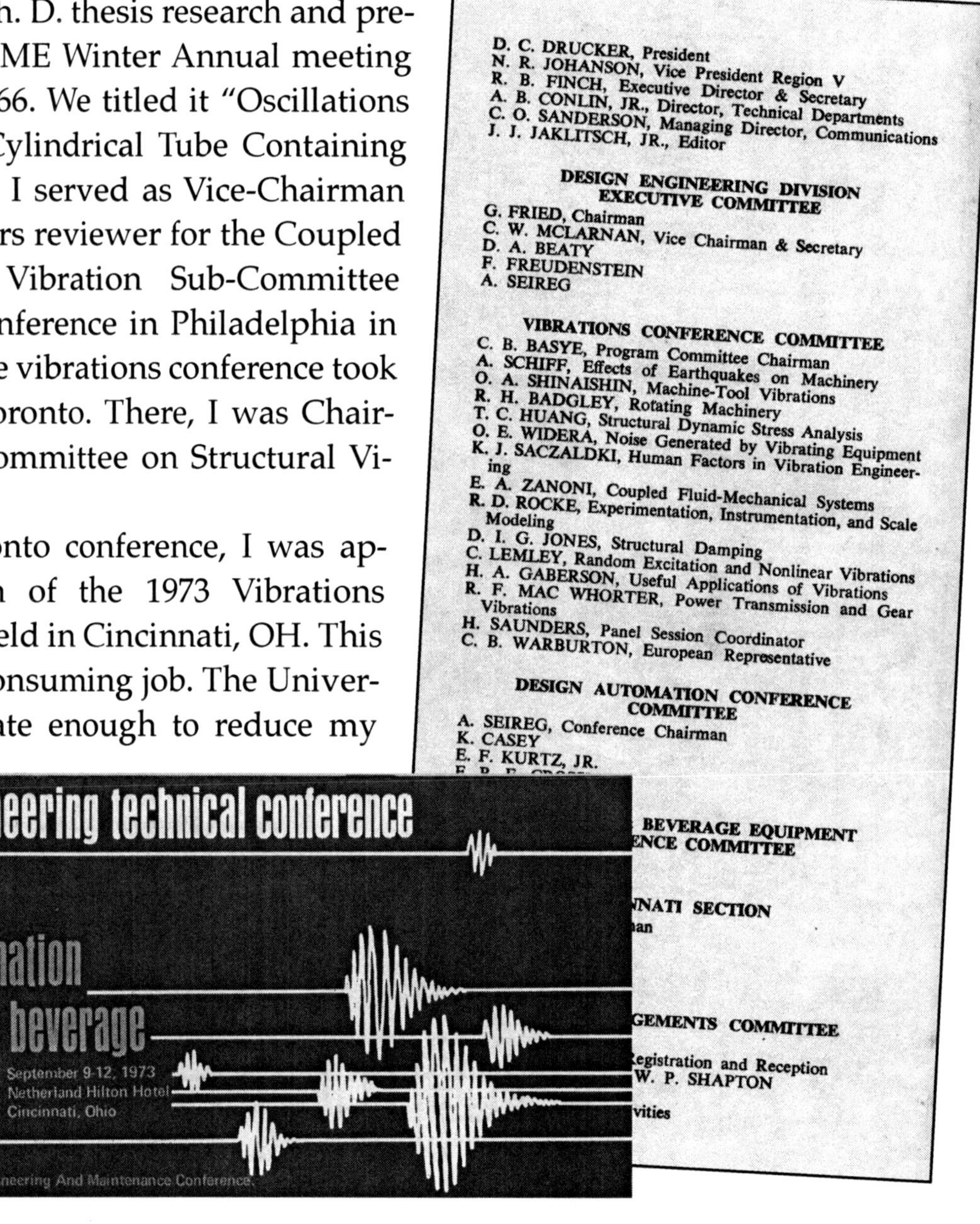
D. C. DRUCKER, President
N. R. JOHANSON, Vice President Region V
R. B. FINCH, Executive Director & Secretary
A. B. CONLIN, JR., Director, Technical Departments
C. O. SANDERSON, Managing Director, Communications
J. J. JAKLITSCH, JR., Editor

DESIGN ENGINEERING DIVISION
EXECUTIVE COMMITTEE

G. FRIED, Chairman
C. W. MCLARNAN, Vice Chairman & Secretary
D. A. BEATY
F. FREUDENSTEIN
A. SEIREG

VIBRATIONS CONFERENCE COMMITTEE

C. B. BASYE, Program Committee Chairman
A. SCHIFF, Effects of Earthquakes on Machinery
O. A. SHINAISHIN, Machine-Tool Vibrations
R. H. BADGLEY, Rotating Machinery
T. C. HUANG, Structural Dynamic Stress Analysis
O. E. WIDERA, Noise Generated by Vibrating Equipment
K. J. SACZALDKI, Human Factors in Vibration Engineering
E. A. ZANONI, Coupled Fluid-Mechanical Systems
R. D. ROCKE, Experimentation, Instrumentation, and Scale Modeling
D. I. G. JONES, Structural Damping
C. LEMLEY, Random Excitation and Nonlinear Vibrations
H. A. GABERSON, Useful Applications of Vibrations
R. F. MAC WHORTER, Power Transmission and Gear Vibrations
H. SAUNDERS, Panel Session Coordinator
C. B. WARBURTON, European Representative

DESIGN AUTOMATION CONFERENCE
COMMITTEE

A. SEIREG, Conference Chairman
K. CASEY
E. F. KURTZ, JR.

BEVERAGE EQUIPMENT
ENCE COMMITTEE

NATI SECTION
an

GEMENTS COMMITTEE

egistration and Reception
W. P. SHAPTON

vities

Program cover from the 1973 ASME Vibrations Conference in Cincinnati, OH.

teaching responsibilities for one semester to allow me time to arrange conference details. I also arranged to be assigned to the Naval Plant Representative Office at McDonnell-Douglas for my annual two-week Naval Reserve duty during this busy time in 1973. This enabled me to read my mail related to the ASME Confer-

University of Missouri - Rolla

8001 Natural Bridge Road
St. Louis, Missouri 63121

ST. LOUIS GRADUATE ENGINEERING CENTER

Telephone
(314) 453-5431

October 1, 1973

Dr. C. Ben Basye of St. Charles recently returned from the fourth biennial Vibrations Conference of the American Society of Mechanical Engineers held in Cincinnati, Ohio. Dr. Basye served as Chairman of the Program Committee for this conference. He was appointed Program Chairman at the third ASME Vibrations Conference in Toronto, Canada in 1971, where he served as Chairman of the Subcommittee on Structural Vibrations.

Authors of the 108 technical papers presented at Cincinnati represented 13 countries from North and South America, Asia, Australia, and Europe. The conference was attended by approximately 500 practicing vibration engineers, researchers, and professors. Basye was responsible for securing three independent technical reviews of each paper offered for presentation, and for selecting approved papers and organizing the program.

Dr. Basye is a Professor of Engineering Mechanics at the UMR Graduate Engineering Center on the UMSL Campus. He has been affiliated with the University of Missouri-Rolla since 1965.

Dr. Basye is also Commanding Officer of the U. S. Naval Reserve Ordnance Division at the St. Louis Naval Reserve Center.

He has been a member of the St. Charles School Board since last April.

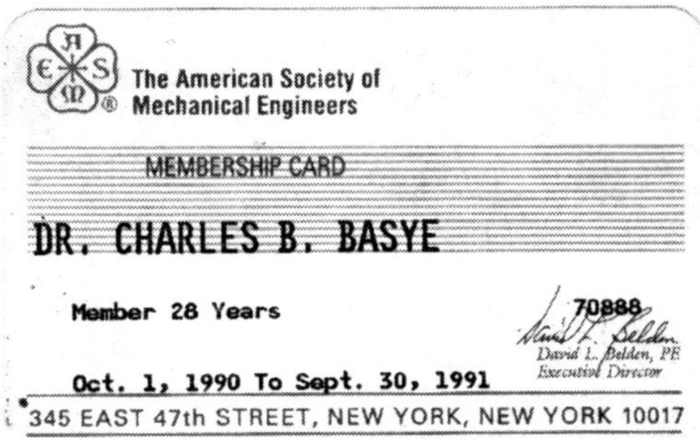

The American Society of Mechanical Engineers

MEMBERSHIP CARD

DR. CHARLES B. BASYE

Member 28 Years

70888

David L. Belden, PE
Executive Director

Oct. 1, 1990 To Sept. 30, 1991

345 EAST 47th STREET, NEW YORK, NEW YORK 10017

A University Press Release concerning the ASME activity, copy of the author's ASME Membership Card

ence at the University office each night and take any necessary action. A copy of the program announcement related to the conference is shown.

Persuading the sub-committee chairmen to serve was a major responsibility. The 15 individuals listed below my name in the copy of the announcement (above), also had a good deal of work to do to ensure the conference' success. Each of these sub-committee chairmen was responsible for getting three independent reviews of submitted papers, and then determining whether the paper should be accepted.

In addition to the Vibrations Conference duties, I served as a member of the ASME Design Engineering Division Vibration and Sound Committee for several years. Part of that time I served as Chairman of that committee.

Activities associated with membership on the St. Charles School Board required both time and attention. During the summer of 1972, a controversy over the content of some junior high school social studies textbooks in the St. Charles School District received coverage in the media. A persistent group of protestors drew attention. One of our sons, fourteen years old in 1972, had told me that some books he had used the previous school year were just nonsense. Being busy, and having complete confidence in the government school people, I ignored both the controversy and my son's comments. I told him that his teachers knew what they were doing, he should do as they said. I make no distinction between what many people refer to as 'public schools' and what I refer to herein as 'government schools.' The heavy, and incompetent, hand of government is deeply entrenched in most aspects of their operation.

Later that summer, as the protestors continued their campaign, I looked into the situation and made a shocking discovery. The books were just as the protestors had described them. The press had portrayed the protestors as well-meaning, but uninformed. The books had been defended by—among others—ten Protestant ministers associated with mainline denominations. One of them was the minister of the church of which we were members. The books were used in courses for which Missouri state law directs—in no uncertain terms—that American history shall be taught. These books were anything but American History. I can make a strong case that the books in question were designed to make our young people ashamed of our country.

I met with the protestors and found them to be "salt of the earth" individuals. They did not possess University degrees, but they had far more common sense that the school bureaucrats and the ministers combined. I publicly sided with the protestors and announced that I would be a candidate for the St. Charles School Board in April of 1973.

We had lived in St. Charles only since 1967 and were not well known. Surprisingly, I was elected. The protestors worked extremely hard on my behalf. Seven candidates ran for two seats on the Board and I received the second highest vote total. The first place vote getter was a pediatrician whose father and grandfather had both served on the St. Charles School Board.

At the first board meeting, I noticed that our treasury had about $1,000,000 in a non-interest bearing checking account. This was great for the bankers, but not for the taxpayers. Since I had been elected by raising such a commotion about curriculum, I decided to not raise the money situation at that meeting. The next monthly financial statement showed the same situation. When we took a break, I called the man responsible for financial matters over to my chair and asked him why we were letting the bankers have free access to such a large amount of money. The School Board President looked over my shoulder and listened to the conversation. I did not get much of an answer but thought that the situation would be corrected before the next board meeting. However, the same situation existed the third month.

I went public and explained that for each of these three months we had approximately $1,000,000.00 in a non-interest-bearing checking account. I read off the exact amounts. I stated that it was not acceptable. For some five minutes not a word was uttered. The minutes for that meeting were presented for approval the next month. They said only that I had raised questions about banking practices. Not a word about the amounts of money involved appeared in the minutes. I objected. The Board President said I could make a motion to change the minutes, but that no one would second it. He turned out to be right.

In 1978, the Superintendent told the Board we should work with some investment bankers from Kansas City and refinance about $7,500,000.00 of bonded indebtedness. He said there was to be no vote of the taxpayers but that the bankers had told him that the School District would be better off financially. The bankers also said that they could make a large sum of money quickly. Our bonding attorney listened to the bankers and publicly told us he thought it was illegal and we should not do it. I asked our Assistant Superintendent for Business Affairs what he thought about it. He responded, publicly, that he did not understand it, but that every banker that he had discussed it with said that we should not approve the Superintendent's plan. In addition, at my request, a St. Charles resident who was the Vice President of one of the largest banks in St. Louis attended the meeting. After hearing the Kansas City bankers, he spent perhaps twenty minutes explaining why we should not approve the Superintendent's plan. The Board nonetheless approved the recommendation.

The next morning, I typed up a request to the St. Charles Circuit Court, asking it to direct the School Board to stop action on this plan. Further, I asked the Circuit Court to direct us to go out for bids if we were allowed to proceed. Things got testy in a hurry. Three of the largest banks in St. Louis let me know, without talking to me, that they would pay my legal bills. Several attorneys from one of the largest law firms in St. Louis replaced my petition with one drafted more professionally, with me as plaintiff. It was apparent I was not alone, even though I had been alone when I filed the document in the Circuit Court. The St. Charles School Board Attorney finally acted responsibly and directed the Board to change course. They rescinded the approval of the Superintendent's plan, saying they did not know what the commotion was about. They claimed they had never intended to proceed anyhow.

There were other incidents in my six years on the Board involving what I would describe as unacceptable action, or lack of proper action, regarding financial matters. I recall one year in which I went through the proposed budget for the next year and identified several hundred thousand dollars that we should not spend. I listed them and requested that we discuss them at the next meeting, before approving the budget. When the budget item came up on the agenda, a board member moved that the budget be approved without discussion. The motion was seconded and passed. The board member who made the motion was the husband of one of the teachers who was active in teacher's union matters. Most Missouri School Board members are good people, but too many believe the myth that Superintendents must almost always be supported.

As bad as some of these financial fiascos were, the lack of basic education in the St. Charles School District was worse. On 10 March 1975, I submitted a report to the other board members. See Reference (38). This report documented the extent to which nonsense had replaced substance in the previous two years at St. Charles High School. Note how many St. Charles High School students were enrolled in each of the following course areas in the 1973-74 and 1974-75 school years.

- Prejudice 449
- Minorities 805
- Suspense and the Supernatural (Witchcraft) 1149
- Minority Voices 423
- Is This the End? 608

I did not find English or History.

Recall how Christine O'Donnell, a 2010 candidate for the U. S. Senate in Delaware, was belittled for stating that she had dabbled in witchcraft while a teenager. Is it not ironic that the incompetent government schools were teaching witchcraft thirty-five years earlier? That is right; 1149 students in St. Charles, Missouri High School were enrolled in this nonsense over this two-year period. As a matter of interest, when I asked—then demanded—access to this enrollment information, I was accused of being a censor. No other member of the St. Charles School Board publicly expressed any concern about the curriculum situation.

I recall talking to attorney Godfrey Padberg in my office in St. Louis one afternoon. I was assisting him in a legal case involving a tractor-trailer accident. I mentioned to him that I was a member of the school board in St. Charles and that I was most concerned regarding the disappearance of history and English in the government schools. He said "The Governor is really concerned about that." His law partner was former Missouri Governor Warren Hearnes. The three of us discussed the situation over lunch shortly after that.

One other incident from my school board activities stands out. The St. Charles District had a "science consultant." It appeared that she may not have done much other than wear hip boots and catch tadpoles in a shallow pond. I suggested eliminating this position as a cost cutting measure. The incumbent in this position was the wife of one of the ministers who had characterized the book protestors as uninformed. She called my boss, the GEC Director Anton (Tone) Brasunas, and stayed on the phone for about an hour. When Tone got off the phone and we went to lunch, he said she told him that I was disgracing the University by my School Board actions.

I later recounted this information to a State Representative in St. Charles. He got excited and was waving his arms. He let loose a few profanities and told me he was one State Representative who wanted to know if any University official ever tried to pressure me because of school board actions. No University official ever did.

In Chapter 17, I will delve much deeper into some of these curriculum problems. Many of our citizens realize that something is seriously wrong with our government schools. However, not very many understand that the dumbing down of our young people is by design. Any reader who will study the references listed in Chapter 17 will understand why we are in this long-existing educational catastrophe.

I have had my Professional Engineer (P.E.) license continuously since receiving

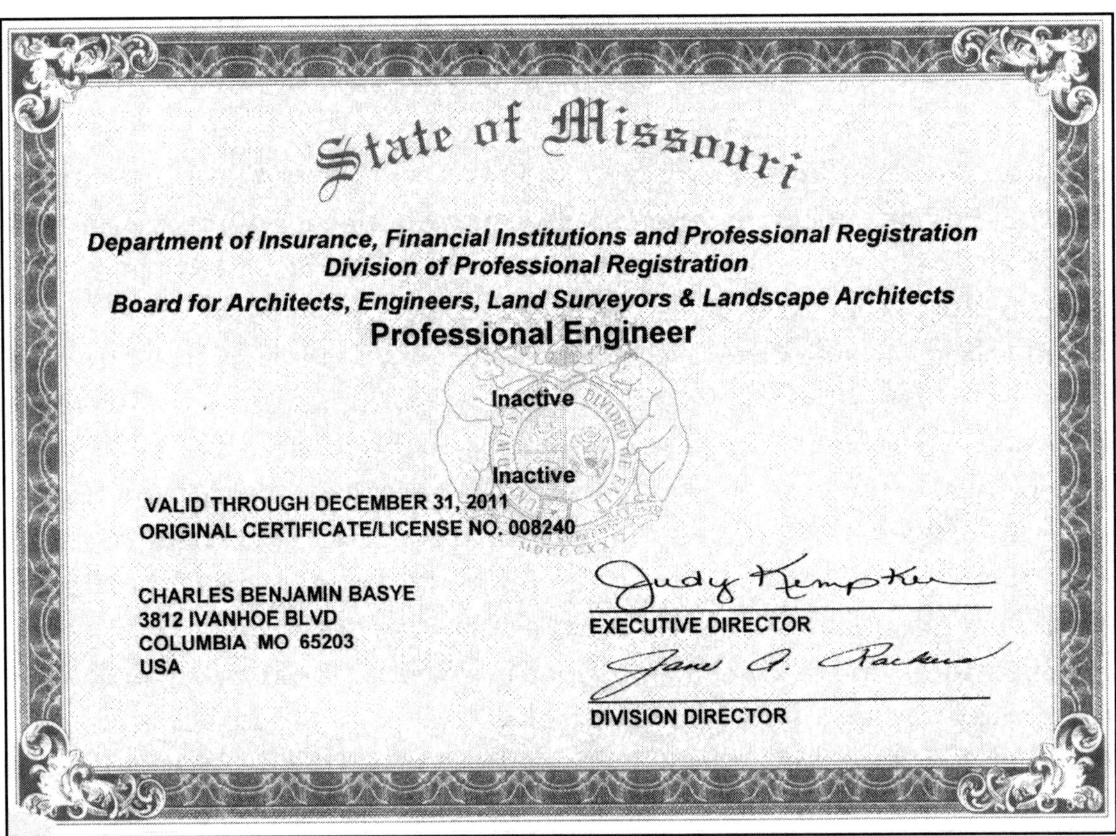
State of Missouri

Department of Insurance, Financial Institutions and Professional Registration
Division of Professional Registration
Board for Architects, Engineers, Land Surveyors & Landscape Architects
Professional Engineer

Inactive

Inactive

VALID THROUGH DECEMBER 31, 2011
ORIGINAL CERTIFICATE/LICENSE NO. 008240

CHARLES BENJAMIN BASYE
3812 IVANHOE BLVD
COLUMBIA MO 65203
USA

EXECUTIVE DIRECTOR

DIVISION DIRECTOR

Missouri State Professional Engineer License - (Inactive)

it in 1957. It is now labeled inactive because I am retired and have not taken some up-date courses required to keep the license active. The University of Missouri presented refresher courses for engineers preparing to take the State P. E. examinations. I served as Director of these courses for 15 years or so before retiring in 1992.

Engineers are eligible to take the State P. E. examination four years after re-

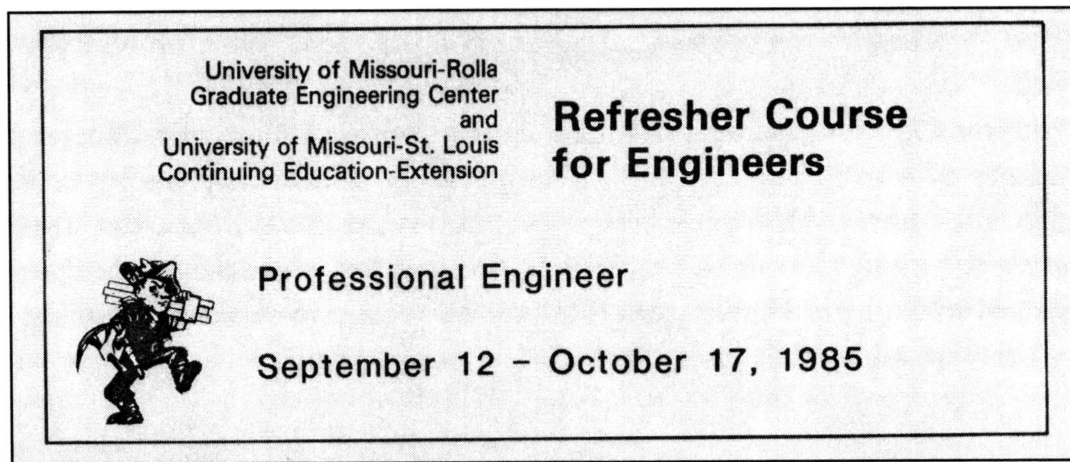
University of Missouri-Rolla
Graduate Engineering Center
and
University of Missouri-St. Louis
Continuing Education-Extension

Refresher Course
for Engineers

Professional Engineer

September 12 - October 17, 1985

Refresher course brochure for Engineering Refresher Coursees

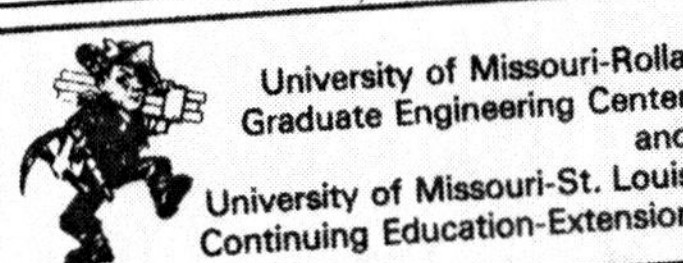

University of Missouri-Rolla
Graduate Engineering Center
and
University of Missouri-St. Louis
Continuing Education-Extension

Refresher Course for Engineers

Professional Engineer Refresher Course

Dates & Time: Tuesdays & Thursdays, September 12 - October 17, 1985, 6:45 - 9:45 pm
Location: J.C. Penney Building on the UMSL campus
Fee: $420 (includes extensive review manual, solutions manual, and sample exam)
Faculty: University of Missouri-Rolla approved faculty

Course topics include the following:

Civil: orientation and mathematics, economic analysis, hydraulics, mechanics of materials, open channel flow, waste water engineering, hydrology, steel design, soils, concrete design, foundations

Electrical: orientation and mathematics, economic anaylsis, time and frequency response, amplifiers, basic electrical circuits and waveform measurement, rotating machines, digital logic, nonlinear electronics, control theory, transmission lines, power systems

Chemical: orientation and mathematics, chemistry, material balance, thermodynamics, fluid mechanics, heat transfer, mass transfer, distillation, separations processes, reaction engineering, economics

Mechanical: orientation and mathematics, economic analysis, thermodynamics, thermodynamic cycles, heat transfer, combustion - fans and ductwork, fluid mechanics, statics - mechanics of materials, heating and air conditioning, machine design, dynamics - modeling engineering systems

Approval to take the Engineer-In-Training examination must be secured from the Missouri State Board of Architects, Engineers, and Land Surveyors before the closing date of July 29, 1985. The address of the State Board is P.O. Box 184, Jefferson City, Missouri 65102; (314) 751-2334. Exam date is October 25, 1985.

Registration: Send the registration form below to the University of Missouri-St. Louis, Continuing Education-Extension, 8001 Natural Bridge Road, St. Louis, MO 63121-4499, Attention: Joe Williams. Please make checks payable to the University of Missouri.

Please register me in PE Refresher ___ Civil ___ Electrical ___ Chemical ___ Mechanical
Name________________ Day Phone________________
Address________________ City & State________________ Zip________
Social Security #________________
FEES ARE PAYABLE BY CASH, CHECK, OR CHARGE. TO CHARGE, FILL IN THE INFORMATION BELOW:
MasterCard or VISA #________________ Exp. Date________
Amount Paid________________ Signature________________

University of Missouri-St. Louis
Continuing Education-Extension
8001 Natural Bridge Road
St. Louis, Missouri 63121

General Information

For Further Information: For further technical information, contact Dr. C. B. Basye at (314) 553-5431. For more information on registering, contact Joe Williams at (314) 553-5961.

Cancellation Policy: The University reserves the right to cancel this program and return all fees in the event of insufficient registration. No fees are returned after a program begins. Refunds may require four to six weeks for processing.

Income Tax Deduction: The cost of continuing education is deductible for federal income tax purposes under certain circumstances. Check with the IRS or your tax adviser.

This Course Is Approved for Veterans' Benefits

Engineering Refresher Coursework topics

ceiving their bachelor's degrees. The front and back of an advertising brochure for one of these courses appears here. Note the topics covered. As Director, I arranged for appropriate people to teach each of these review topics for the four areas of engineering—civil, electrical, chemical, and mechanical. I also taught several of the review sessions.

While working at the GEC, I participated in a variety of consulting activities. The University had (and has) a written policy, in the Policy Manual, relating to faculty consulting. Faculty were (and are) permitted to consult one day per week, Not much more in the way of detailed rules existed. A reasonable amount of consulting was encouraged. Each year, each faculty member was required to document—in rough terms—his or her consulting activity for the past year. Since most of my teaching was at night, I had considerable latitude regarding day schedules. I was in the University office most of the time, but did have the flexibility to use weekends for class preparation—as opposed to some of the day hours—if I chose to do so. This flexibility enabled me to perform consulting duties if they required day work. There was never a problem being available when one of the advisees needed assistance.

I took part in perhaps 400 to 500 consulting cases between 1969 and 1995. Some were brief, involving perhaps a few hours. Sometimes I concluded a discussion with a decision that I should not get involved. Many cases involved investigating an accident or failure, then submitting a report. My clients included perhaps as many as thirty insurance companies and fifty law firms. I consulted for law firms located in Nebraska, Kansas, Missouri, Illinois, Alabama, Utah, and Indiana. I was deposed, under oath, probably in excess of 100 times. Most of these cases involved opinions related to accidents or product failures. I gave live testimony in both civil and criminal cases in excess of sixty times. Some cases were in state courts, some in federal courts. I offered opinions in behalf of both plaintiffs and defendants. From my perspective, determination of the truth was the guiding principle.

I participated in investigations conducted on behalf of Union Electric, American Motors, Peabody Coal, Walmart, Durbin Durco, Southwest Mobile Systems, Emerson, John Deere, Boone Electric Cooperative, a Japanese manufacturer of hydraulic jacks, a manufacturer of large hydraulic presses, and others.

One consulting job involved a study of large and unsightly cracks in large steel castings. These castings were part of the support structure that connected the wheels to the trailer bed of large flat-bed trailers developed to haul the largest tank in the U. S. Army inventory. Cracks developed in the complex geometry of the casting when the steel shrank as it cooled during the casting process. The Army was naturally concerned. Some of their engineers stated that the casting had "failed."

I made a written and oral presentation to engineers and managers at the Aberdeen Proving Ground in Maryland, and at an Army Command near Detroit. I presented a discussion and fracture mechanics analysis. I explained that there can be more than one definition of "failure." These parts had indeed failed if failure means that cracks exist. They had not failed—and cracks were acceptable—if the parts did not break, and continued to function for an acceptable time. In fact, the Army engineers at Aberdeen loaded one of the large tanks on a trailer with the cracked castings and drove for 6,000 miles over the test track. No castings broke, although there was some growth in some of the cracks.

In another case, one of the most well-known insurance companies in America asked me to determine the cause of the breaking of a tie rod on an automobile. A college student was driving the car, which suddenly hit a station wagon from behind. The station wagon went out of control and ran into a pickup truck on the highway shoulder. Two highway workers were eating lunch in the truck when it was hit. Meanwhile, the student's car broke off a wooden highway sign post and next took out over 100 feet of chain link fence before running into a porch on a house and starting a fire. Investigating police had removed the broken tie rod and secured it in their evidence locker. I had permission to inspect the tie rod, but could not remove it from police custody. I inspected it and concluded that the tie rod had suffered a fatigue failure, which caused the student to lose control. Everything else then transpired. I gave the insurance company a report with my conclusion.

All was quiet relative to this situation for perhaps two years. Then multitudes of lawyers became involved. A trial lasting three weeks and three days took place in an Illinois courtroom. While I maintained that the failure was caused by metal fatigue, the automobile manufacturer claimed that the tie rod broke due to an impact of the car with the station wagon, or with the post, or with the fence, or with the porch. The automobile manufacturer had three technical experts: one of their design engineers; a Ph. D. in metallurgy; and, a Professor of Engineering Mechanics from a Big Ten University. I was the lone technical expert contending that it was a fatigue failure. The other three said that it was an impact failure. I was on the witness stand for one and one-half days. All twelve jurors agreed with me as to cause of failure. However, one juror concluded that since the car had about 66,000 miles on it, the manufacturer should not be blamed. Cases such as this are difficult for jurors to understand. Experts, under oath, contradict each other.

Another case in which I participated was tried in a Birmingham courtroom. It involved an interstate highway collision between two semi-tractor trailer vehicles.

I testified as to casual factors. Before calling his engineering expert to the stand to refute my testimony, a Birmingham lawyer told the jury at great length how smart his expert was. The lawyer must not have known that "his" engineer had received 14 "D's" and "F's" from Georgia Tech. The lawyers on my side had a copy of the engineer's transcript. When he got on the stand, he was asked to explain each "D" and "F." It was not a pretty scene. Watching the lawyers keep a straight face was something to behold.

One unsettling aspect of these trials is that they are usually not searches for the truth. Instead, they are dominated by legal maneuvers intended to sway jurors, rather than to enlighten them. The famous Russian dissident Aleksandr I. Solzhenitsyn published *Words of Warning to America*. He stated: "At the present time it is widely accepted among lawyers that law is higher than morality... That is not the case. The opposite is rather true! Morality is higher than law! ... morality is always higher than law."

I have investigated fifteen or more motorcycle and bicycle accidents involving collisions with cars, trucks, or farm tractors. Most people do not understand that the drivers of these vehicles can be alert and responsible and still move in front of a motorcycle they should have seen. Drivers are conditioned to look for cars or trucks; many look right past the bicycle or motorcycle, never seeing it. This happens over and over, usually with tragic consequences for the motorcycle occupant.

Four letters of thanks or appreciation from attorneys related to legal cases follow. The first was written in 1978 and the last in 2008. Criminal defense Attorney Mike Frank wrote the first. Mike was defending Ken Dempsey, a police officer accused of burglary. Mike and I were convinced of Ken's innocence. The St. Louis jury agreed with us. Mike and I worked on the case until 2:00 a.m. on the morning I testified. Mike cried for several minutes when the jury reported "not guilty." Mike asked me a series of questions and suggested that I answer quickly because the Prosecuting Attorney would likely object and the Judge might not let me answer. I answered almost before Mike finished his questions. Finally, the Prosecutor asked the Judge to direct me to not answer any questions until he could think about it and decide whether or not he wanted to object. The Judge was wagging his finger in my face and telling me not to answer until the Prosecutor had time to think. Later, I told Mike that the Judge was smiling as he was telling me to slow down and Mike said "He was telling you to keep doing what you had been doing." By this time in the trial, the Judge was probably convinced, as Mike and I were, of Ken's innocence.

MICHAEL M. FRANK
ATTORNEY AT LAW, INC.
SUITE 926T PARKWAY TOWER BUILDING
225 SOUTH MERAMEC
CLAYTON, ST. LOUIS, MISSOURI 63105

MICHAEL M. FRANK
HOWARD E. MCNIER

TELEPHONE
(314) 721-4403

December 19, 1978

Dr. Ben Basye
3100 Mockingbird
St. Charles, Missouri 63301

Dear Ben:

Thank you. Thank you for being you. Thank you for being just a good person who believes in honesty, apple pie and the American Way. I just want you to know how very much I appreciate all that you did for Ken Dempsey this past week. With actions like yours, Dave Garin's and Tim Cavanaugh's, Ken Dempsey may once again be able to function in the society of men.

May you and your family have a very Merry Christmas and a Happy New Year, and may God continue to shine on people such as you.

Best regards,

Mike

Michael M. Frank

MMF:bas

Enclosure

Thank you letter from Attorney Michael Frank for my assistance with the Dempsey trial

Overland Police Chief Acquitted Of Burglary

Overland Police Lt. Kenrick F. Dempsey, the highest-ranking police officer to go on trial for a crime in St. Louis County in a decade, was acquitted of burglary Friday.

"I'm giving you another chance to wear a uniform," juror Bernie Wilkins told a weeping Dempsey moments after the verdict. "I want you to wear one and I don't care where, just do it."

Dempsey collapsed at the counsel table and embraced his attorney, Michael Frank, as both broke into tears.

Dempsey was charged with second-degree burglary, carrying a 10-year prison term, after he was arrested in a police stakeout inside a furniture store April 13.

A succession of command-rank officers in the 44-man Overland police department testified against Dempsey in the five-day trial in the courtroom of Circuit Judge Herbert Lasky.

Assistant county prosecutor Sean O'Hagan told jurors Dempsey was a "bad apple" who had been caught "red-handed" in the stakeout.

Dempsey took the stand in his own defense, portraying himself as the victim of a vicious conspiracy that left him separated from his wife and seeking psychiatric help.

Dempsey was suspended on the day of his arrest. He has not drawn any of his annual salary of $13,000 since that date.

The 20-year veteran of police work was the key witness in the federal trial of thrill-show promoter Hershey Moss last spring in federal court. Dempsey testified he tipped investigators when Moss offered to pay him $2,000 to kill motorcycle stunt driver Maurice Smith. Moss was convicted of conspiracy and fraud.

Overland Police Lt. Lyle Bennett testified last week he had set up a stakeout at the Blackwell-Wielandy Co. furniture store at 1450 Ashby Road after Sgt. Ralph Crump reported he received an anonymous tip that a break-in would occur.

Bennett testified that he and three other detectives were inside the store when they heard scratching noises on a locked door. Dempsey then entered and went to an office cash drawer.

As Dempsey was preparing to leave, Bennett identified himself, pointed a double-barreled shotgun at Dempsey and arrested him, saying he had pried open the door with a knife.

"Yes I did, Lyle, but I didn't take any money," Bennett testified Dempsey responded.

Bennett and other officers testified that money in the cash drawer had been dusted with a special fluorescent powder. Although no money had been taken, when Dempsey's hands were placed under an ultraviolet light an hour later, they showed the presence of the powder, Bennett testified.

County police experts testified that a pocketknife taken from Dempsey after his arrest was probably the one used to pry open the furniture store door, based on scratches on the lock discovered after the incident.

Dempsey, who denied ever having admitted guilt, said he was set up in the stakeout when he investigated an insecure door, and said Bennett had "planted" the fluorescent powder on his hands.

"I'm not a thief," Dempsey told jurors.

The jury deliberated 2½ hours, taking just one ballot.

"If it had been up to me it wouldn't have taken 2½ minutes, but others wanted to look everything over," said juror Wilkins after the verdict.

As night watch commander, Dempsey said he had discovered an insecure door at Blackwell-Wielandy a week before his arrest. He made out a report on the incident, which was introduced into evidence in the trial, and informed Crump.

Dempsey told jurors he did not believe that Crump, an old rival in the department, had ever received an anonymous tip but had seized on Dempsey's report to set him up for the burglary charge.

Dempsey testified that he had spent 20 years in police work, starting in the city, working in Florissant, for McDonnell Douglas Corp. as a security guard where he had a top-secret clearance, and finally with Overland.

He said other officers were jealous over his good arrest record and his promotions.

"Are you saying that the Overland Police Department, almost to a man, has conspired to put you in the bag by supposedly framing this crime just because they thought you did too good a job?" O'Hagan asked in cross-examination.

Dempsey responded that "a lot of them" did.

Defense attorney Frank wept for 10 minutes after the verdict was returned. Asked if Dempsey was a close friend, Frank answered:

"He's just a good cop."

Newspaper article on the Dempsey matter

LAW OFFICES

ROBB & ROBB

MARK TWAIN TOWER
SUITE 1500
106 W. 11TH STREET
KANSAS CITY, MISSOURI 64105

TELEPHONE
(816) 474-8080

March 14, 1986

C. Ben Bayse, Ph.D., P.E.
3100 Mockingbird Drive
St. Charles, Missouri 63301

RE: 1986 UMKC/KCMBA "EXPERTS" SEMINAR

Dear Ben:

I very much appreciate your participating in the UMKC/CLE Experts Seminar last week. I heard numerous favorable comments about your segment of the program. I thought that you did a great job.

It was again a pleasure working with you in connection with this Program. By all accounts, it was a large success.

Best personal regards.

Yours very truly,

GARY C. ROBB
PROGRAM CHAIRPERSON

GCR:jmb

cc: Michael J. Baker, Esq.
Director UMKC/CLE

P.S. Your expense vouchers have been forwarded, and will be promptly remitted.
Regards G.

The letter from Attorney Gary Robb concerns my participation in a Continuing Legal Education Seminar. UMKC and the Kansas City Metropolitan Bar Association were also involved.

HARLAN HELLER
BRENT D. HOLMES
H. KENT HELLER
DAVID STEVENS
FRED JOHNSON
JASON M. CROWDER
COLLEEN MANNIX

LAW OFFICES OF
HELLER, HOLMES & ASSOCIATES, P.C.
A PROFESSIONAL CORPORATION
1101 BROADWAY
P. O. BOX 889
MATTOON, ILLINOIS 61938-0889
(217) 235-2700
FAX NO. (217) 235-0743

September 9, 1997

C. Ben Basye, Ph.D., P.E.
Consulting Engineer
15001 West Hwy. 40
P.O. Box 128
Rocheport, MO 65279-0128

Re: Mikel S. Berryman
Our File No. 10457

Dear Professor Basye:

Thank you for the wonderful job you did in the Berryman matter. Thank you even further for re-arranging your schedule at the last moment to accomodate the pace at which the trial was going.

I am quite pleased to tell you that based primarily upon your testimony the jury found in favor of our client and against the defendant and awarded damages in the sum of $3,250,000.00.

Once again, from both Scott and I, thank you.

Very truly yours,

Kent Heller

H. Kent Heller

Kathy

HKH/kjs
a:bas10457.ltr/kjs97-35/090997

cc: Mr. Scott Berryman

The issue in the Berryman case referred to by Attorney Kent Heller was which of two occupants in a serious accident was driving. The jury apparently believed my opinion instead of that of a Highway Patrol accident reconstruction expert.

SCHNACK LAW OFFICES
510 VERMONT STREET
QUINCY, ILLINOIS 62301-2902

ANDREW C. SCHNACK III
KENT R. SCHNACK
RYAN C. SCHNACK

Telephone 217-224-4000
Fax 224-8565

LOREN SCHNACK, OF COUNSEL

Sender's Email Address:
slo@adams.net

September 2, 2008

C. Ben Basye
3812 Ivanhoe Blvd.
Columbia, Missouri 65203

RE: Thomas R. Smith v. Mathew R. Likes and J. Wesley DeMoss
Adams County No.: 06-L-74

Dear Dr. Basye:

Thank you again for all your assistance. As always, you are an absolute pleasure to deal with and I hope to heavens that I never find you on the other side of a lawsuit. I will be in touch if I am not successful in striking Plaintiff's expert's Affidavit.

Please feel free to call if you have any questions.

Thanking you for your consideration, I am

Very truly yours,

SCHNACK LAW OFFICES

Kent

Kent R. Schnack /sab

KRS/sab
enclosure

P.S.: Please be sure and stop by if you are ever in town.

The case referred to by attorney Kent Schnack involved a slow moving farm implement hit by a fast-moving automobile.

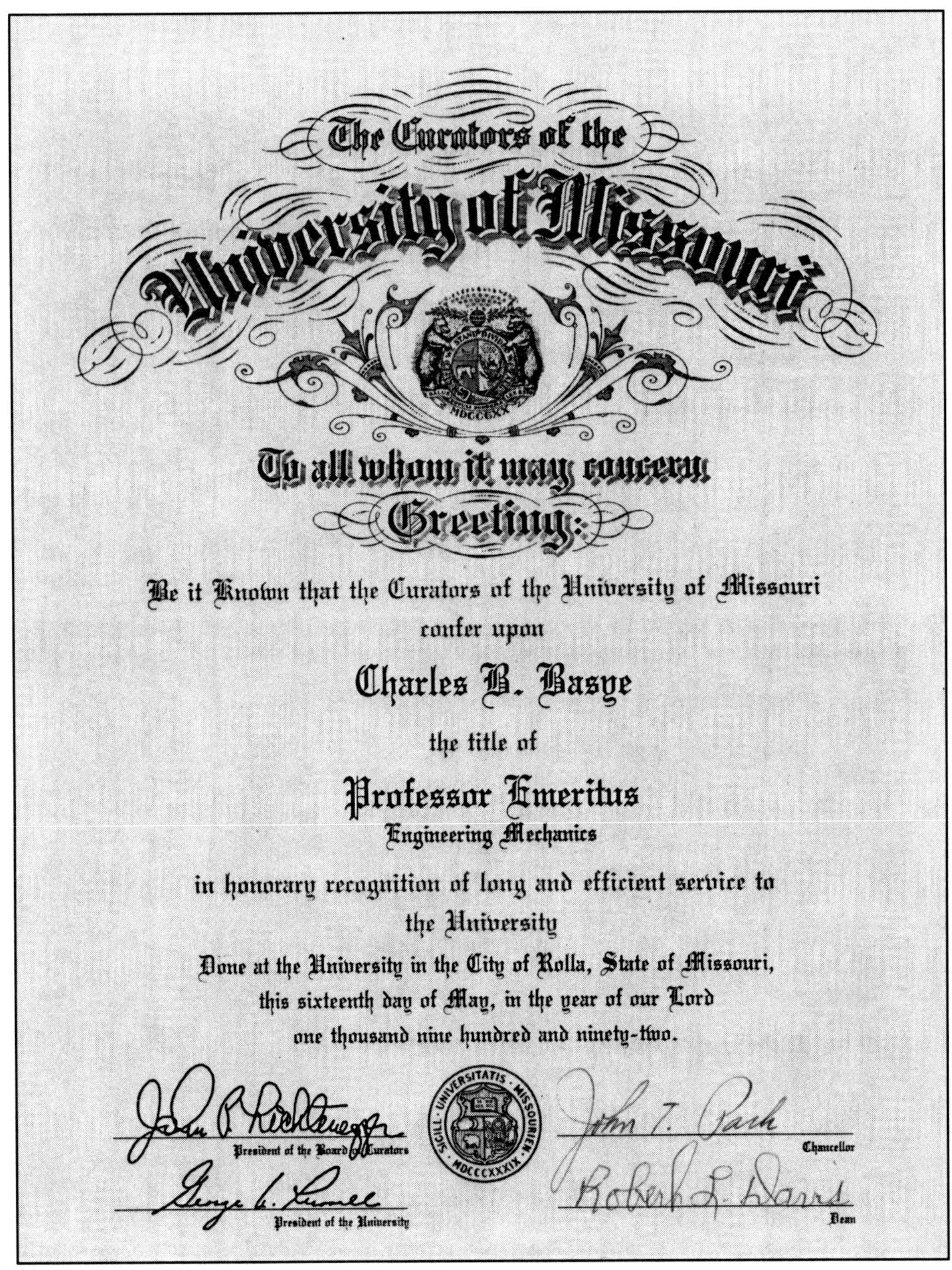

The Curators of the
University of Missouri
To all whom it may concern:
Greeting:
Be it Known that the Curators of the University of Missouri
confer upon
Charles B. Basye
the title of
Professor Emeritus
Engineering Mechanics
in honorary recognition of long and efficient service to
the University
Done at the University in the City of Rolla, State of Missouri,
this sixteenth day of May, in the year of our Lord
one thousand nine hundred and ninety-two.

President of the Board of Curators
President of the University
Chancellor
Dean

I retired from the University of Missouri at the end of the Spring Semester in 1992, with the title of Professor Emeritus. By previous arrangement, I was employed to teach on a part-time basis until 1995.

Chapter 15: Retirement, 1995 to the Present

My effective date of retirement was in 1992, but I taught on a part-time basis until 1995. Friends and colleagues at the GEC presented me with a plaque at a retirement luncheon in St. Louis. A photograph of the plaque is shown.

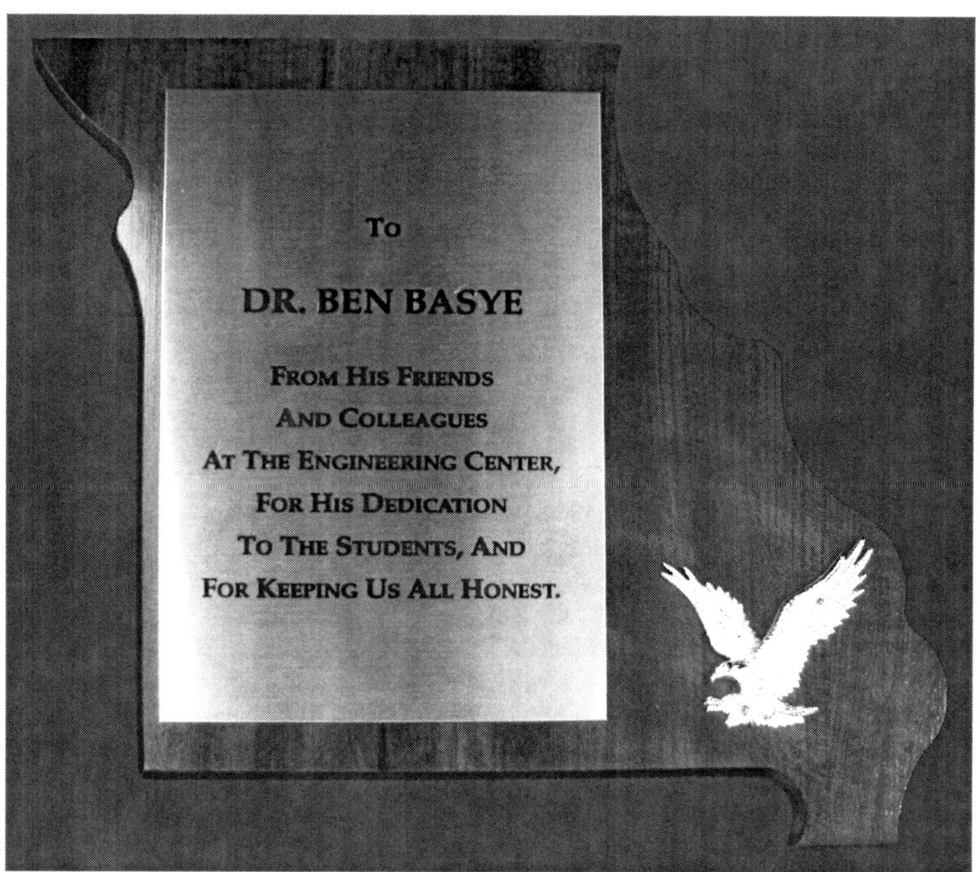

Retirement plaque from friends at the GEC

Joanne and I built a house on our farm on Highway 40, adjacent to the town of Rocheport. We moved into the new house on the last day of January 1993. The house is shown below. In 1998, we contracted with Morton Builders to build two buildings close to the house. One of those is shown in the right part of the photograph and the other one is barely visible through the trees in the left part. We added the Morton carport in the center of the photograph in 1999. It was a beautiful home and we enjoyed it immensely. However, the time came when we had to face the fact that we were no longer young. I was mowing approximately ten acres. Even with the John Deere tractor that was quite strenuous. Therefore, we sold the retirement dream home in 2010, after having it listed on and off since 2007. We moved to a Villa in Columbia, where a homeowners association takes care of lawn upkeep and snow removal.

Author's home at 15001 Highway 40, Rocheport, MO

Even though we no longer live in the country, we still have farm property close to Rocheport. Three of our sons own farm property close by. Our oldest son, George, owns the farm I grew up on. Our next son, Randy, owns the farm which great grandfather Michael Mauzy Basye purchased in 1852. Union School is located on a corner of it. Chuck, our third son, owns the farm directly across Highway 40 from our retirement farm.

The author relaxing with Sylvester and Thomas

In addition to keeping active around the farms, I continued consulting activities when asked to do so, but only when I found the issue interesting. I participated in the investigations of several serious accidents involving motorcycles colliding with farm vehicles. The accidents usually resulted in the death of the motorcycle operator. I took on some other consulting cases as well.

The photograph shows me on the farm with two of my best friends, Sylvester and Thomas. They both came out of the woods and liked our place. We liked having them around. They spent about ten years with us before using up their nine lives.

I filed as a Republican candidate for the Missouri State Senate in 1996. I did not get elected, but spent only about $1,000. Two Democrats spent about $200,000 in their side of the primary. In 1999, I filed for the Columbia School Board but did not win.

Our son Randy operates his farm in accordance with Quality Deer Management parameters. He feeds the wildlife and gets interesting pictures on his infrared-actuated cameras. Two of his are photographs are below. They were taken on the farm which Michael Mauzy Basye bought. It has been continuously owned by members of our family for 160 years.

Deer and turkeys frequent Randy's feeder

Our 50th wedding anniversary took place on 12 December 2004. To celebrate this event, son Randy and daughter-in-law Debby took Joanne and me to Chicago. Our youngest son, Scott, prepared a delicious meal. He graduated from the Institute of Culinary Education in New York City several years ago. His menu is reprinted here.

Happy 50th Wedding Anniversary
Charles B. and Joanne Basye
December 12, 2004

Amuse Bouche

Shrimp Cornets
Tomato Bisque w/ Tuscan Olive Oil and Fresh Thyme

Krug 'Grand Cuvee' Champagne, Reims, France

First Course

Harvest Salade
Endive, Radicchio, Nueske's Smoked Bacon, Organic Dried Cranberries, 12 yr Comte, Toasted Pecans
Grainy Mustard Vinaigrette

Paul Hobbs, Russian River Valley Chardonnay, 2002
Sonoma, California

Second Course

Hand-Harvested Maine Diver Scallop over Cauliflower puree, Roasted wild mushrooms, with Fresh Umbrian winter truffles

Domaine Gros Freres Clos de Vougeot, Grand Cru, 2002
Cote de Nuits, Burgundy, France

Main Course

Boeuf "Duo"
Braised Short Rib of Beef in Bordelaise w/ Horseradish Crème Fraiche
Dry Aged Prime New York Strip 'Au Poivre'
Curried Carrot Batonnet
Haricot Vert with Mushroom and Bacon

Jayson Pahlmeyer, Proprietary Red, 1997
Napa Valley, California

Executive Chef: Scott Kennedy Basye *Chicago, IL*

Joanne and Ben Basye 50th wedding anniversary menu

On Memorial Day, 1999, I was attending a ceremony at the Boone County Courthouse, in Columbia. Knowing something was wrong, I drove to the Boone County Hospital Emergency Room. I had a heavy feeling in the left part of my chest and was perspiring. It was about a one-mile drive through the streets of Columbia to the Hospital. The excellent staff took care of the situation. A stent was inserted within an hour or so. As far as my health is concerned, things have gone pretty well since then. Joanne has had a broken hip and a knee replacement. We are most thankful for the excellent medical care. Many Americans are convinced that our excellent health care is in danger from attempts by the Federal Government to take it over. I am in agreement with them.

The year 2003 marked the fiftieth anniversary of my graduation from the University of Missouri, with the B. S. degree in mechanical engineering. Classmates Darrell Kirkendall, Don Williams, and Owen Hornkohl stayed with us at our Rocheport farm the night before the celebration at the University. Ruth Kirkendall and Sue Williams were there as well. It was a wonderful visit after fifty years.

I have been active in the Military Officers Association of America, or MOAA, an organization formerly known as The Retired Officers Association of America. I have been active as a member of the local chapter, called the Mid-Missouri Chapter of MOAA. About 11 years ago, I served as Chapter President. I have also been active as a member of the Missouri Council of Chapters of MOAA for about ten years and was President of the Council for the year of 2005. The Council President represents the state organization each spring at a three-day meeting in Washington, D. C. One of our actions during the meeting consists of visiting the offices of Missouri Representatives and Senators to discuss items of concern related to the U. S. military.

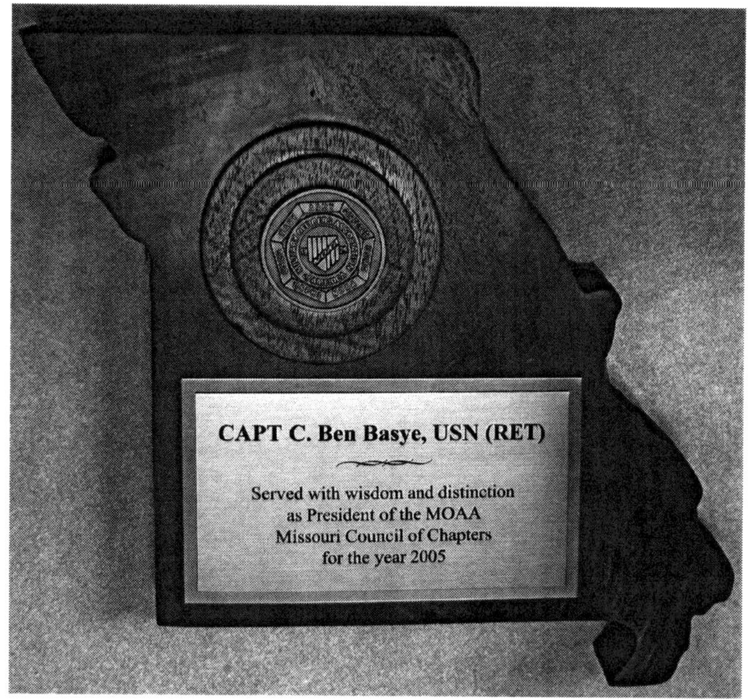

Appreciation Plaque for Service as MOAA Council President, 2005

The Mid-Missouri Chapter participates in a Memorial Day parade in Columbia each

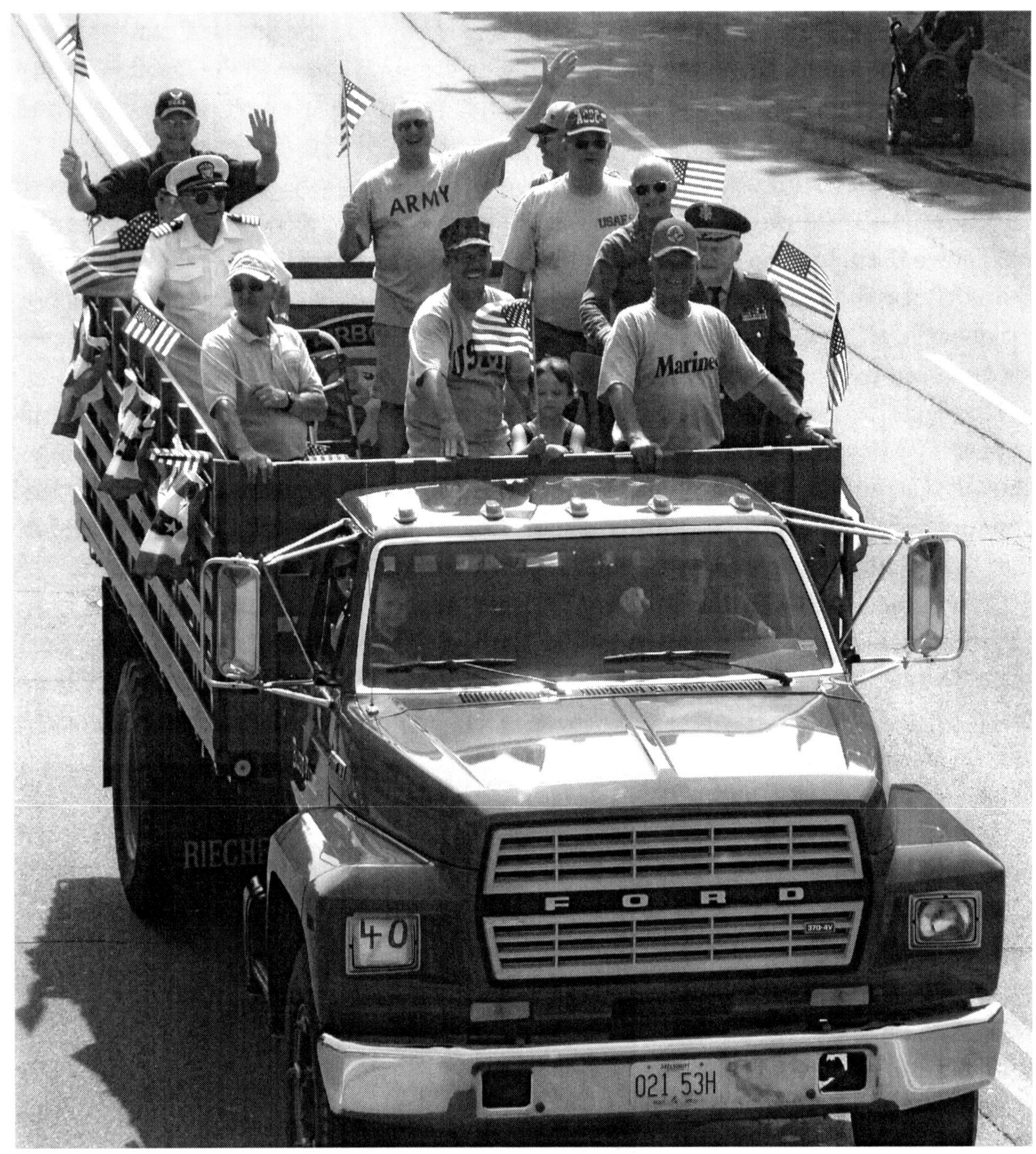

Memorial Day Parade, 31 May 2010,
Randy Basye, son of author, driving truck; Randy Basye, grandson of author, passenger;
Brianna Basye and Brian Basye, great-grandchildren of author, passengers

Memorial Day Parade, 31 May 2010, from the left: Dennis Bogle, USMC; Roger Jaeger, USA; Joe Casler, USAF; Tim Springer, USAF (Ret); Jim Harding, USAF (Ret); the author; Joe Korb, USA; Mike Terry, USMC; Bill Reilly, USA (Ret); Chuck Basye, USMC; and Ray Letourneau, USN

LTCOL Jim Harding USAF (Ret) and the author in 2010 Memorial Day parade

year. The photographs show Lieutenant Colonel Jim Harding, USAF (Ret) and me in the parade on Broadway on 31 May 2010. Jim flew 31 missions over Europe as a B-17 Flying Fortress navigator during World War II. He passed away on 17 February 2011 at age 91.

PART 4. Critiques and Conclusions

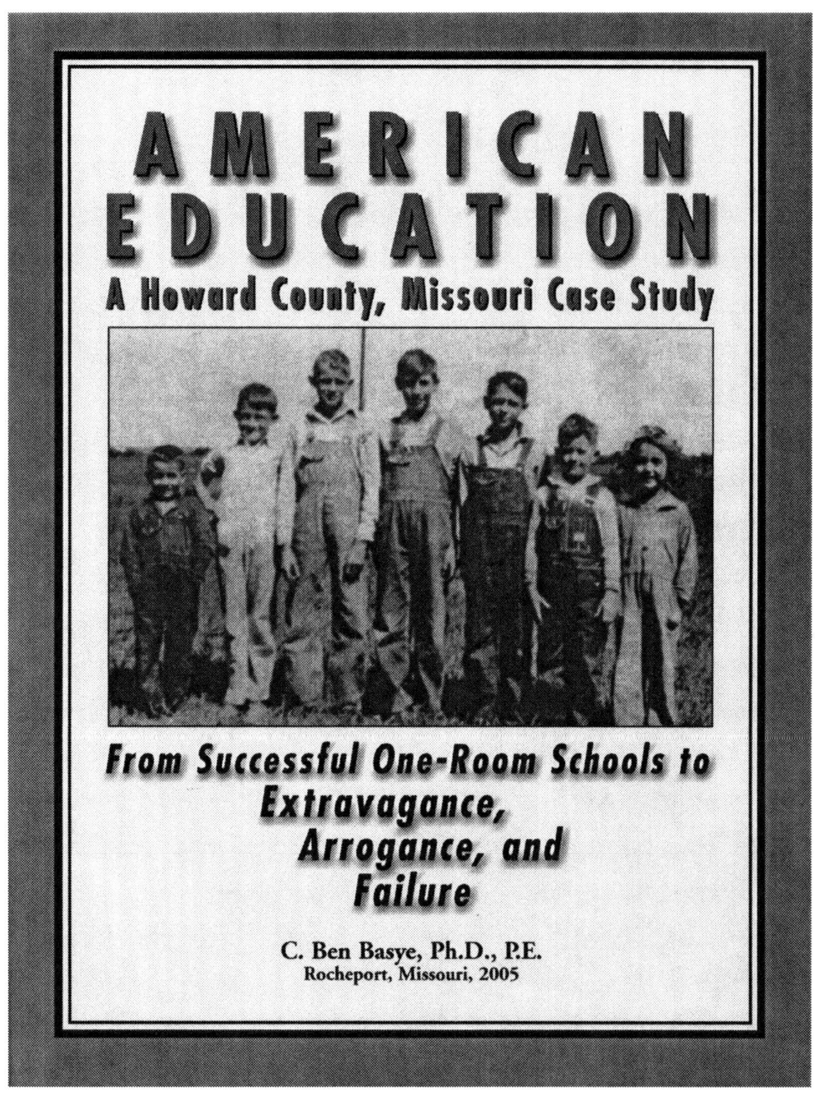

Chapter 16. Critique of the "New Military"

In the previous chapters, I have recounted my life's journey. My military service, which totaled more than four decades, was obviously a major component of that journey. This service provides part of the background for this chapter, in which I will critique the present U. S. military and compare its culture with that of the traditional American armed forces. I will begin with a review of some current literature. I will comment first on books and other sources related to general societal trends in this country. Then will follow with sources specific to military policy, culture, and current effectiveness.

The author of Reference (10), Balint Vazsonyi, lived under the Nazis when Germany occupied his native Hungary. After Germany's defeat came life under the Soviet Communists. Vazsonyi thus has first-hand experience of the horrors of socialism and the loss of freedom. He documents how Americans' founding principles are being replaced by government-mandated group rights, redistribution of income, and multiculturalism. He classifies this country's founding principles as rule of law, individual rights, guarantee of property, and a common American identity. His brilliant book was featured in The American Legion Magazine in August 1999. A VETVOICE letter to the editor in the December issue of that magazine said that the review of his book "may be the most important article ever published in The American Legion Magazine." Vazsonyi describes the detrimental effects of disturbing societal trends on our military. See pages 239, 40, 41.

Martin L. Gross has authored more than a dozen books, including several bestsellers. In Reference (12), titled "The End of Sanity," he introduces a descriptive label, "The New Establishment," which has woven itself into the very fiber of our nation. The destructive effects of this movement have weakened America as never before. On pages 5, 6, 7, and 8, Gross discusses how this movement has infected the U. S. military. Pages 98 to 105 elaborate on the destructive effects of the large-scale introduction of women into the U. S. military. He acknowledges, as we all do, the excellent service women have provided in supplemental roles.

Professor Samuel P. Huntington of Harvard is the author of Who Are We? (Reference 14), and a dozen other books. His sub-title is The Challenges to America's National Identity. He discusses the ideologies of multiculturalism and diversity and the promotion of group rights at the expense of individual rights. See page 18. He also notes the fact that large numbers of top leaders of American corporations tend to disavow identification with the United States. See page 7. Unfortunately, many top military leaders are pushing the destructive 'diversity' agenda. Professor Huntington's many activities included serving as a consultant to the State Department, the National Security Council, and the CIA during the Johnson and Carter Administrations.

Kate O'Beirne includes the military among areas of our country being damaged by the radical feminist assault. Attorney O'Beirne in Reference (13) documents significant aspects of the harm done to our military capability by lowered standards associated with women in the military.

Dr. Christina Hoff Sommers, in Reference (15), The War against Boys, documents the fact that girls are being given unwise special attention and treatment in many parts of our society. The Boy Scouts are under attack but not the Girl Scouts. The U. S. military is also involved in counterproductive acts and reduced standards for women in the military. In some respects, some of these acts could be described as "a war against service men." They could especially be described as a war against white service men.

Dr. Gerald L. Atkinson is a decorated former U. S. Navy carrier aviator. He is an accomplished retired executive of high-technology research and development companies. In Reference (4), Atkinson describes a "breakdown of trust" in naval aviation, resulting from an attack by radical feminists and their allies in the Clinton administration, Congress, the mass media, and in the high ranking officer corps of the Navy itself. It is an attempt to 'feminize' naval aviation. Affirmative action and reduced standards for selected minorities and females have done—and continue to do—tremendous harm. As bad as the Clinton administration was, the Obama administration is even worse. Sadly, George W. Bush did absolutely nothing to address these problems in his eight years as President.

Brian Mitchell, a decorated infantry officer and intelligence agent, wrote Reference (5). In his opinion, military women are not fit to fight and the military brass knows it. He reveals the farce associated with new, sensitive drill instructors and how one National Guard fighter wing was disbanded to cover up the failure of a showcase female pilot. He also reveals how enrollment of women has seriously damaged the morale, traditions, and standards of West Point, Annapolis, and the Air Force Academy.

Stephanie Gutmann, the author of Reference (6), is a freelance journalist who has written extensively on sexual politics for a variety of publications. She shows that the complete integration of women into the military is physically and sociologically impossible. Our present course is a sure setup for battlefield disaster. She states

Our armed forces are deeply mired in an expensive, resource-draining, time-consuming, morale-flattening project, one that has nothing to do with military readiness and everything to do with politically correct politics. That project has used quotas, double standards, and coercive policies to recruit greater numbers of women, promote them faster, and put them closer to combat with little thought to the fact that this is, in effect, an attempt to meld two dissimilar populations—men and women—in an institution that requires conformity, interchangeability, standard issues, known quantities.

She refers to 'fem fear' on the carrier USS Stennis. Nine times out of ten, it is the man, not the woman, who gets in trouble. See pages 226-227. Colonel David Hackworth USA (Ret) concluded "What the British longbow did to the French army at Crecy in 1346, the failed military policy on gender integration has done to the U. S. armed forces at the end of the twentieth century: near total destruction." See the back cover of Reference (6).

Laurence C. Baldauf, Jr., a 1955 Naval Academy graduate, entered naval aviation in 1956. Both his father and father-in law were admirals. He is the author of Reference (7), Bah Bah Blue Sheep: A Critique of Military Yes-Men. Baldauf became disillusioned during the Vietnam War, which he concluded was a moral war but also an illegal war. He was convinced that we were not in the war to win and that there was no provision for victory. In January 1966, having completed his obligated term of service, he submitted his resignation from the Navy. The Navy initially refused his resignation request and some eighteen months of controversy followed. He was finally discharged in June 1967. He concluded that before the finest young men our country is capable of producing (the naval aviators he associated with) reach flag rank, the true leaders will be "weeded out." They will either be killed in warfare or training, resign in disgust, or be forced to retire. Baldauf quotes General MacArthur in a speech before the Massachusetts Legislature on 15 July 1951 as follows

Men of significant stature in national affairs appear to cower before the threat of reprisal if the truth be expressed in criticism of those in higher public authority. For example, I find in existence a new and dangerous concept that members of our armed forces owe primary allegiance and loyalty to those who temporarily exercise the authority of the executive branch of government, rather than to the country and its constitution which they are sworn to defend.

Reference (11) is available on the internet. Its author was, at the time, a thirty-nine-year- old single white male, with 17 years of distinguished, varied, and responsible Army service. His recommendations included the return of Officers and NCO Clubs, which have been discarded. He is convinced that, should we face a resolute enemy in open combat, the results would be catastrophic. He discusses the never ending stream of things such as "African-American Month" and "Asian-Pacific American Months" which accentuate differences. He recommends that we have "American Soldier Year" and be done with it. He laments the teaching of military people to see themselves not primarily as soldiers, but as females or African-Americans who happen to be soldiers. He further states that we have taught them not to be polite and respectful, but instead to carry chips on their shoulders, to search for some offense. He concludes that the hypersensitivity to race and gender issues are contributing to the destruction of morale.

Vice Admiral J. C. Harvey, Jr. in the fall 2007 issue of "Shift Colors" wrote that "Only 28% of American youth are even eligible for military service, based on test scores, fitness, and moral character." The test score debacle can best be addressed by correcting the failure of government schools, as discussed in the following chapter. The destruction of the family is a significant factor related to moral problems among America's young people. O'Beirne in Reference (13) discusses this on pages 9-16. She quotes Robert Rector of the Heritage Foundation, "The collapse of marriage is the principal cause of child poverty and a host of other social ills."

Army Major H. R. McMaster wrote Reference (8) while doing historical research at the University of North Carolina. He titled the book Dereliction of Duty/Lyndon Johnson, Robert McNamara, the Joint Chiefs of Staff and the Lies That Led to Vietnam. Michael Barone, in praising the book, wrote "A chilling indictment.... There have been many books on Vietnam, but none that examines so closely and intensively how Lyndon Johnson, Robert McNamara, and Maxwell Taylor systematically conspired to prevent the Joint Chiefs of Staff from performing their duty." Admiral David McDonald was a member of the Joint Chiefs of Staff as the Chief of Naval Operations. He later wrote "Maybe we military men were all weak. Maybe we should have stood up and pounded the table...I was part of it and I'm sort of ashamed of myself too. At times I wonder, why did I go along with this kind of stuff"? See Reference (8), page 262. He was referring to not protesting more vigorously when unwise civilian bullying of the Joint Chiefs occurred.

The widespread utilization of women in the military merits scrutiny. General John A. Vessey, Chairman of the Joint Chiefs of Staff told the House Armed Services Committee, "The greatest change that has come about in the United States forces in the time that I've been in the military service has been the extensive use of women....That's even greater than nuclear weapons, I feel, as far as our own forces are concerned." See Reference (5), page xi.

Commander Atkinson, in Reference (4), argues in no uncertain terms that 'affirmative action' quotas for women and minorities exist in naval aviation, and, the results have been disastrous. One former U. S. Navy flight instructor he quoted pulled no punches: "I'm getting out. It just isn't fun anymore. All of this affirmative action bull—t is just too damn much to take. The Navy is selling its soul." Atkinson proves that standards for Navy pilots have been lowered to help females and minorities. He notes that 100% of the group of five female pilots trained in combat aircraft failed in a deployment on the USS Abraham Lincoln. See pages 46 and 47 of Reference (4).

In addition to authoring Reference (4), Dr. Atkinson wrote a 120 page report titled "Sensitivity Training and the 'Socialization' of the U.S. Military." He documents the extent to which members of our 'New Military' are being subjected to this disgusting thought control 'sensitivity training.' This claptrap, akin to what was prominent in Stalin's Soviet Union and in Hitler's Germany has no legitimate place in the United States Military.

One of the first female Navy carrier pilots was Kara Hultgren. On 25 October 1994, she was attempting to land her Grumman F-14A Tomcat jet fighter on the USS Abraham Lincoln in the Pacific Ocean west of San Diego. The weather was clear and calm. She was killed and the official Navy position was that it was an engine failure. However, many Navy pilots (anonymously) did now agree with the Navy position. They maintained that she had received special treatment. Being on active duty, they could not publicly take issue with the official Navy position. One stated that she was "an accident waiting to happen." It later came to light that she had received four downs in flight training and another female pilot had received seven downs. Two downs usually result in the pilot trainee being washed out. Sometimes, even one down has resulted in dismissal. These females were not washed out, however. See pages 288-302 of Reference (5).

Mitchell, in Reference (5), stated that with the exception of the medical professions there is no real need for women in the military. He correctly points out that every other soldier, sailor, and airman is a potential combatant and women are not up to that job. He also correctly observes that our present course threatens to leave the American military no more disciplined, no more efficient, no more fearsome, no more military than the United States Postal Service. See pages xvi-xvii.

World renowned Israeli military historian Martin van Creveld, commenting on the foolhardy policies of the United States relative to women in the military, stated "For you, the military is not a question of life or death....So you can afford to make all kinds of social experiments, which we cannot...The very fact that you have this debate may itself be construed as proof that it's not serious. It's a game. It's a joke." See Reference (5), page 215. Pages 185-188 of Reference (5) include an enlightening discussion of Israeli experiences regarding women in the military. Mr. Creveld has lectured or taught at many strategic Institutes in the Western world, including the U. S. Naval War College. He has authored 22 books on military history and strategy. His books have been translated into 20 languages. See Wikipedia.

Mitchell includes an extensive discussion of the Tailhook scandal of 1991 in Las Vegas. See his Chapter 12. Former Reagan Navy Secretary James Webb, who was elected to the U. S. Senate from Virginia as a Democrat in 2006, expressed his thoughts about Tailhook. He concluded

Tailhook should have been a three- or maybe a five-day story. Those who were to blame for outrageous conduct should have been disciplined, and those who were not to blame should have been vigorously defended, along with the culture and the mores of the naval service. Instead, we are now at four years and counting, and its casualty list reads like a Who's Who of naval aviation. See page 245.

Tailhook became a political purge.

Mitchell correctly concludes that "The simple facts are that women are no longer needed in the military and their expanding presence is destroying the military's body and soul. The widely known but unaccepted truth is that most of what our senior civilian and military leaders tell us about women in the military is a lie." These lies include: military women are meeting the same standards as men, the presence of women has only had a positive effect on military readiness, and victimization of women is a product of a patriarchal culture. Mitchell points out that the feminization of the American military is no longer a story of reluctant admirals and generals forced to act against their better judgment. Instead, these senior military individuals are either true believers in the military's unmaking or they are unprincipled opportunists. See pages 341-344.

ADM Thomas H. Moorer former Chairman of the Joint Chiefs of Staff and former Chief of Naval Operations endorses the massage of Reference (4) by stating

This book presents solid evidence of what we have long suspected. The Clintons and their Boomer elitists are irreparably damaging the U. S. Navy. If the radical feminists are allowed to continue their agenda, the proud fighting Navy which won the war of the Pacific will no longer be capable of similar victory.

Obama is even worse than Clinton, in my opinion.

William S. Lind, military historian and host of 'Modern War' on NET-TV and former staffer to Senators Gary Hart and Robert A. Taft, Jr. stated "Commander Atkinson discloses the U. S. Military's biggest secret, the Stalinist atmosphere in which America's fighting men must now work and suffer, forbidden to say what they know is the truth: that women have no legitimate place on a battlefield or a warship." Lind was endorsing the powerful message of Reference (4). He purposely made a chauvinistic joke when addressing some Marine Corps Captains so as to observe the reaction. He described some billets which women, with spiffy little uniforms, could be assigned to in the feminized Navy. The Captains were terrified because their careers could be in danger from just listening to this. They were most familiar with the current Navy practice of 'sensitivity training,' like that used by Stalin.

The Chief of Naval Personnel, Vice Admiral Gerald L. Hoewing wrote an article in the Spring/Summer 2004 issue of Shift Colors, a newsletter for Navy retirees. He said that "I don't think there are too many things more important to readiness than our diversity." He said that diversity must include background, age, talent, religion, and of course, our race and gender.

U. S. Army Chief of Staff George Casey appeared more concerned about 'diversity' than the victims of Muslim jihadist Major Nidal Malik Hasan. See Human Events of 16 November 2009, page 1. Thirteen Americans were dead and thirty-eight more were wounded when Nidal shouted "Allahu akbar" before gunning them down inside the Army's Ft. Hood. Casey stated; "Our diversity, not only in our Army, but in our country, is a strength. And as horrific as this tragedy was, if our diversity becomes a casualty, I think that's worse."

U. S. Navy Chief of Naval Operations Gary Roughead was interviewed for a feature article in Military Officer Magazine in October 2009. He was asked to share his views on diversity. He responded "I strongly believe that as an organization you are better off with diverse perspectives. That is the power of diversity. It can be working with NGO's, for example, or mixing genders on board ships as I did a number of years ago. If you look at the Navy today, it looks like America, but if we look at just the officers, I see a bunch of white guys."

An anonymous 0-6 (Navy Captain or Army/Marine Colonel) wrote "Ft. Hood Killer at Work in Annapolis." This author notes that the current Superintendent of the U. S. Naval Academy states his number one priority is to increase diversity. Joint Chiefs Chairman ADM Mike Mullen claims that diversity is a "strategic imperative." This anonymous officer argues that gender-based political correctness has fostered a poisonous atmosphere. A double standard exists when punishing males and females guilty of identical offenses. Males were frequently dismissed while females generally received light punishment. In one five year period, every male midshipman accused of sexual assault but acquitted in a military court martial was still kicked out.

The American Legion Magazine for April 2010 has an article entitled, "Stealth Jihad," written by Frank Gaffney. Gaffney notes that two authors of a so-called independent review of the Ft. Hood massacre committed by Muslim Major Hasan, which was 86 pages long, did not contain the words Islam, Islamic terror, Shariah, jihad, or Muslim Brotherhood. The two authors were Vernon Clark, appointed to be Chief of Naval Operations by Bill Clinton, and Clinton's former Army Secretary, Togo West. Gaffney described the West-Clark report as an outrageously egregious example of unilateral disarmament in the battle of ideas.

Professor Emeritus Bernard Lewis has a Ph. D. degree in the history of Islam. He lectured on "Freedom and Justice in Islam." This was published by Hillsdale College in Imprimis in September 2006. He quotes Osama bin Laden:

In this final phase of the ongoing struggle, the world of the infidels was divided between two superpowers-the United States and the Soviet Union. Now we have defeated and destroyed the more difficult and the more dangerous of the two. Dealing with the pampered and effeminate Americans will be easy.

Although bin Laden did not refer to the fact that the U. S. military has been feminized and that top military leaders have such a hang-up on diversity, he was certainly aware of these facts, as are his successors.

Earlier, I referred to the article "Ft. Hood Killer at Work in Annapolis." This article, published in November 2009, notes that Naval Academy officials promote the fact that 35% of the freshman class is composed of favored minority groups: Hispanic, black, Asian/Pacific Islander, and Native American. Twenty percent are female. Admissions officials privately acknowledge that they are directed to dramatically increase these percentages each year. One Naval Academy professor has reported that the nonwhite candidates are graded against easier admissions requirements than whites. The author has been told by active duty military recruiters that minority volunteers are desired over whites.

Reference (5) contains an extensive discussion of the negative consequences of sending our women to war. Sally Quinn, wife of Washington Post editor-in-chief

Ben Bradlee, asked: "If we can't win a war without our mothers, what kind of a sorry fighting force are we? Even the evil Saddam Hussein doesn't send mothers to fight his war." One female Army sergeant testified to extensive sexual activity on mixed sex guard duty and the complete lack of discipline. See Pages 195-214. On page 288, it is revealed that at least thirty-nine women (probably more) left the USS Eisenhower during a six-month cruise because of pregnancy. Some Army women were reported to be selling black market condoms for $40 or $50 each. See page 206. One of the latest hare-brained ideas is to start assigning women to serve on submarines.

Columnist Walter Williams, in a column published in the Columbia Daily Tribune on 7 October 1998, reported that 58% of single Air Force women and 48% of single Navy women were pregnant at one base.

In December 2009, Army Major General Anthony Cucolo issued an order that was intended to address the apparent widespread sexual activity among his troops in Iraq. His order would permit punishment of Army women who became pregnant and their sexual partners. It only took about a week for his order to be rescinded by General Raymond Odierno.

Only about 12% of Army females could throw a hand grenade beyond its burst radius. That means that 88% of Army females would be subjected to the effects of any hand grenade they threw. Only 12% of Navy females could carry a two-person stretcher which is required during shipboard emergencies.

The Air Force's aggressive affirmative action policies led to a class-action lawsuit which cost it $10,000,000 to settle. The Air Force had illegally forced eighty-three white male Lieutenant Colonels to retire. Those promotion billets were needed to permit promotion of women and other non-white-males. See Human Events, 6 November 1998.

The Naval Academy, the Military Academy, and the Air Force Academy have lowered their academic standards. This is discussed in Reference (4) on page 46. It was reported that female military officers, both Navy and Air Force, who had liberal arts degrees and no engineering background, were useless when assigned to billets requiring engineering judgment. Gross discusses the same problem on page 100 in Reference (12). This point is further discussed by Atkinson in Reference (4) on page 88. A former engineering professor at Annapolis told of a rallying cry of midshipmen, "Poly-Sci, QPR high!" This refers to the taking of political science courses to bolster the quality point rating by taking these relatively easy political science courses. The Political Science Department was headed by a female Navy officer. Traditionally, students at the military academies studied engineering or related science.

Another incident shines light on the warped value system of the "New Navy." Devout Christian LCDR Kenneth Carkhuff had been described as a "community superstar" on his fitness report. In August 1994, he told his commanding officer that he believed that it was morally wrong to expose women to combat. One week later, Carkhuff was told that if he did not resign within 24 hours, he would be forced out.

The modern military services' new value system has negatively and drastically affected recruiting. I actively assisted the St. Louis Navy recruiters several decades ago. I presented a "Loyalty Day" talk in the Missouri State Capitol building on 3 May 1975. See page 139. Congressman Richard Ichord was scheduled to be the speaker but was unable to leave Washington, D. C. At the last minute, he informed the Navy recruiters, who were responsible for the speech, and they asked me to replace Congressman Ichord. To deliver the speech, I drove a Camero sports car, which belonged to the Navy Recruiters, to the state capitol. The car had a large image of Navy wings of gold on each side. I did several other things to help the recruiters over the years. However, I would now find it most difficult to encourage a white male to enter military service, in light of the misguided policies of civilian and military bureaucrats, as documented here and elsewhere.

I write this chapter with deep sadness. It comes from the realization that a decades-old—actually centuries-old—successful military culture is under assault not only by feminist zealots but by uniformed military leadership. If only one of the high ranking military officers would publicly announce his resignation due to the shortcomings of present military personnel policy, it might cause some long needed reevaluation. As author Stephanie Gutmann wrote in Reference (6), page 277, quoting ex-naval officer Patrick Vincent: the brass "refused to defend their own culture"; they even began to systematically criminalize the warrior spirit. LCDR Baldauf in Reference (7) wrote "Moral courage is the lacking ingredient in today's high-ranking military leaders. Many of them have excellent combat records, but without exception they are all .....sheep." What other explanation could explain their unacceptable behavior? Professor Harry V. Jaffa (Imprimis, June 2004) noted that diversity is a main feature of political correctness which appears to be unable to distinguish right from wrong. What a sad time for the United States of America.

Chapter 17. Critique of American Education

Many Americans know that something is seriously wrong with our education system. Indeed, we have more system than education. It is also unfortunately true that our education system is deliberately dumbing down our young people. This almost treasonous behavior has been going on for decades.

How could such an assertion be true? Any reader of this book with sufficient interest can determine the truth rather easily. Review the titles of References (17) through (36) to begin with. Most of these books should be available in local libraries. But it is even easier than that. Reference (23), probably the most important and enlightened analysis of this national tragedy, is available on the internet. Go to JohnTaylorGatto.com and bring up The Underground History of American Education. Read Mr. Gatto's letter of resignation from his position as a New York school teacher. This is in 'I Quit, I Think' in the Prologue. That letter starts "Government schooling is the most radical adventure in history. It kills the family by monopolizing the best times of childhood and by teaching disrespect for home and parents." It ends, "I can't teach this way any longer. If you hear of a job where I don't have to hurt kids to make a living, let me know. Come fall I'll be looking for work." Gatto sent the letter to the Wall Street Journal, swallowed hard, then quit. A week after the Journal published his letter in July 1991, he had received invitations to speak at NASA, the Western White House, Columbia Graduate Business School, and Apple Computer, among other venues. After nine years he had spoken in all 50 states and seven foreign countries. It is high time to tell the truth, to cut through the fog and hot air put out by proponents of the failed government schools. John Gatto has been doing an outstanding job of exposing the truth.

Gatto's classic work, Reference (23), offers numerous revelations. In 1973, the president of the National Education Association (NEA) said "Dramatic changes in the way we raise our children are indicated, particularly in terms of schooling...

we will be agents of change." In 1989 another education bureaucrat told all 50 governors "What we're into is a total restructuring of society." In 1997, still another education bureaucrat discussed a condition which he called "over-education." He wrote: "We must continue to produce an uneducated social class that will do... 'the scut work.' "(Note; I use the word 'scut' here, but an abbreviation for the 'N word' was used in the quoted source). See "Change Agents Infiltrate" on page 46.

On page 52, Gatto reveals the continuing drop in literacy from 96% in 1941 to 81% in 1952 to 73% in 1970. On pages 101 and 102, he discusses the strenuous opposition of the citizens of America to compulsory attendance in government schools. The 1934 version of "Public Education in the United States" includes "The history of compulsory-attendance legislation in the states has been much the same everywhere, and everywhere laws have been enacted only after overcoming strenuous opposition." This sounds like the Obama Democrats' government-run health care.

NEA reports from 1911 and 1918 are noted on page 108. These reports reveal a conscious abandonment of textbooks intended to train the mind. The reports savagely attacked the traditional "bookish curricula." History was to be replaced by something called "social studies." The 1918 NEA report decreed that specified behaviors, health, and vocational training were the central goals of public education. Mental development, character, and godliness were not.

On page 177, Gatto attributes the undermining of the idea of school as an oasis of mental development to the rise of the field of educational psychology, mainly between 1901 and 1911. There was a growing distrust of government schools. The Dean of Columbia Teachers College said "If school cannot be made to drop its mental development obsession the whole system should be abolished." See page 178.

On page 193, Gatto discusses obstacles to the goal of using American schools to remake society. The first obstacle was local control, exercised by thousands of local school boards. The camouflage of consolidation for economy's sake dramatically reduced the number of school boards, and thus school board members. The comparatively few school board members now in office are relatively easy to control. It is rare indeed for a school board member to have the ability to correctly analyze the serious problems which exist and to also have the courage and capability to do anything meaningful to solve them. While most school board members are good people, they are nearly universally worthless, I believe, as far as successful problem solving is concerned. Since school board members are almost worthless, it follows that boards made up of these individuals must also be practically worthless.

The second obstacle noted by Gatto was the influence of good teachers as role models. Old-fashioned teachers knew what was important, and they taught it.

As late as 1930, there were still almost 150,000 one-room/one-teacher schools in America. The army of high salaried, non-teaching principals, assistant principals, coordinators, and other parasitic bureaucrats did not yet exist. Forcing today's teachers to use approved texts and to conform to all of the bureaucratic rules ensures that they cannot stray far.

The third obstacle was the neighborhood context of schools. Neighborhood schools make undermining traditional society harder. As Gatto points out, James Conant, an influential member of the Carnegie commission stated that a reason for the Russians to successfully launch Sputnik before the U. S. did something similar was the small size of American schools. So, Americans thereafter built larger schools. This made it easier for the de-intellectualized curriculum to be foisted upon unsuspecting students and their parents. Meanwhile, the number of teachers as a percent of school employees was falling from 95% in 1915 to some 50% ninety years later. From 1960 to 1990, the number of school administrators grew 342%. Costs shot up by about the same percentage amount.

Section 192, starting on page 308 of Reference (23), lists eight ways schools wreck havoc on our children. The reader can review these on the internet.

John Gatto discusses the tragic case of Benson, Vermont, beginning on page 345. There, the voters turned down a proposed school budget twelve times. Benson had four one-room schools, four teachers and no administrators. The voters evidently believed school matters were proceeding in an acceptable fashion. However, the Vermont State Senate forced Benson to pay the amount that the voters had rejected a dozen times. After all, there were no wheelchair ramps. After the state intervention, the voters had to support the following non-teaching bureaucrats: a superintendent, an assistant superintendent, a principal, an assistant principal, a nurse, a guidance counselor, and a librarian. Teachers jumped in number from four to eleven. An unknown number of other personnel were employed. It was also necessary to supply space and furniture for these non-teaching parasitic bureaucrats.

Gatto points out an embarrassing fact in a footnote at the end of the Prologue: "For instance, school superintendents as a class are virtually the stupidest people to pass through a graduate college program, ranking fifty-one points (on the Graduate Record Examination) below the elementary school teachers they normally "supervise", and about eighty points below the secondary school teachers, while teachers themselves as an aggregate finish seventeenth of twenty occupational groups surveyed."

I authored Reference (1) titled *American Education / A Howard County, Missouri Case Study: From Successful One-Room Schools to Extravagance, Arrogance, and Fail-*

ure in 2005. Most of Reference (1) is a history of one-room Union School which I attended as a child. This school was built on a corner of a farm owned by my great-grandfather in 1892. He permitted the school to be built on his farm with the clear understanding that the school lot was always part of his farm when not used "for school purposes." The use of the school for school purposes ceased in 1945, so individuals possessing traits of honesty and positive character would readily acknowledge the historical truth. This truth was acknowledged until the early part of this century. The Fayette School Board made a belated claim of ownership of the school lot at the request of a clique of individuals, not one of whom had any legitimate right to the Union School property. The Fayette School Board claimed ownership based exclusively on a deed filed in 1915. That deed was established to be a forgery with 100% certainty in Reference (1). This interesting and disgusting situation is covered extensively in Reference (1). Not one member of the Fayette School Board or their high-priced attorney has exhibited any public interest in revealing how they can claim ownership of this real estate. Their silence regarding this important point continues to be deafening. Fayette, Missouri's failed School Board claimed ownership at the behest of the clique so that the School Board could then turn the Union School property over to the clique.

Chapter 11 of Reference (1) was titled "The Government Education Disaster – National, State, and Local Trends." Much of the content of that chapter is repeated here. Dr. Loren E. Klaus, President of Shawnee College of Ullin, Illinois, said, "We have developing today an educational-political complex more dangerous to our freedoms than any military-industrial complex imaginable." Dr. Klaus stated his case to 4218 delegates at an educational conference in Columbus, Ohio in September 1976. A full page article in a Missouri School Boards Association News item in September 1976 recounted Dr. Klaus's address. Today, words and actions of governors and presidents illustrate that Dr. Klaus was indeed a visionary. How often we hear governors, presidents, and state and national legislators tell us we must have more money for education? The truth is that we have been down that road too many times. The more money we provide for government education, the worse the results. The taxpayers of the United States have absolutely no responsibility to continue to pay the exorbitant taxes which permit the unionized government school people to mislead our students instead of educate them. We have no responsibility to continue to support the exorbitant retirement pay for these people, starting at such an early retirement age. The unionized government school people wish to be referred to as professionals. Professionals do not act like the thugs and public employee union members who occupied the Wisconsin State Capitol Building in February and March of 2011.

I will now briefly review some of the literature referred to in the List of References. As noted above, Reference (23) is available on the Internet. It is probably the best reference available today. Reference (27) was written by Thomas Sowell, a senior fellow at the Hoover Institution at Stanford University. It is entitled Inside American Education: The Decline, The Deception, The Dogmas. Dr. Sowell writes "Our educational establishment—a vast tax-supported empire existing quasi-independently within American society—is morally and intellectually bankrupt." He points out (correctly) the positive aspects of permitting people with educational backgrounds other than college of education training to teach in our schools.

Reference (28) is entitled Dumbing Down Our Kids: Why American Children Feel Good About Themselves, But Can't Read, Write, or Add. Author Charles Sykes, points out the sad fact that our students rank at, or near, the bottom of international tests in mathematics and science. While the educational establishment points the finger at families, society, and television, the real culprit is the educational establishment itself.

Reference (18) is an analysis of education expenditures and results for all 50 states and the District of Columbia. For 1996, the top three of the fifty-one in student achievement spent less than did the bottom three in achievement. The top three in achievement had a higher pupil-teacher ratio than did the bottom three. The two states with the lowest teacher salaries had higher achievement than did the two states with the highest teacher salaries. To summarize:

- More money spent on government education does not improve student achievement
- Lower pupil-teacher ratio does not improve achievement
- Higher teacher and administrative salaries do not improve achievement.

In Reference (41), Polly Williams, an accomplished black woman and Wisconsin state representative, spoke on the topic "Inner-City Kids: Why Choice is their only Hope." She stated "—the public schools are failing to educate our children. Sixty per cent of all Milwaukee ninth graders do not complete high school, and of the 40% who stay in school and walk across the stage, only 10% can read." She also revealed that 62% of government school teachers and administrators refuse to send their own children to the government schools. Over opposition of teachers unions, the NAACP, and the bloated government education establishment, Polly Williams and others got a parental empowerment bill passed. Up to 1,000 students could receive $2,500 worth of tuition vouchers for private schools. If the government monopoly can be broken in Wisconsin, there is hope elsewhere.

It is apparent that the public school curriculum has changed significantly. History, mathematics, English, and reading are not given the attention that decades and centuries have proven they deserve. John Gatto, in Reference (23), explains the reason for these almost treasonous changes. Reference (42) is a publication of the National Education Association (NEA). On page 19, these NEA authors say "Should we teach plane geometry at all?' On page 42, they say "Euclid designed his geometry as an exercise in logical problem solving in an age when there weren't many interesting problems to solve; ever since, youngsters living in an utterly fascinating world, youngsters who know more at 15 than Euclid did at his death, have struggled to make triangles congruent." It is noted that Euclid lived some 300 years before Jesus Christ, and that he wrote a book that was used as a text as late as 1903. Think of it – Euclid wrote a book that was used as a text some 2200 years after being written. This NEA publication concludes that today's fifteen-year-old knows more than Euclid.

The NEA publication also states (page 42) "Who came first, Abraham Lincoln or Millard Fillmore? Most adults don't know and most students don't care – though they might if both men had been related to some inquiry into the historical process, such as whether great men shape their times or hard times create great men." This would appear to illustrate the contempt of the NEA for history, as well as its contempt for one of our greatest presidents.

In February 2005, I received a letter from Major General Milnor Roberts of the World War II Veterans Committee. General Roberts said, "Sixty years ago, as a young infantry captain, I hit the beach at Normandy during the momentous D-Day battle." The purpose of his letter was to express concern over the fact that our upcoming generation is not aware of the sacrifices made that day. He said "A recent survey of high school students at a well-regarded public school revealed that 73% could not even say whom America fought in World War II." He continued "And when it came to Pearl Harbor – 7 December 1941, the date 'which will live in infamy' – 91% of students could not name that day. Tragically, 75% of Stanford University students also could not name that day." Results were similar at the Ivy League universities.

General Roberts pointed out that the U. S. Department of Education sponsored the development of revised history standards in 1994. The World War II material in these standards centers on "multi-cultural" groups. America is harshly criticized for using the atomic bomb, even though this action saved hundreds of thousands of lives. Roberts noted that one popular high school history textbook includes five pages on the U. S. dropping the atomic bomb. Every single highlighted quote is

DR. C. BEN BASYE FOR

ST. CHARLES BOARD OF EDUCATION

TUESDAY, APRIL 3, 1973

Why the overwhelming majority of American citizens who have inspected "Promise of America" vigorously oppose its use as an eighth grade history text.

1. **Legalized abortion and marijuana are presented as social accomplishments in the year 2000.**
2. **The theme of class hatred and prejudice runs throughout the books. Many chapters dwell upon violence and insulting language. For instance, terms are used such as "dirty Polack," "nigger," "bastards," and "Sonofabitch." A brief examination of these books might lead one to conclude that the long overdue coverage of minority history, conspicuously lacking in many texts, has been objectively included. However, a more thorough examination reveals a continuous portrayal of a sick America with overwhelming racism, poverty, intolerance, welfare, and injustice. Not only is the white race treated in an insulting fashion, but minorities as well.**
3. **These books contain too much controversial material--especially when the audience is made up of impressionable youths in their early teens. Volume I of the series is supposed to cover American life before 1800. Actually, pages 77 to 80 give a detailed case study of a high school "rebellion" where the students took over their school. Another "case study" describes a 16 year old boy's "rebellion" against his father (pages 74 to 76). The text is very sympathetic to the idea of rebellion. For instance, the Teacher's manual for "Promise of America" (Teacher Tactics, page 16), gives the teacher these instructions, "Stress that rebellion involves going against a recognized authority, in this base a son against his father. This case is analogous to the underlying causes, symptoms, and spark of the American Revolution..." Note that this "case study" of the boy rebelling against his father is obviously slanted. The father is depicted as a selfish, unreasonable, bossy man who struck his son. Why must a so called history book throw one more obstacle between child and parent?**
4. **Many important and great figures of American history have been ignored or neglected in order to describe the undesirables. For instance, Benjamin Franklin is given one short sentence in Volume I. The authors devote six entire paragraphs of the same volume to George Rockwell and the American Nazi party. To further illustrate the imbalance, note that, with three exceptions (Kennedy, Wilson, and Lincoln) photographs of America's presidents are not included. However, space is found for Al Capone, Hitler, Stalin, American Nazis, numerous protestors, several Klan photographs and drawings, many homeless and welfare families, race riots, Socialist-workers parade, Malcolm X, Stokely Carmichael, Black Panthers, extensive coverage of Ressurection City, extensive coverage of poverty (only U.S. poverty, never poverty in Socialist or Communist countries), and extensive emphasis of revolt and rebellion situations.**
5. **There are huge gaps in history as well. The textbooks present history as a series of class struggles: blacks versus whites, men versus women, youth versus age, etc. All of history is equated to class struggle. The political, economic, geographic, military, and technological aspects of history are ignored to a great extent.**
6. **The series has been defended on the grounds that it is a "noble effort" to present "controversial matters" to the eager, developing minds of our children. Most eighth graders do not yet have the maturity and self confidence to resist the subtle flattery of example after example that depict the young as "good" and the old as "bad." Why widen the generation gap any further? Why provide a negative influence that could separate a child in the emotional throes of puberty from the authority and influence of his parents?**
7. **Further, "Promise of America" tells our young people that a permanent U.S. Army is dangerous to liberty. Most Americans will agree that this statement is untrue and uncalled for. All informed authorities agree that America must remain militarily strong. See, for instance, "The Shifting Balance of Military Power, Supplemental Statement to Report of Blue Ribbon Defense Panel", U.S. Government Printing Office, 9-30-70.**

Above, Analysis of a series of books called "Promise of America"; These were used as textbooks for eighth grade history in St. Charles, Missouri and other locations in 1973. See Balint Vazsonyi's warning on page 185.

critical of the United States. General MacArthur rates one sentence while there is an entire chapter on "The War and Civil Rights." Admiral Nimitz is not mentioned. One sentence describes Iwo Jima, and that is to criticize America's strategy.

Remember that the author of Reference (10), Balint Vazsonyi, lived under both the German Nazis and the Soviet Communists before leaving his native Hungary. On page 232, he states "Nowhere does the battle rage as fiercely as in education." He expresses deep concern that the founding documents of our country have been removed from the classroom, and that civics classes have disappeared along with George Washington's birthday. No history—no national memory—no identity. There will be no American anything. This appears to be the primary purpose of the 'National Standards in United States History' sponsored by Bill Clinton's Education Department in 1994. Historian Vazsonyi stated "The elimination of a nation's true history, expertly practiced in the Soviet Union and the Third Reich, guarantees commissars an uncontested field as they bring up generations with blanks instead of history in their heads."

Recall the discussion on page 144 of the controversial books in the St. Charles, Missouri School District. These books were being used where Missouri State Law specified in no uncertain terms that history shall be taught. The book series was called "Promise of America." An analysis of these books appears on the previous page. I used this analysis as an election handout when I ran for the St. Charles School Board in 1973.

In 1975, I shared information on curricula trends in our public schools with several senior members of the University of Missouri administration. Chancellor Raymond L. Bisplinghof, of the University of Missouri-Rolla, in a private letter to me, stated "I read with interest your critique of 'Promise of America' and I must say that I was appalled to learn that such a book is used in our public school classrooms. But I was even more appalled the other day when I read in a St. Louis paper that a professor of education from the University of California (Berkley) proposed at a meeting of the NEA that reading and arithmetic be made optional in the grade schools. It seems to me that such a step would make such schools virtually worthless to society."

Chancellor Bisplinghof was one of the most outstanding and accomplished engineers in the United States. Reference (35), an eight-page document dated 23 August 1971, is known as "The Powell Memorandum." Its author was Lewis Powell, a past Chairman of the Virginia State Board of Education. Powell wrote this document at the request of the United States Chamber of Commerce. Powell was later nominated to be a Justice of the Supreme Court and was approved by the U. S. Senate with only one dissenting vote. Powell discusses the broad attack on our American economic system. He wrote, "Yale, like every other major college, is graduating scores of bright young men who are practitioners of the 'politics of despair.' These young men despise the American political and economic system…their minds seem to be wholly closed. They live, not by rational discussion, but by mindless slogans."

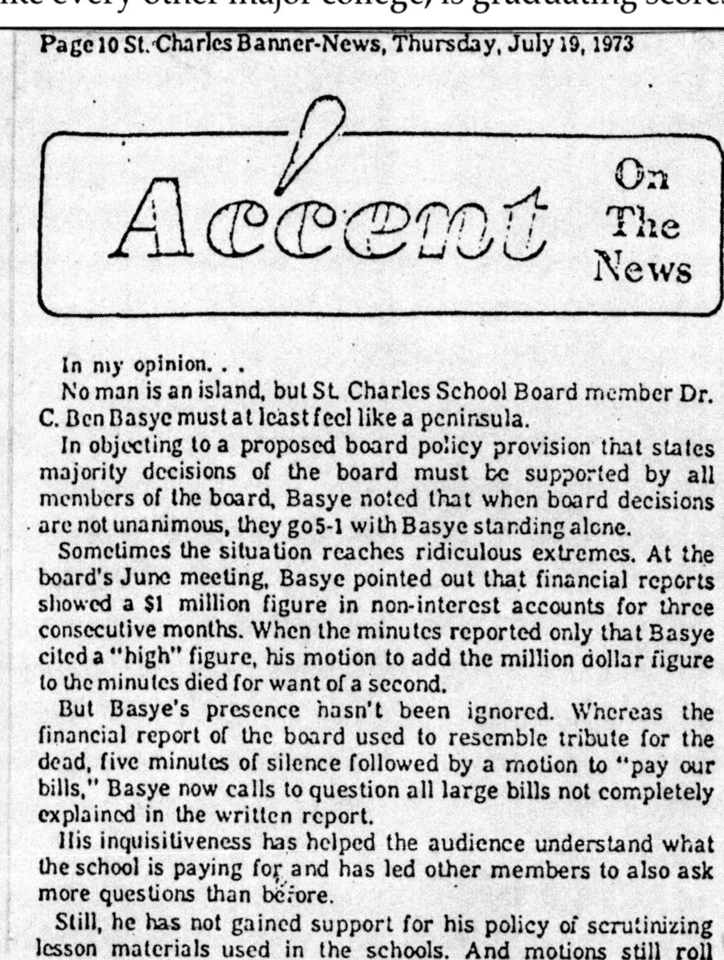
Page 10 St. Charles Banner-News, Thursday, July 19, 1973

Accent On The News

In my opinion. . .

No man is an island, but St. Charles School Board member Dr. C. Ben Basye must at least feel like a peninsula.

In objecting to a proposed board policy provision that states majority decisions of the board must be supported by all members of the board, Basye noted that when board decisions are not unanimous, they go 5-1 with Basye standing alone.

Sometimes the situation reaches ridiculous extremes. At the board's June meeting, Basye pointed out that financial reports showed a $1 million figure in non-interest accounts for three consecutive months. When the minutes reported only that Basye cited a "high" figure, his motion to add the million dollar figure to the minutes died for want of a second.

But Basye's presence hasn't been ignored. Whereas the financial report of the board used to resemble tribute for the dead, five minutes of silence followed by a motion to "pay our bills," Basye now calls to question all large bills not completely explained in the written report.

His inquisitiveness has helped the audience understand what the school is paying for and has led other members to also ask more questions than before.

Still, he has not gained support for his policy of scrutinizing lesson materials used in the schools. And motions still roll through the board, not unanimously, but unanimously minus one.

— Steve Hornbostel, staff writer

News article from the St. Charles Banner News of 19 July 1973

The next topic I review is Reference (45), Missouri Senate Bill 380, known as the "Outstanding Schools Act." In 1992, Democrat Mel Carnahan campaigned for governor by proclaiming that our public schools were underfunded. He proposed that he be elected governor; he would then make a case for higher school taxes. He hoped to convince citizens to support higher taxes. However, when he became governor, there was no vote of the citizens. Democrats controlled the State House and Senate. They imposed the $310 million tax increase without a citizens' vote. What happened next? Raises of three per cent plus $200.00 per year were proposed for the 54,000 state employees. At the same time, Carnahan proposed 15% pay raises for 354 bureaucrats in the State Department of Elementary and Secondary Education. Senate Bill 380 has done more harm than good. One of the most unwise parts of the bill is a requirement for at least sixteen hours of state approved orientation and training for anyone elected to a school board. We definitely need capable people on school boards. We need people who can do their own thinking and who have the courage to advocate what is right, even if they stand alone. We do not need sheep who support whatever the majority advocates, or what the Superintendent tells them to.

I confronted the "me-too"type of school board decision-making almost four decades ago. See the news article on page 186.

The "No Child Left Behind" Act (NCLB) is the centerpiece of George W. Bush's federal education program. Bush signed this document on 8 January 2002. Chapter 5 of Reference (32), titled Ed Fraud 101, contains an excellent 22 page analysis of NCLB. Accompanying the act has been an explosion of federal government spending for education. Human Events placed this tab at a yearly value of $64 trillion on page 8 of its 14 February 2005 issue. While Bush bragged about this amount, he was criticized by democrats for not wasting even more.

From Reference (32), page 63, we note "Because NCLB hinges on adequate yearly progress, the lower the initial standards set by the states, the easier it is to show sufficient progress. Since the passage of NCLB, many states have redefined failure downwards. Some states set their NCLB baselines at levels that should be satisfied by any random selection of people not in a mortuary."

It should be clear to anyone who takes a rational look at this situation that the U. S. Department of Education should be abolished. It was brought to life by Jimmy Carter to please the NEA. Columnist Michelle Malkin, in the Washington Times, labeled the Department of Education the "Department of Embezzlement." She described a sixty-four- page federal grand jury indictment. She wrote "This million dollar criminal enterprise is just the tip of the iceberg of fraudulent federal spending . . . . Federal education aid has been embezzled to pay for luxury cars, real estate, diapers, and rent."

Instances of unacceptable spending and other questionable behavior by government school officials are plentiful.

St. Louis Superintendent of Schools Jerome B. Jones spent $25,403 for twenty-one trips between 1 July 1985 and 8 May 1986. This was more than the superintendents of Atlanta, Miami, Milwaukee, Houston, and Kansas City, combined, spent for the same period. According to the St. Louis Post Dispatch, one member of the St. Louis School Board had to file suit to be permitted to examine district financial records. The Kansas City School Board relieved its superintendent for questionable expenses, according to the Columbia Daily Tribune of 2 February 1995. The St. Charles, Missouri Superintendent spent $109 for a radar detector (fuzz buster) for his district furnished automobile. He removed the money from the building fund without the knowledge or permission of the School Board. The St. Louis media reported on this when it occurred in the late 1970's.

The Columbia Daily Tribune of 23 April 1993 reported on an audit of Central Missouri State University by State Auditor Margaret Kelly, and the response to the audit by the university. The audit found that CMSU was missing millions of dollars of equipment, including 58 cars and trucks. Uncollected student fees totaled $3.5 million. The auditor said university officials made "extravagant and inappropriate" spending. Included were

1. An estimated $7.9 million subsidy over five years for the athletic program
2. More than $2.8 million on a public radio and television station
3. $11,309 from 1989 to 1992 to upgrade airline tickets, including a ticket for University President Ed Elliott's son.

University officials characterized the audit as "outdated and politically motivated."

The Moberly Monitor-Index and Evening Democrat of 18 November 1996 included an article titled "High-Ranking Springfield School Official Resigns." The official, Conley Weiss, was one of two individuals with the title of Superintendent. Weiss resigned one week after the school board terminated a $491,000 contract he had negotiated for consulting work over a five-year period. The contract was signed without knowledge of the school board.

The St. Louis Post Dispatch of 9 January 1996 titled an editorial "$330,000 Worth of Irresponsibility." It concerned management practices of the Special School District of St. Louis County. The $330,000 was paid to an individual who had been hired as superintendent, then demoted to another job despite his contract.

On 30 October 1990, the St. Louis Post Dispatch led with the editorial "A Lesson in Greed." It concerned the St. Louis Junior College District management practices. The editorial stated "The way district officials hid these automobile purchases from the Board of Trustees helps destroy what little financial creditability the college may have left." The Chancellor of the St. Louis institution was paid $13,000 as a consultant for a college in Virginia (while he was on vacation). Later, the president of the Virginia college won a no-bid $5,000 consulting job from the St. Louis institution.

The Columbia Daily Tribune raised questions regarding a severance package for Marshall Gordon, President of Southwest Missouri State University. He had approved $7,000,000 in unplanned spending related to cost overruns for a performing arts center. The severance package was estimated at some $400,000. He was to continue with full pay and benefits for a time during which he could take leaves of absence at will. He was to be reimbursed $37,000 for university-related entertainment expenses and $50,000 for "miscellaneous transition expenses."

I now turn my attention to Reference (33), The Shadow University – The Betrayal of Liberty on America's Campuses, by Alan Charles Kors and Harvey A. Silvergate. The authors examine the overwhelming influence of "political correctness" and group rights on college campuses. Washington Post columnist Nat Hentoff endorsed the book as follows; "Many of America's colleges and universities, including the most prestigious, have largely abandoned a respect for free speech, due process, honesty from on high, and the very concept of intellectual freedom." He said that these two authors have created the most far-reaching and in-depth report on the appalling state of American higher education.

Reference (34), The Diversity Myth –Multiculturalism and the Politics of Intolerance at Stanford, by David A. Sacks and Peter A. Theil, vividly reveals the nature of a cultural revolution on campus and details the changes necessary to reverse the tragic disintegration of American colleges and universities and to restore academic excellence. The book documents the tremendous harm done as Stanford 'revised' a Western Civilization requirement, and replaced it with what has become known as 'multiculturalism'. Sadly, such unwise and disastrous trends are all too commonplace in higher education today. Similar foolishness has even become entrenched in the bureaucracy of the U. S. military as noted in the previous chapter.

The Iowa State Daily reprinted Reference (39) from the New York Times in 1961. It included "The old problem of teaching versus research by college faculty members has again come into the limelight. The central problem here can be stated simply: Professors and instructors at universities are normally judged – and promoted or not promoted—on the basis of their published research. Is not the first-rate teacher capable of firing the imagination of his students and really teaching them his field worthy of more respect and advancement than the mediocre teacher whose research output is some piece of unimaginative drudgery that is of the most marginal importance?"

Author Charles T. Sykes presented a talk at Hillsdale College in 1989. See Reference (40). The topic was the same as the preceding paragraph, namely, the exaggerated importance given to faculty research. Sykes revealed the situation at Harvard, where three of the last four recipients of a teaching award had been denied tenure. The pattern is the same at other universities. Sykes stated "The academic culture is not merely indifferent to teaching, it is actively hostile to it. In the modern large university, no act of good teaching goes unpunished." The author, as a senior professor and member of a tenure review committee in the University of Missouri system, has heard candidates for tenure criticized by "His problem is, he spends too much time with his students." While some university research is important, much of it is worthless. Government sponsored research does, however, bring in money for overhead. It supports more non-teaching bureaucracy.

The Reader's Digest of November 1998 reveals that the National Science Foundation awarded a professor $107,000 to tell dirty jokes. The same professor and a colleague had earlier received a $170,000 grant to study "cognitive consequences of emotions." Other awards by the same government agency included $221,000 to study why men do not smile as often as women, and $72,000 to study the history of the fax machine.

The Columbia Daily Tribune of 17 December 1991 listed these examples of questionable federal research grants:

- $27,000 to find out why inmates want to escape from prison
- $31,000 for a study of the hearing ability of parakeets
- $46,000 to determine how long it takes to cook eggs
- $50,000 to prove that sheep dogs protect sheep
- $107,000 to study the mating habits of the Japanese quail
- $192,000 to study drunk fish and rats
- $219,000 to teach college students how to watch television.

"Administrative bloat" is another problem. The 7 October 1992 issue of the Chronicle of Higher Education discussed a controversy over a $2,400,000 retirement benefit for David P. Gardner, retiring President of the University of California. The 12 February 1992 issue of the Chronicle noted that in 1950, colleges spent 27 cents on administration for every dollar spent on instruction. In 1988, the amount spent on administration was 45 cents. The Democrat-Leader of Fayette, Missouri of 9 February 1991 noted that the number of employees in the Missouri Department of Elementary and Secondary Education (DESE) jumped from 695 in 1973, to 1909 in 1990. That same department had eleven employees in "public information." In 1994, one campus of the University of Missouri (not the largest campus) had a chancellor, a deputy to the chancellor, two assistants to the chancellor, five vice-chancellors, three associate vice-chancellors, and one assistant to a vice-chancellor. In addition, there were the deans, associate deans, assistant deans, and directors.

Remember the warning about the educational-political complex on page 181. The Columbia Daily Tribune of 6 January 2005 contained a front page article titled "Wilson lands at MU after four terms in Missouri House." Former State Representative Vicky Riback Wilson reportedly worked for the interim vice provost for undergraduate studies in the Graduate School. One might ask why there is a vice provost for 'undergraduate' studies in the 'Graduate School.'

The failed Kansas City experiment became notorious nationally. Federal Judge Richard Clark took it upon himself to mandate tax increases without action by either taxpayers or the State Legislature, in hopes of solving desegregation problems. A Columbia Daily Tribune editorial on 30 March 1997 began, "After nearly 20 years and $1.6 trillion the court-ordered grand experiment in the Kansas City School District is a palpable failure." This failed program was featured on the 60 Minutes TV program on 27 February 1994. The Economist of London, England had an article on the failed Kansas City school program in its 28 August 1993 issue. "According to the bulk of liberal pundits, the best way to fix America's faltering schools is to spend more money on them," the article began. The Economist concluded "Educational reformers should forget about their money spending schemes and start thinking, instead, of some more hard-headed ways to raise educational standards."

Referring to the arrogance of Federal Judge Clark in ordering the exorbitant spending, which produced little of value, the Free Market of June 1990 stated, "This was not a dispute between two levels of government, but rather between the taxpayers and all government." Further, "The ruling also illustrates the flaw in government–controlled education. The government near monopoly on education must be broken by allowing parents to withdraw their support for the state schools and spend their money on private market-sensitive schools."

The Fayette, Missouri Advertiser, on 5 July 1995, reprinted an opinion piece from nationally syndicated columnist Stephen Chapman. Chapman's article was titled "Lessons from Kansas City's Failure." He concluded, "The experience offers powerful evidence that the perennial 'remedy' of the educational establishment is not just futile but fraudulent. In the absence of drastic reforms, more spending means more waste."

It is easy to document other areas of wasteful, illegal, or unnecessary spending. The 30 January 1992 USA Today reported that auditors accused such well-known universities as Penn State, Syracuse, M. I. T. , and Carnegie-Mellon of overcharging taxpayers millions of dollars for doing government research. Stanford was found to have spent federal research grant money for depreciation of a yacht, and for part of the cost of the university president's wedding. When the Stanford abuses came to light, the behavior of other institutions changed. See Reference (27). M. I. T. returned $731,000. Duke, Cornell, and Dartmouth lowered their claims. Undergraduate students would probably get a better education if there was less research money available to universities. The Columbia Daily Tribune reported that six faculty members in the University of Missouri's Research Animal Diagnostic Laboratory received bonus payments totaling $824,687 over and above their salaries in fiscal 2002.

The Columbia Daily Tribune of 26 July 2004 listed the high salaries of Columbia School District administrators. Twelve of these bureaucrats were paid more than $100,000 per year. This was seven years ago – how much worse is it now? Twenty-five were paid more than $85,000 per year. When are citizens going to finally decide that they have taken enough? When are the citizens going to demand an end to the overspending? The fact that the government schools are not educating our children makes this gross over-spending even more unacceptable.

Dr. Robert J. Herbold, the author of Reference (44), wrote "We need to support new routes for teacher certification in order to increase the number of teachers qualified to teach math and science." The Chronicle of Higher Education, on 3 January 1988, said "If we are to have a sufficient number of teachers of adequate quality, we must break the monopoly that the schools of education have on teacher certification. A 10-year moratorium on certification requirements was proposed. During that moratorium, the schools would be free to recruit qualified college graduates with majors in academic subjects, whether or not they have had any education courses. I believe that if we could get this experiment under way in one state, the improvement of its educational program would be so swift and dramatic that parents and taxpayers in the other forty-nine would demand and get its establishment there." Dr. John Silber, President of Boston University, wrote the preceding proposal. State certification of government school teachers has never been about the qualification of individuals. It has always been about protecting the monopoly position of schools of education. University professors of science, mathematics, engineering, physics, and chemistry are not "certified" by the state. The 18 December 2002 minutes of the Fayette School Board noted that a $1500 check was presented to a Fayette teacher for receiving National Teacher Certification. Can't we understand that if state certification is of zero value, and it is, then national certification is even more deplorable?

The fact, and it is a fact, that the dumbing down of the students of the United States by the government school system is deliberate is reprehensible. It could even be described as treasonous. It is probably also true that many teachers may not realize that this dumbing down is deliberate. However, this does not reduce the seriousness of the situation. If the government schools are not concentrating on reading, writing , arithmetic, history, civics, and other components of basic education that served the people of the United States so successfully for the decades before the educational psychologists, the NEA, and others gained significant influence, then the government school system probably should be destroyed. America was much more literate before the government school system was forced upon its citizens than it is today.

One encouraging trend is the monumental growth of home schooling. The American Legion Magazine of September 2008, on page 57, includes an article titled "Home Sweet Homeschooling." It includes "As recently as 1980, homeschooling was illegal in 30 states. Not until 1993 was it legal in all 50 states. But it has exploded in the past 20 years, educating just 50,000 U. S. kids in 1985, 300,000 by 1992, and 850,000 by 1999." By 2007, the number of home-schooled children was 1.5 million. The article lists some Americans who were homeschooled. These included George Washington, John Quincy Adams, Abraham Lincoln, Theodore Roosevelt, Woodrow Wilson, and Franklin D. Roosevelt. Also John Jay, Thomas Edison, Robert E. Lee, Booker T. Washington, Mark Twain, and Andrew Carnegie were homeschooled.

Reference (37), issued by the Intercollegiate Studies Institute, is entitled The Shaping of the American Mind – The Diverging Influences of the College Degree & Civic Learning on American Beliefs. Some of its findings were:

- College seniors failed a basic test on History.
- Freshmen did better than seniors.
- 71% of Americans failed the basic Civic Literacy test.
- College graduates are ignorant of America's Founding History and Constitution.
- Over 70% of Americans agree that colleges should teach America's history.

A front-page article in the New York Times of 12 August 1975 was headlined "'Crisis' noted in teaching of U. S. History." The article starts "The teaching of American history in the nation's public schools 'is in crisis,' a special report by the Organization of American Historians warns." Reference (19), was written in 1953, fifty-nine years ago. Professor of History Arthur E. Bestor of the University of Illinois titled his book Educational Wastelands: The Retreat from Learning in Our Public Schools. Recall the courses listed earlier in this book in St. Charles, Missouri. The St. Charles School District did not teach any English or history but found time for such courses as "Prejudice," "Minorities," "Witchcraft," "Minority Voices," and "Is This the End?"

Go to city-journal.org on the Internet. Look up Heather MacDonald's article, "Why Johnny's Teacher Can't Teach" and Sol Stern's piece, "Radical Math at the DOE." DOE stands for the New York City Department of Education. MacDonald begins with "American's nearly last-place finish in the Third International Mathematics and Sciences study of student achievement caused widespread consternation this February, except in the one place it should have mattered most: the nation's teacher education schools."

Stern documented the radicalization of math education. He quoted a Professor of Math Education, Maryilyn Frankenstein of the University of Massachusetts. Frankenstein proclaimed that instead of traditional math, math teachers should make clear that in a truly "just society," food would "be as free as breathing the air."

Reference (31) is David Horowitz's The Professors/The 101 Most Dangerous Academics in America. Horowitz describes what higher education has sunk to in the case of these 101 radicals. In the opinion of the writer, we, as a society, have permitted significant nonsense to replace substance in higher education in the establishment of departments such as "Women's Studies" and "African-American Studies." "Hispanic Studies" is also part of the mix.

What can and should the beleaguered parents and citizens of America do about this situation? Knowledgeable people who have followed the failure of our government school system for years are convinced that the system is beyond repair. They are probably right. America would be better off if the government school system, with its monopoly, did not exist. Since it so difficult to abolish the monstrosity, what else could be considered?

Some suggestions which should improve things follow.

First, at the federal level:

- Abolish the United States Department of Education.
- Rescind George W. Bush's No Child Left Behind Act.
- Pass a federal law that prohibits federal judges from setting tax rates.
- Cut federal education spending to zero. This should be a state function.
- Target federal research grants to the most important areas. Make the grants to state governments and incorporate meaningful reporting and performance requirements.

Second, at the state level in Missouri:

- Rescind Carnahan's Senate Bill 380.
- Decrease the size and influence of the State Department of Elementary and Secondary Education. It is probably overstaffed be a factor of at least ten.
- Abolish all "certification" requirements of government school personnel.
- More money means less quality as far as the government schools are concerned. Therefore, cut the amount spent significantly
- Pass a state law that prevents state judges from setting tax rates.

- Realize that government school people probably are less qualified than any other segment of society to decide what should be taught. To facilitate citizen knowledge of educational materials, pass a state law, with steep penalties for non-compliance, mandating that all curricula materials, including all textbooks, be displayed for easy inspection by anyone interested.
- Pass a state law that prohibits government school teachers and/or administrators from serving on school boards while they are employed in a different district.
- Pass a state law prohibiting service on a school board if any employee of the district is related within the fourth degree by blood or marriage to the board member. The present law which only prohibits board members from voting to employ relatives is completely ineffective
- Pass a state law which prohibits any individual from serving as a superintendent if any employee of the district is related to the superintendent within the fourth degree by blood or marriage.
- Use extreme caution before electing any retired K-12 school teacher or other retired school bureaucrat to any school board.

I have a few final comments. Some readers probably think I am an angry man, given the tone of some of these statements. Those readers are correct. We should all be angry. For decades, the government schools have been deliberately dumbing down the helpless young people of this great country. It is far past time to continue tolerating this. School bureaucrats have responded to legitimate parental complaints in a condescending "we know best" tone. It is abundantly clear that the government school people do not 'know best'. There are many outstanding and dedicated people employed in government education. You know them and I know them. This does not change the facts, however. Too much harm has been done by government schooling and it continues being done. Remember the book, The Underground History of American Education, by the brilliant author, John Taylor Gatto. Purchase it or read it on the internet. Americans must inform themselves, then get involved. We owe our children and their future, our country, and the memories of past Americans nothing less.

Chapter 18. Conclusions

I originally intended this book primarily as an autobiography. However, many aspects of American life are rapidly changing in a destructive direction and I have a deep concern for the future of our country. Having the background and experience to analyze some of these changes, I have added a critique of our failed government education system and a critique of a misguided and ruinous feminization of our military to the autobiography. Other equally serious problems are beyond the scope of this book. These would include the destruction of our families, the passing away of our culture and moral order, illegal and overwhelming massive third world immigration, collapsing birthrates and the shunning of the important task of motherhood by our young women.

The early part of my life's journey, as documented in these pages, occurred before America strayed so far from the path laid out by the founders. Opportunities existed. Along with others of my generation, I took advantage of them. Citizens of this great country have traditionally looked upon themselves first and foremost as individuals. And they were evaluated as individuals. Contrast this 'way it ought to be' with today's emphasis on groups instead of individuals, with attention to outcomes instead of opportunities, with the hang-ups on diversity and multiculturalism, with affirmative action and quotas rating higher than merit, and with the attack on the white male in so many areas of government, education, and even in our military.

Recall the quotes in Chapter 16 from several of our highest ranking uniformed military officers regarding their preoccupation with diversity. The Chief of Naval Operations expressed concern that naval officers are "a bunch of white guys." If the fact that Navy officers are a bunch of white guys is unacceptable, why haven't high ranking white officers stepped aside to enable their replacement by lessor qualified women and minorities? Should we, as a society, be upset that most professional and university basketball players are "a bunch of Negro guys?" Of course we should not. These Negro players have proven to be the best and they have earned the right to play. Through the centuries, there were good reasons for almost all military tasks to be carried out by men, and not women. These reasons are as valid today as they have ever been. The exaggerated emphasis on military diversity and feminization is seriously harming our military. It must cease!

If women meet the same physical standards as men in our 'new military', why aren't women performing as NFL defensive backs? Why not assign women to serve as NBA point guards? The answers are obvious to any right-thinking American but apparently not obvious to civilian and military bureaucrats pushing the destructive feminization agenda. Yet we are assigning America's precious young women to perform military tasks which they are not capable of performing. And their presence is extremely counterproductive in many situations. It is past time for sanity to return regarding women in our military.

Contrast the preoccupation with diversity of today's high ranking military officers with the thoughts of some of our most successful senior World War II officers. Fleet Admiral Ernest J. King was the Commander-in-Chief of the United States Fleet and Chief of Naval Operations. When he was asked if, as had been reported, he had said "When they get in trouble, they send for the sons-of-bitches" he replied that he had not but would have if he had thought of it. Fleet Admiral William F. Halsey is reported to have said that he never trusted a man who did not drink and cuss. They were both naval aviators and they understood the importance of traditional military culture. They understood that that culture is worth defending from misguided attacks. Sadly, it appears that there is to be no place in the feminized and politically correct "new military" for individuals who some might have described as "sons-of bitches." America formerly, for decades and even centuries, understood that these individuals have been of extraordinary value when the going gets tough. America is destined to pay an awesome price for the wrong-headed and misguided politically correct idealism associated with the feminization of our military. In fact, we are already paying that price as is pointed out in Chapter 16.

We need to reflect on such historical military experiences as the Bataan Death March, the Battle of Midway, the Battle of the Bulge, D-Day, Iwo Jima, Korea, Viet Nam, the sinking of the Indianapolis and so many others. Has America sunk to the level that we meekly accept subjecting young women to such experiences? Have we completely lost our mind? Recall that Martin van Creveld, the world-renowned military historian, described the feminization of the United States military as a game, or a joke. Women and men are equally important, but they are different. Women have no legitimate place on a battlefield, on a combat airplane, or on a warship.

Chapter 17 constitutes a critique of the failed government education system in the United States. Most Americans are unaware that the dumbing down of our helpless students is by design. Most influential decision makers realize, and affirm, that education requires mastery of traditional subjects such as English, mathematics, writing, history, and spelling. However, insufficient effort is expended on those areas. Chapter 17 will enlighten interested readers as to the magnitude of the education crisis. School Boards should be leaders in addressing the education crisis but they are much more likely to be part of the problem. Recall the failure of the St. Charles School Board when they were informed that things such as witchcraft had replaced history? Recall the continuing failure of the Fayette School Board to acknowledge the proven truth regarding the ownership of the Union School lot? It is easy to conclude that Mark Twain may have been right. In "Following the Equator: / A Journey Around the World", Twain wrote "In the first place God made idiots. This was for practice. Then he made School Boards."

I am no hero and make no claim to be one. I have not been shot at in anger by enemies of our country. However, as documented in this book, I have flown with and / or been an associate of many heroes, namely United States Navy pilots noted in this book. Included would certainly be Harvey P. Lanham, Lilburn Edmonston, Cliff Fanning, Ed Pawka, Dick Bates, Jim Verdin, Bill Bauhof, Sport Horton, Dave Tatum, and others. It is appropriate to call these heroes eagles; thus the sub-title of this book was selected to be "I Flew with Eagles."

Will America survive as the free country that so many have sacrificed so much for? The ultimate sacrifice by several members of the United States Navy for this, the greatest country in history, is documented herein. Below is a montage of several of the U. S. Navy fighter pilots referred to in this book who made the ultimate sacrifice many decades ago. Their memory, as well as the memory of so many others who have made that ultimate sacrifice over the last two plus centuries, deserves much better from 21st century America than is represented by the dumbed-down education system or by the politically correct feminized military. As Vazsonyi stated "Whether the United States survives as the beacon it has been will depend on the willingness of Americans to contemplate anew the reasons for its success, and to make decisions accordingly." The hour is late and many Americans appear to be asleep. Will we awaken in time? The issue is in doubt.

George Basye

Jesse Brown

Hal Avants

J.B. Morris

Babe Edmonston

Jim Verdin

The finest that this country or any country is capable of producing.

List of References

1. Basye, C. Ben, American Education: A Howard County, Missouri Case Study/ From Successful One-Room Schools to Extravagance, Arrogance, and Failure, self-published, 2005.
2. World Book Encyclopedia, Volume 4, 1963.
3. Solzhenitsyn, Aleksandr I., "Words of Warning to America," from Educating for Liberty: The Best of Imprimis, 1972-2002, page 265.
4. Atkinson, Gerald L., From Trust to Terror: Radical Feminism is Destroying the U. S. Navy, Atkinson Associates Press, 1997.
5. Mitchell, Brian, Women in the Military: Flirting with Disaster, Regnery, 1998.
6. Gutmann, Stephanie, The Kinder, Gentler Military: Can America's Gender-Neutral Fighting Force Still Win Wars? Scribner, 2000.
7. Baldauf, Laurence C., Jr., Bah Bah Blue Sheep: A Critique of Military YES-MEN, Cabrillo Press, 1968.
8. McMaster, H. R., Dereliction of Duty: Lyndon Johnson, Robert McNamara the Joint Chiefs of Staff and the Lies that Led to Viet Nam, Harper Perennial, 1997.
9. Walt, Lewis W., America Faces Defeat, Apollo Books, 1972.
10. Vazsonyi, Balint, America's 30 Years War: Who is Winning? Regnery, 1998.
11. Carson, Jim, Letter to Center for Strategic and International Studies from Aviation Regiment CMR 477 Box 1551 APO AE 09165 dated 27 March 2001. (Available on Google, "American Military Culture").
12. Gross, Martin L., The End of Sanity: Social and Cultural Madness in America, Avon Books, 1997.
13. O'Beirne, Kate, Women Who Make the World Worse, Sentinel, 2006.
14. Huntington, Samuel P., Who Are We? Simon and Schuster, 2004.
15. Sommers, Christina Hoff, The War Against Boys: How Misguided Feminism is Harming Our Young Men, Simon and Schuster, 2000.
16. McNamara, Robert S., In Retrospect: The Tragedy and Lessons of Vietnam, Random House, 1995.
17. Armbruster, Frank E., Our Children's Crippled Future: How American Education Has Failed, Quadrangle/New York Times Book Company,1977.
18. Barry, John S. and Rea S. Hederman, Report Card on American Education: A State-by-State Analysis, 1976-1998, American Legislative Exchange Council, 1998.

19. Bestor, Arthur E., Educational Wastelands: The Retreat From Learning in Our Public Schools, The University of Illinois Press, 1953.
20. Blumenfeld, Samuel L., The Whole Language OBE Fraud: The Shocking Story of How America is Being Dumbed Down by Its Own Education System, Paradigm, 1995.
21. Gatto, John Taylor, Dumbing us Down: The Hidden Curriculum of Compulsory Schooling, New Society Publishers, 2002.
22. Gatto, John Taylor, Ed., The Exhausted School: Bending the Bars of Traditional Education, Berkley Hills Books, 1993, 2003.
23. Gatto, John Taylor, The Underground History of American Education: An Intimate Investigation Into the Prison of Modern Schooling, The Oxford Village Press, 2006.
24. Gross, Martin L., The Conspiracy of Ignorance: The Failure of American Public Schools, Harper Collins, 1999.
25. Kozol, Jonathan, Illiterate America, Anchor Press/Doubleday, 1985.
26. Marshner, Connaught Coyne, Blackboard Tyranny, Arlington House, 1978.
27. Sowell, Thomas, Inside American Education: The Decline, The Deceptions, The Dogmas, The Free Press (Macmillan), 1993.
28. Sykes, Charles J., Dumbing Down Our Kids: Why American Children Feel Good About Themselves, But Can't Read, Write, or Add, St. Martins Press, 1995.
29. Williams, Joe, Cheating Our Kids: How Politics and Greed Ruin Education," Palgrave Macmillan, 2005.
30. American Legion Magazine, September 2008, page 57.
31. Horowitz, David, The Professors: The 101 Most Dangerous Academics in America, Regnery, 2006.
32. Bovard, James, The Bush Betrayal, Palgrave Macmillan, 2004.
33. Kors, Alan Charles and Harvey A. Silverglate, The Shadow University: The Betrayal of Liberty on America's Campuses, The Free Press, Simon and Schuster, 1998.
34. Sacks, David O. and Peter A. Theil, The Diversity Myth, 'Multiculturalism', and The Politics of Intolerance at Stanford, Independent Institute, 1995.
35. Powell, Lewis F., Jr., Attack on American Free Enterprise System, U. S. Chamber of Commerce, 23 August 1971.
36. Los Angeles Times, "The Decline of American Education," 15, 16, 17 August 1976.
37. Intercollegiate Studies Institute, "The Shaping of the American Mind," December 2009.

38. Basye, C. Ben, "Educational Trends in the Nation and in our St. Charles Public School System," 10 March 1975.
39. Iowa State University Daily (reprinted from the New York Times), "Research vs. Teaching; Problem for Professors," Ames, Iowa, 15 March 1961.
40. Sykes, Charles J., How Colleges are Failing Our Students, Imprimis, Hillsdale College, 1990.
41. Williams, Polly, "Inner City Kids; Why Choice is Their Only Hope," and J. Patrick Rooney, "Private Vouchers; A New Idea in Education Reform," Imprimis, Hillsdale College, 1992.
42. Greenleaf, Warren T. and Gary A. Griffin, Schools for the 70's and Beyond; A Call to Action, National Education Association, 1971.
43. Roberts, Milnor, "Letter regarding Revisionist History in American Schools," World War II Veterans Committee, February, 2005.
44. Herbold, Robert J., "K-12 Establishment is Putting America's Industrial Leadership at Risk," Imprimis, Hillsdale College, 2005.
45. Missouri General Assembly, Senate Bill 380, "Outstanding Schools Act," 87th General Assembly.
46. United States Congress, "No Child Left Behind Act," Signed by President George W. Bush, 8 January 2002.
47. Buchanan, Patrick J., The Death of the West: How Dying Populations and Immigrant Invasions Imperil Our Country and Civilization, St. Martin's Press, 2002.

About the Author

The author, C. Ben Basye, was born on a farm close to Union School in Howard County, Missouri. He was one of the last six graduates of one-room Union School. He holds a B. S. degree in Mechanical Engineering from the University of Missouri and the M. S. degree in Theoretical and Applied Mechanics and Ph.D. in Theoretical and Applied Mechanics and Applied Mathematics, both from Iowa State University. Basye also attended the Universities of Nebraska and Wyoming, as well as Central Missouri State University and Brown University.

Basye is Professor Emeritus of Engineering at the University of Missouri-Rolla. He taught 18 different graduate engineering courses at the University of Missouri-Rolla Center in St. Louis. He has also taught engineering at Iowa State University and has served as faculty advisor for more than 400 graduate engineering students.

He holds the rank of Captain, Retired Reserve, U. S. Navy.

Basye's leadership positions include service to the American Society of Mechanical Engineers and President of the St. Charles County School Board. He was President of the Missouri Council of Chapters of the Military Officers Association of America in 2005, and is a Life Member of the Military Officers Association of America. He has been a member of the American Legion for 37 years.

Index

CPSIA information can be obtained at www.ICGtesting.com
Printed in the USA
LVOW09*0418100414

381075LV00002B/2/P

9 781936 688241